ROUTLEDGE · E

GENERAL EDITOR

C000176708

JOHN MILTON

Selected Shorter Poems
and Prose Writings

ROUTLEDGE · ENGLISH · TEXTS
GENERAL EDITOR · JOHN DRAKAKIS

WILLIAM BLAKE: *Selected Poetry and Prose* ed. David Punter
EMILY BRONTË: *Wuthering Heights* ed. Heather Glen
JOHN CLARE: *Selected Poetry and Prose* ed. Merryn and Raymond Williams
JOSEPH CONRAD: *Selected Literary Criticism and The Shadow-Line* ed. Allan Ingram
CHARLES DICKENS: *Hard Times* ed. Terry Eagleton
JOHN DONNE: *Selected Poetry and Prose* ed. T. W. and R. J. Craik
HENRY FIELDING: *Joseph Andrews* ed. Stephen Copley
BEN JONSON: *The Alchemist* ed. Peter Bement
ANDREW MARVELL: *Selected Poetry and Prose* ed. Robert Wilcher
JOHN MILTON: *Selected Poetry and Prose* ed. Tony Davies
WILFRED OWEN: *Selected Poetry and Prose* ed. Jennifer Breen
ALEXANDER POPE: *Selected Poetry and Prose* ed. Robin Sowerby

Forthcoming

Robert Browning	*Selected Poetry* ed. Aidan Day
Geoffrey Chaucer	*The Wife of Bath's Prologue and Tale and the Clerk's Prologue and Tale* ed. Marion Wynne-Davies
Joseph Conrad	*Heart of Darkness* ed. John Batchelor
George Eliot	*The Mill on The Floss* ed. Sally Shuttleworth
Thomas Hardy	*The Mayor of Casterbridge* ed. J. Bullen
Gerard Manley Hopkins	*Selected Poetry and Prose* ed. R. J. Watt
James Joyce	*Dubliners* ed. Stan Smith
D. H. Lawrence	*Selected Poetry and Prose* ed. John Lucas
Christopher Marlowe	*Dr Faustus* ed. John Drakakis
Mary Shelley	*Frankenstein* ed. Patrick Lyons
Percy Bysshe Shelley	*Selected Poetry and Prose* ed. Alasdair Macrae
Edmund Spenser	*The Faerie Queen Book 1 and Selected Poems* ed. Elizabeth Watson
Virginia Woolf	*To the Lighthouse* ed. Sandra Kemp
William Wordsworth	*Selected Poetry* ed. Philip Hobsbaum
W. B. Yeats	*Selected Poetry and Prose* ed. Graham Martin

JOHN MILTON

Selected Shorter Poems and Prose Writings

Edited by Tony Davies

ROUTLEDGE · LONDON AND NEW YORK

First published in 1988 by
Routledge
11 New Fetter Lane,
London EC4P 4EE

Published in the USA by
Routledge
in association with Routledge,
Chapman & Hall, Inc.
29 West 35th Street,
New York NY 10001

Printed in Great Britain by
Richard Clay Ltd, Bungay, Suffolk

British Library Cataloguing in
Publication Data
Milton, John, 1608–1674
    John Milton: selected shorter poems and
    prose writings. – (Routledge English texts).
    I. Title   II. Davies, Tony, 1940–
    828'.409   PR3553
    ISBN 0-415-00668-6

Library of Congress Cataloging in
Publication Data
Milton, John, 1608–1674.
    [Selections. 1988]
    Selected shorter poems and prose writings /
John Milton: edited by Tony Davies.
    p. : cm. – (Routledge English texts)
    Bibliography: p.
    ISBN 0-415-00668-6 (soft)
    I. Davies, Tony, 1940–   . II.
    Title. III. Series.
PR3553.D38   1988
821'.4 – dc 19
    ·

*To the memory
of my mother,
15. xi. 1914–2. v. 1986*

Contents

Introduction

The poetry and prose in this selection were all written and, with a handful of exceptions, published within a period of little more than thirty years, between 1629 and 1660; but those thirty years were probably the stormiest and most eventful in the entire history of these islands, before or since. 'The highest of times', the philosopher Thomas Hobbes called them. For the politician and historian Clarendon they were the years of the 'Great Rebellion'. Later historians, though using different names – the English Civil Wars, the Puritan Revolution, the English Revolution – have continued to debate the political morality, the underlying causes, the wider significance of a passage of events seen by some contemporaries as an interlude of criminal insanity, by others as an example of the highest principle and courage, by some as a bloody violation of justice and traditional decency, by others as the prelude to a New Jerusalem. The only thing that no one has disputed then or since is the high drama and radical excitement of a 'world turned upside down'. In 1629 Charles I dissolved an angry and uncooperative Parliament and embarked on an 11-year experiment in absolute sovereignty, an experiment that was to end in civil war, political revolution, and his own death under the executioner's axe. In 1660, to the accompaniment of well-orchestrated public celebration and much private bitterness and disillusion, the army and Parliament that had fought, tried, and condemned him, agreed to restore his son to the throne they themselves had abolished eleven years before.

1

All these events John Milton followed closely, at first as a private citizen and onlooker (though an increasingly impassioned and committed one), later as a participant and chronicler. In the summer of 1629 he was an unknown postgraduate at Cambridge, approaching his twenty-first birthday and expected, having taken his BA that Easter, to proceed smoothly to his MA and then to ordination and a career of respectable obscurity as an Anglican parson. In 1660 two of his books were burnt by the public hangman, and only the intervention of some influential friends saved Milton himself from trial and punishment (perhaps even death) as a heretic and revolutionary. No writer's work, however private, can be properly enjoyed or understood if it is uprooted from the history and the society in which it is produced. But this is doubly true of Milton, a poet of high ambition and idealistic aims who was also a pamphleteer, propagandist, and paid employee of the new republic, himself a leading actor – or at least an important minor one – in that 'extraordinarily wordy revolution' in which writers and intellectuals played a part scarcely less significant than politicians and soldiers. One historian has calculated that 'well over 22,000 sermons, speeches, pamphlets and newspapers were published between 1640 and 1661', an unprecedented torrent of print that testifies to 'a clash of ideas and of ideologies, and the emergence of radical concepts affecting every aspect of human behaviour and every institution in society from the family to the Church to the State' (Stone 1972: p. 49). The contours of Milton's work, the rhetorical rhythms of his writing, even the choices of genre, form, image, are shaped and imprinted by the urgency and turbulence of the period and the vivid excitements of his own reactions to it. Later poets living through revolutionary epochs, like Blake, Wordsworth, and Shelley, have felt strong kinship and solidarity with Milton; but that tradition of English radicalism has almost gone now, at least in poetry, and if we want to find something like it in our own century we must turn to tragic visionaries of war, love, and revolution like the Chilean Neruda, the Scots MacDiarmid, the Nigerian Soyinka. There, as in Milton, we can feel the double articulation of the radical stance: the deep search for the 'root' in language, culture, history (something utterly different from the bogus traditionalism of the Olde Tea Shoppe, Victorian values, and the 'British Way of Life'), and an impassioned commitment to renewal and fundamental change.

The relationship (we might call it the 'dialectic') between the two senses of *radical* is never an easy or uncomplicated one. 'Without contraries is no progression', declared Blake (Blake 1959: p. 44); and in writing of this kind there is always a strain, a feeling of tensed energies at once sustaining and subverting the arching spans and dangerous equilibrium of the language, like a suspension bridge or a high-wire act. A lot of the excitement and pleasure of reading comes from that. With Milton, it works through the syntax, with its coiled springs of inversion and deferral, its great teetering piles of subordinate clauses, its booby-trapped conjunctions. It works, too, through the abrupt, sometimes bizarre bilingualism of old and new, past and present, pagan and Christian, high Latin eloquence and low Saxon abuse. Above all it works through the ideas (though it is still considered bad form in some academic circles to suggest that poetry has anything to do with ideas; and in any case it is misleading to separate them out as though they can be studied independently of the language and forms that embody them). For Milton, writing, whatever the genre or occasion, is (to borrow a term from the Russian critic Mikhail Bakhtin) a 'dialogical' activity, a form of internalized argument, conversation, or debate.[1] 'Out of the quarrel with others', wrote W. B. Yeats, 'we make rhetoric; out of the quarcel with ourselves, poetry.' But although the notion of poetry as a 'quarrel' nicely captures the dialogical tension of his work, the contrast between public and private voices, outer and inner speech, which plays an important part in the romantic idea of the poet, will not work with a Renaissance writer like Milton, whose poetry is as public, as *forensic*, as his prose, both being projected outwards to an active and concretely envisaged readership. Nothing could be drearier, or more false, than the Victorian idea that reading Milton is like eavesdropping on the solitary musings of a 'great mind', enthroned in magisterial isolation. Much more, it is like being caught up in an animated open-ended argument as it moves, developing all the while, from place to place, from genre to genre, with now one voice and one theme dominating, now another. Not surprisingly drama exerts a powerful attraction, though it was never a practical possibility, Milton being a generation too late for the theatre of Marlowe, Jonson, and Shakespeare, and excluded by age, politics, and blindness from that of Dryden and Etherege. In addition to a masque (*Comus*) and a neo-classical tragedy (*Samson Agonistes*), the other texts are often shadowed by dramatic forms and aspirations. *Paradise Lost* was first conceived as a tragedy. *Lycidas* is a 'monody', a kind of dramatic *scena*, as full of voices as Caliban's isle. The Nativity poem stages the birth of Christ with all the baroque (some think inappropriate) splendour of a Jacobean masque, complete with antimasque of pagan monster-deities. The sonnets plead, buttonhole, dispute. A virtuoso of forms, Milton is as far as possible from being a purely formalistic writer. The Ludlow masque, the little madrigal on the Circumcision, the sonnet on his blindness are as substantive, as fully committed to the public debate about liberty and virtue, as the *Tenure of Kings and Magistrates* or the *Christian Doctrine*. We can disagree with the ideas, just as we can dislike the poems. But to pretend that they are quite separate things, or that ideas have got nothing to do with our appreciation of 'literature', trivializes both.

This counterpoint of voices and arguments happens on a number of levels. Some are integral to the text, like the succession of witnesses at the inquest that forms the heart of *Lycidas*. Others, like the intervention of Phoebus in the same poem or the reply of Patience in the blindness sonnet, recall the intensely dramatic character of Puritan spirituality, with its inner colloquies of the divided self, body against soul, passion against reason. Sometimes the debate or conversation is with other writers, a complex allusive 'intertext'[2] of Virgil and Spenser and Shakespeare and the author of the Psalms or the Book of Revelation. These can look daunting, especially when piled together into a great heap of learned-sounding footnotes. But Milton's relationship with his sources and references (which, like Ben Jonson, he treats as 'guides, not commanders') (Jonson 1975: p. 379) is the opposite of a dusty academicism, being intensely active and metamorphic, so that, while a footnote can give a source for the blind Fury, or the rejuvenated England

4

'shaking her mighty locks', it cannot begin to explain what strange transformations they have suffered in the process of being drawn into the orbit of Miltonic compulsions. Much the same goes for the citation of 'authorities' in the prose writings. All seventeenth-century authors do this: it gives an air of solid research, and suggests that you have a good majority of the respectable dead on your side. But Milton's use of the convention is idiosyncratic and flexible (unscrupulously so, some of his editors have thought), dictated by the interests of his readers and the rhetorical needs of the argument rather than by some static notion of unchanging and authoritative tradition.

At another important level, the implied debate is with contemporaries – not some generalized 'reading public' but specific groups, concretely envisaged: the Puritan aristocracy (*Comus*), the dissident Presbyterian intelligentsia (*Lycidas, Of Reformation*), the libertarians and root-and-branch radicals in army and parliament (*Areopagitica, The Tenure*), the Rota republicans (*The Ready and Easy Way*), the 'audience fit though few' of sober and virtuous dissenters, dignified and hopeful in defeat (*Paradise Lost*) – a succession of 'overlapping circles' (Christopher Hill's phrase) within which the writer's individual tonality, though never fully submerged into a mere representativeness, interacts and resonates with other voices, denouncing or defending the bishops, pleading for or against the prerogative of kings, championing or deriding the Good Old Cause, questioning and justifying the ways of God to men.

These levels of the texts – levels of correspondence that lock them into history and culture – can be elusive and difficult for modern readers, especially perhaps the classicism, for which Milton is notorious. "Tis Latin, 'tis Greek English', said his eighteenth-century' biographer Jonathan Richardson of Milton's language (Darbishire 1932: p. 313); and Samuel Johnson grumbled about his 'train of mythological imagery, such as a College easily supplies' (Johnson 1906: p. 116). The Victorian critic Mark Pattison put it particularly dispiritingly when he wrote of the 'lofty strain which requires more effort to accompany, than the average reader is able to make', concluding with satisfaction that 'an appreciation of Milton is the last reward of consummated scholarship' (Pattison 1902: p. 215). Though intended as the highest praise (Pattison is rescuing Milton from Blake and the Chartists and claiming him as the special property of the 'cultivated' few), this perfected the deadly representation of Milton as a pompous pedant and intellectual bully (George Eliot's brutal portrait of Pattison himself, the Reverend Casaubon in *Middlemarch*, is seen by the idealistic and deluded young woman who marries him as a figure of Miltonic grandeur). This is the Milton attacked by Eliot and Leavis and, in different terms, Empson, and defended by C. S. Lewis and A. N. Wilson: orthodox, patriarchal, and dull.

We do not have to accept this version of Milton, though, to see that he remains a difficult writer. More than three centuries divide our intellectual and cultural landscapes from those of a seventeenth-century intellectual who wrote comfortably in four languages and combined an intimate knowledge of classical and biblical literature with a passion for theological debate and an energetic absorption in contemporary politics (one of his enemies called him *Johannes Polypragmaticus* – 'Jack Busybody') (Parker 1968: I, 390). For most of us, Milton's lifelong arguments with Plato, British history, and the Book of Genesis are a matter for dutiful research rather than enthusiastic participation, and although a footnote or a scholarly treatise may help me to understand what his mortalism and Arianism *mean*, they are unlikely to make me feel on my pulses why they *mattered* (though two men were burnt alive at Smithfield for refusing to disavow the second of those when Milton was 3 years old).[3]

Nevertheless, the difficulties can be and have been made too much of. Milton described poetry as 'more simple, sensuous and passionate' than prose, and although the meanings of all three words have drifted a little since he wrote, it is certain that he regarded poetry, however complex its surface detail and elaboration, as a basic mode of discourse, not 'subtle and fine' like the intellectual operations of rhetoric but impacting directly on the primary senses and emotions through what Wordsworth called 'the grand elementary principle of pleasure' (Wordsworth 1977: I, 880). And the elusive networks of intertextual and contextual reference, though we may only be able to reconstitute them patchily and with difficulty, can serve as a useful reminder of two things: first, that the isolated text, the

6

'words on the page' of the practical critic, is in almost every way an artificial and impoverishing notion, and certainly a historically specific one, derived from nineteenth-century ideas about originality, authenticity, and organic form; and second, that we later readers have our 'intertextualities' too, our semantic landmarks and codes of familiar reference, which we can no more put on hold when we read an older writer like Milton than we can somehow assume at will the cognitive universe of a seventeenth-century reader. We read Milton, willy-nilly, as a contemporary of *ours*, not his: not because of some peremptorily unhistorical notion of the topical 'relevance' of his writings to a late-capitalist society like our own – one of the great pleasures of reading older writers comes from the exercise it gives to historical imagination – but because in the last resort it will always be *our* purposes and preoccupations that will determine how much and what kinds of interest those writings continue to provide.

Milton's family was middle-class and comfortably off, his mother the daughter of a wealthy merchant tailor, his father a scrivener, an occupation somewhere between an accountant, a solicitor, and an investment broker. The family was Protestant, even (to use a vague term) Puritan: John Milton senior had been disowned by his own father, a Roman Catholic of the old school, for reading an English Bible, still in the 1580s a symbolic act of Protestant independence; and he hired as a private tutor for his own son the Presbyterian minister Thomas Young, later to be one of the leaders of the attack on the Anglican hierarchy. At St Paul's School (from 12 to 16) and Christ's College, Cambridge (from 16 to 23) the younger Milton read Greek and Latin and also (less conventionally) Spenser and Sidney. Just as important, he read John Foxe's *Acts and Monuments* (1554), a history of the English Reformation known popularly (and it *was* popular, in its seventh edition by 1610) as the 'Book of Martyrs'.

For Milton's generation, as for his parents', the Protestant Reformation meant not only the heroic recovery of the true faith and pure word of God (hence the nickname 'Puritan' for enthusiasts of the reformed churches) after centuries of Popish superstition; it meant too, at least for the prosperous classes and for ambitious *petit bourgeois* like the Miltons, the emergence of England – or 'Britain' as the Tudors liked to call it, exploiting their Welsh ancestry – as a self-conscious, expansive, and independent political entity. The break with Rome, set in train for his own reasons by Henry VIII and doctrinally consolidated under his children Edward and Elizabeth, was a political as much as a theological event; and the establishment of a national church with the secular sovereign at its head as 'Defender of the Faith' – ironically, a title conferred on Henry for defending the papacy *against* Luther – provided a powerful institutional symbol of emergent nationhood and a focus for patriotic as well as pious sentiments and aspirations. Indeed, the Church of England operated as an important institution of secular as well as doctrinal orthodoxy; and the state – for the Henrician reforms and the Reformation settlement had established for the first time in England a 'state' in the modern sense: a professional civil service and a range of governing agencies – played its reciprocal part in enforcing religious alongside social conformity.

Milton seems to have been destined for a career in the church, an obvious choice for a young man from a pious and respectable family who had no interest in law or medicine, and who showed no inclination to follow his father into business. But by 1632, when he left Cambridge and returned to live with his elderly parents, now in retirement in the suburban riverside village of Hammersmith, the established church was already locked into that doctrinal and political confrontation with its own Puritan members which within a decade was to drive thousands of conscientious Protestants out of church and country and to lead to its own bloody dissolution. After dispensing with Parliament in 1629, in part because of its refusal to countenance a Declaration enforcing religious conformity, Charles I ruled directly through the prerogative courts and the Star Chamber; and his key agent throughout this period of personal rule, in effect his Prime Minister, was William Laud, Bishop of London and from 1633 Archbishop of Canterbury. Laud, who packed the church and the universities with his own appointees, embarked with the king's support on the wholesale harassment and persecution of religious and political dissent through the establishment of an authoritarian regime of absolute sovereignty backed by the power of the state and legitimated by the orthodoxies of the national church, an aim embodied in the notorious *Constitutions and Canons* of 1640, which required every 'Parson, Vicar, Curate, or Preacher' to read out four times a year an 'explanation of the Regal power' elaborating the doctrine that 'the most High and Sacred order of Kings is of Divine right, being the ordinance of God himself, founded in the prime Laws of nature, and clearly established by express texts both of the old and new Testaments'. Failure to do this was punishable by fines, suspension, and excommunication. But Laud's animus against dissenters went a good deal further than that. In 1630 the Presbyterian Alexander Leighton was hauled up before the Star Chamber and High Commission for publishing a pamphlet against the bishops, fined ten thousand pounds (far more than he would ever have possessed in an entire lifetime), and then, in his own words, 'received thirty six stripes with a terrible Cord. After which, he stood almost two houres on the Pillory, in cold Frost and Snow, and suffered the rest; as cutting off the Eare, firing the Face [branding on the cheek with the letters 'SS', for 'sower of sedition'], and slitting of the Nose.' Similar atrocities were suffered by other Puritans who dared to criticize Laud and his fellow bishops in public. Henry Burton and John Bastwick were both fined, mutilated, and branded, and the unsuppressible William Prynne had his ears hacked off not once but *twice*, first in 1634 and again (the remaining stumps) in 1637. Revulsion at the brutality of these punishments and admiration for the courage of the victims combined with suspicion of Laud's pro-Spanish foreign policy and his own supposed leanings to Catholicism to mobilize popular feeling against him, and behind him the court and king, rapidly drifting out of contact with political reality. To this gathering social and ideological crisis the ruling elite could respond only with harsher repression (Stone 1972: pp. 117–35; Yale: I, pp. 34–48).

All this while Milton was living at home, in Hammersmith and later at Horton in Buckinghamshire. He had been writing poetry for a decade or more and some Latin hexameters had been published while he was still an undergraduate. But his first English poem, sixteen lines of conventional piety about Shakespeare, was printed in 1632. About this time, too, he contributed some lines to a pastoral entertainment for the dowager Countess of Derby at Harefield House, with music by his friend Henry Lawes; and Lawes may have been responsible for the commission a couple of years later of a full-scale masque for the family of the countess's stepson, the Earl of Bridgewater, recently appointed Lord Lieutenant of Wales (in effect a colonial viceroy). Performed in Ludlow Castle in the autumn of 1634, it was published, anonymously, in 1637, in which year Milton wrote *Lycidas* for a collection of Latin and English elegies in memory of his Cambridge acquaintance Edward King, published the following year. Donne's friend Sir Henry Wotton thought well of the masque; and the placing of *Lycidas* at the climax of the other King elegies suggests that Milton was already regarded as a significant poet. At any rate the two poems seem to signal a change of direction in Milton's plans. True, the Attendant Spirit who presides over the masque is a clerical figure, beneath the Arcadian disguise; and *Lycidas* sits firmly in the tradition of Protestant pastoral in its concern with the priestly vocation and the crisis in the church. But the shepherd of pastoral equivocates between priest and poet, and the commissioning and publication of the two poems, together with the fervent Christian-Platonic aspirations expressed in the texts themselves, suggest that poetry has decisively supplanted the ministry as a focus for his ambitions. By 1642 he could declare publicly his determination 'to be an interpreter and relater of the best and sagest things among mine own citizens throughout this island in the mother dialect; that what the greatest and choicest wits of Athens, Rome or modern Italy, and those Hebrews of old, did for their country, I in my proportion, with this over and above of being a Christian, might do for mine' (Yale: I, pp. 811–12). He intended, that is, to join the exalted company of Homer, Virgil, Tasso, and the author of the Book of Job: to become the epic poet of Protestant England.

This is a *political* as much as a personal ambition, and there is less contradiction between the 'Poet soaring in the high region of his fancies' and the pamphlets written with his 'left hand' in the 1640s than some of his biographers have suggested. Epic is a child, and an analogue, of revolution. In particular, it is a poetry of emerging imperial city-states and nations: Athens, Rome, England. Plunging *in medias res*, into the thick of the present, it straddles with its arching spans of narrative both past and future. For Milton, it is also a medium of *cultural* revolution, a discourse of the free and virtuous citizen, 'of power beside the office of a pulpit to inbreed and cherish in a great people the seeds of virtue and public civility, to allay the perturbations of the mind and set the affections in right tune ... to sing the victorious agonies of martyrs and saints, the deeds and triumphs of just and pious nations doing valiantly through faith against the enemies of Christ' (Yale: I, pp. 816–17).

This conception of the moral and political function of poetry is centrally Puritan, linking him with Spenser and Sidney as securely as it separates him from Donne or Herbert. But the European tone, the sense of belonging to a cosmopolitan intelligentsia, must reflect his visit in 1638–9 to France and Italy, where, armed with letters of introduction and his own unquenchable confidence, he met and talked with a number of eminent intellectuals including Hugo Grotius, Giambattista Manso, Lucas Holstein, and the great scientist Galileo. Manso, now almost 80, had been a friend and patron of poets like Tasso and Marini. The other three all exemplified in different ways both the easy internationalism and the treacherous ideological instability of counter-reformation Europe: the scholar Holstein, curator of the Vatican Library, born in Protestant Hamburg but now a Roman citizen and Catholic convert; the historian and jurist Grotius, political émigré from his native Holland, living in Catholic Paris as ambassador of the Protestant queen of Sweden; the astronomer Galileo, 75 years old and almost blind, famous throughout Europe but condemned to inactivity and forbidden to publish by the Inquisition. These encounters no doubt confirmed Milton's conviction that Mediterranean Europe, and Italy in particular, remained the fountainhead of modern as of ancient art and learning; 'for the sun, which we want, ripens wits as well as fruits', he wrote later, 'and as wine and oil are imported to us from abroad, so much ripe understanding and many civil virtues be imported into our minds from foreign writings and examples of best ages' (Yale: V, p. 450). But they must also have strengthened his hatred of the 'grim wolf', the Roman Catholic Church, documenting it with vivid testimonies (that of Galileo in particular) to the two great evils flowing from the secular power of priests, in Laud's London as in Peter's Rome: the persecution of innovation and dissent, and the suppression of knowledge through censorship.

While Milton was in Italy Charles I had launched the first of his two disastrous attempts to impose a Laudian regime on the Church of Scotland, whose General Assembly had recently abolished bishops, prayer book and church courts and covenanted instead for a system of elders ('presbyters') presiding over a network of regional assemblies or 'synods'. The pathetic failure of the two 'Bishops' wars' of 1639 and 1640 established the Scots experiment as a model of church reform for English Puritans and confirmed Presbyterianism as the first wave of organized ideological resistance to Stuart and Laudian absolutism. Leighton, Prynne, Burton, Bastwick were all Presbyterians, root-and-branchers in religion but politically conservative. In the early 1640s Milton might have called himself a Presbyterian too, and *Of Reformation* retains at least a tactical allegiance to the idea of monarchy. But his stance was already divergent. In the pamphlets of 1641–2 both the logic of the argument and the pull of the rhetoric are driving beyond the attack on prelates to a much wider critique of social authority and 'an end to all earthly tyrannies', and the anticlericalism there directed at the bishops will shortly embrace the Presbyterians too: 'New Presbyter is but old Priest writ large' (Carey, *CSP*: p. 296).

In any case, Milton's conception of religious and civic duty was grounded less in salvationist Puritanism, with its Calvinist emphasis on righteousness and calling, than on classical ideas of justice and liberty, with their strong republican connotations: 'Love Virtue, she alone is free.' Like the Florentine humanists, he thought of Christianity as a continuation and synthesis of the Graeco-Roman world, not its negation. The 1644 pamphlet

12

Of Education constructs a curriculum almost exclusively classical, fulminates against 'ignorantly zealous divinity', and among some fifty Greek and Latin authors mentions the Bible briefly just three times, for the moral parts of the Old Testament and the gospels (*after* Plato, Xenophon, Cicero, Plutarch), for the Mosaic law, and for Hebrew practice on Sundays (Yale: II, pp. 362–415). As for monarchy, immediately after his return from Italy he began to copy into his private notebook examples from English history of the greed, injustice, and deceitfulness of kings, adding that 'commotions for these reasons want not a stout captain, as a plebeian wittily answered the Duke of Norfolk (sent against the commons in Suffolk and asking that who was their captain) that "Poverty was their captain and his cousin Necessity"' (Yale: I, p. 487).

Milton's politics, wrote the eighteenth-century Tory critic Samuel Johnson, were those of 'an acrimonious and surly republican' (Johnson 1906: p. 112). William Blake, whose own political views were the opposite of Johnson's, described him as 'of the Devil's party', a phrase often used in the later eighteenth century to denote republican supporters of the American and French revolutionaries (Blake 1959: p. 44). Shelley, from a similar perspective, reminded his readers that 'the sacred Milton' had been 'a bold enquirer into morals and religion' (Shelley 1971: p. 206). These are not literary judgements, of course, and there is no mechanical relationship between someone's political views and his opinion of Milton's poetry. But the two are often strongly interconnected, even in critics who would deny the connection and insist on their critical objectivity. Thus the language in which Johnson condemns the pastoral mode of *Lycidas* as 'easy, vulgar and therefore disgusting' betrays a *political* valuation inside the literary one (Milton's poetry, like his politics, subverts the distinction between 'polite' and 'vulgar' discourse), and reveals the deep interweaving not only in Johnson but in neo-classical criticism generally of social and aesthetic values. Or again, when Eliot attacks Milton's poetry as a 'Chinese wall', casting a baleful shadow over later poets from Dryden to Swinburne and cutting off the arterial flow of cultural vitality from the Elizabethans, he is advancing a histor-

13

ical hypothesis and a political position in the guise of a literary judgement: that the death of Charles I, and with him of the last vestiges of feudal authority, ushered in a wasteland of corrupt and 'dissociated' modernity whose portentous symbol is *Paradise Lost*, a poem so dissociated that it has to be read twice, first for the 'sound' and a second time for the 'sense' (Eliot 1957: p. 143).

These two examples are meant to suggest ways in which our literary responses and choices reflect our wider 'theories' about the world, theories that we may not always be fully aware of. These are often quite inconsistent; and some of the most interesting Milton criticism happens when different bits of the theory start banging into each other. This occurred quite a lot in the century or so after Milton's death, when he was becoming institutionalized as 'the sacred Milton', the English Virgil, but before his political activities and opinions had faded safely into history. This provoked some painfully ambivalent responses:

> These sacred lines with wonder we peruse,
> And praise the flights of a seraphic muse,
> Till thy seditious prose provokes our rage,
> And soils the beauties of thy brightest page.
>
> (Thomas Yalden, 1698)

One way out of the dilemma, hinted here, is to *aestheticize* Milton by insisting on a formal distinction not only between poetry and prose but between the poetry (or 'Poesy') and its *content*. So in another poem of this period the old regicide is allowed into Heaven, in spite of his 'studied treason and self-interest stained', simply because he is a poet:

> 'twas verse alone
> Did for my hideous crime atone,
> Defending once the worst rebellion....
> Till Paradise Lost wrought Paradise Regained.
>
> (Alexander Oldys, 1700)

– a sentiment echoed more than two centuries later by Auden, writing of another poet whose life and work evoke sharply contradictory responses:

14

Time that with this strange excuse
Pardoned Kipling and his views,
And will pardon Paul Claudel,
Pardons him for writing well.

('On the death of W. B. Yeats')

Milton's early biographers, Toland and Richardson, had commented on his poetry, naturally enough. But this neo-classical formalism, useful as a tactical manoeuvre to enable people who hated Milton to agree that he was of course a 'great poet', released the first wave of serious Milton criticism, John Dennis's discussion of his 'sublimity', later developed by Burke, and Addison's eighteen *Spectator* essays on *Paradise Lost* (Shawcross 1970: pp. 125–36, 147–220). Johnson stands outside this development, prevented by the integral 'life & letters' format of the *Lives of the Poets* as much as by his own critical temperament from bracketing out the historical and political Milton. The romantic poets and critics, too, insisted that Milton's republican and libertarian principles were intrinsic to his poetry; and the discovery in 1823 of the theological treatise *De Doctrina Christiana* gave Macaulay a chance to reassert the inseparability of poetry and prose, writer and work:

> Nor do we envy the man who can study either the life or the writings of the great poet and patriot without aspiring to emulate, not indeed the sublime works with which his genius has enriched our literature, but the zeal with which he laboured for the public good, the fortitude with which he endured every private calamity, the lofty disdain with which he looked down on temptations and dangers, the deadly hatred which he bore to bigots and tyrants, and the faith which he so sternly kept with his country and with his fame.
>
> (Macaulay 1901: p. 56)

Macaulay's essay offers a Milton part Whig saint, part Carlylean hero. Bombastic and inaccurate though it is, it represents none the less an important counter-tradition of Milton criticism, a tradition extending in our day to the pioneering work of the Marxist Christopher Hill, significantly, like

Macaulay, a historian rather than a literary critic. But the dominant literary-critical consensus has remained, since the eighteenth century, unhistorical and formalist. Leavis, who thought it 'deplorable' that students of literature should 'devote any large part of their time to solemn study of Milton's "thought"' (Leavis 1962: p. 23), ignored his ideas and concentrated the attack on his *style*; and Christopher Ricks's answering defence of *Milton's Grand Style* (1963) remains, as its title suggests, largely within the chosen ground, not challenging the essential premise (Ricks is far more formalistic in this respect than his mentor William Empson) that a writer's language can be treated as a disembodied, free-floating entity, devoid of context and innocent of history.

That quarrel is history itself, now. But the issues have not gone away, and are not likely to. The great bulk of Milton criticism continues to turn its face from history (except, in a narrow sense, literary history), and his 'thought' remains as little studied on literature courses as Leavis would have wished. Whatever view we take of this, it should be remembered that the neo-classical and formalist separation of 'style' from 'content', literature from practical life (as expressed in Auden's disillusioned maxim 'Poetry makes nothing happen'), stands in sharp contrast to the position of Milton himself, who from an early age was 'confirmed in this opinion, that he who would not be frustrate of his hope to write well hereafter in laudable things ought himself to be a true poem, that is, a composition and pattern of the best and honourablest things' (Yale: I, p. 890), and who never ceased, even under censorship, repression, and defeat, to think of writing as a mode of action in the public and political world.

Milton was a millenarian. That is, he believed that the Christian era would culminate in a great confrontation between good and evil in which the forces of Antichrist would be routed, Christ would return in judgement, and the Saints – the redeemed People of God – would live for a thousand years under the beneficent monarchy of Christ (King Jesus, as the Fifth Monarchists called him), until at last space, time, the physical universe would all pass away, to be replaced by the eternal kingdom of God. These beliefs, derived from a number

16

of cryptic passages in the prophetic Book of Daniel, the gospels, and the Book of Revelation, have been widespread among Christians of all kinds from the early church down to the present day. But for Milton and his contemporaries in the 1630s and 1640s they had a special urgency and relevance, when like many other people he was convinced not only that the Last Judgement was imminent but that the English were the chosen people of God (the Jews having fallen out of favour after the crucifixion), and that the New Jerusalem of the Saints would be built, as another millenarian poet was to put it a century and a half later, 'in England's green and pleasant land' (Blake 1959: pp. 109–10).

It is never easy to know what we mean when we say that people 'believed' something like this. For some fundamentalists, the biblical prophecies are literally true, and have only to be correctly interpreted to yield the exact time and place of the Last Judgement. Many sectaries, though, understood them as largely metaphorical, as symbols of their own activism and conversion, like Winstanley's 'Christ rising in sons and daughters' (Hill 1975: pp. 142–50). Milton probably read the apocalyptic texts in a more allegorical and 'literary' way (he thought of the Book of Revelation classically, as 'the majestic image of a high and stately tragedy', with a sevenfold structure of scenes and choruses); but in 1641 he looked forward confidently to the day when Christ, 'the eternal and shortly expected King', would 'put an end to all earthly tyrannies, proclaiming [his] universal and mild monarchy through heaven and earth'.

Many members of the Parliament that met in November 1640 shared these millenarian hopes, either literally or as a metaphor for divinely guided social change and personal regeneration; and the speed of events, as the political pressures and frustrations of the Laudian interlude broke surface in a great eruption of pamphlets, petitions, and remonstrances, must have seemed to substantiate them even before the first skirmishings of Armageddon at Edgehill two years later. As the historian Lawrence Stone has remarked, 'the outbreak of the war itself is relatively easy to explain; what is hard is to puzzle out why most of the established institutions of State and Church – Crown, Court, central administration, army, and

episcopacy – collapsed so ignominiously two years before'
(Stone 1972: p. 48). Within a week of the first sitting of the
new Parliament, Prynne, Bastwick, and Burton were out of
jail. Before the end of December their arch-enemy Laud was
under arrest, charged with treason, and by the time *Of Reformation* was on the bookstalls in May 1641 he was in the Tower of
London. With him there was the Earl of Strafford, the King's
closest adviser; and on 12 May, when Strafford was led to
execution in front of an angry crowd, Charles was powerless to
help him. In July thirteen of Laud's bishops were impeached,
and the courts of Star Chamber and High Commission, twin
pillars of royal-episcopal absolutism, were abolished. In
November Parliament presented the king with the Grand Remonstrance, a summary in 206 articles of the grievances against
him. Instead of trying to negotiate, Charles, who seems actually to have believed the Tudor nonsense about divine right and
the quasi-feudal fiction of a doting and obsequious populace,
tried to re-establish his dwindling authority by coming in person to the Commons to arrest five of the leading members.
Rebuffed by the Speaker, he left London for the north, hoping
to raise support and get his hands on the arsenal at Hull.
Parliament responded by seizing control of the local militias,
and in September, less than two years after the first sitting, a
parliamentary army set out towards Nottingham, where the
king had raised his standard as a formal declaration of war.
From this moment until 1660, when the Restoration drove him
into retirement, Milton's writings are a direct commentary on
the progress of the revolution, the unfolding 'reforming of
Reformation'; and every question, public or private, is viewed
in its relation to the national struggle. Education, he tells
Samuel Hartlib, is 'one of the greatest and noblest designs ...
for the want whereof this nation perishes' (Yale: II, p. 363).
Parliament, harassed in the early years of the war by royalist
propaganda, must refuse the temptation to introduce censorship lest it also 'suppress all this flowery crop of knowledge
and new light sprung up and yet springing daily in this city'
(see p. 103, l. 722). When the Presbyterians in the Westminster
Assembly threaten their own version of episcopal hierarchy, or
their allies in Parliament seek to reverse the fierce logic of the

18

revolutionary process they themselves set in motion, waverers must be urged 'not to startle from the just and pious resolution of adhering with all their strength and assistance to the present Parliament and Army in the glorious way wherein Justice and Victory hath set them' (see Yale, III, 194). Progressively disillusioned first with the Presbyterian dissidents he had supported in 1641–2, then with the Long Parliament whose 'valorous and happy counsels' he had praised in 1644, then with the Council of State whose overseas correspondence he handled in the 1650s as Latin Secretary, and perhaps finally with the English people themselves whose defence in 1652–4 procured him a European reputation and (some said) cost him his sight, Milton's texts retain an apocalyptic register but retreat steadily from the wide-ranging readership and millennial certainties of the early 1640s. Even before Cromwell's death in 1658, the revolution of the Saints had lost its way in a wilderness of disunity, constitutional improvisation, and political crisis; and by 1660, as God's Englishmen seem bent on 'choosing them a captain back for Egypt', the active constituency of his discourse has dwindled from people to Parliament to Rump to Council to a handful of armchair republicans in a London coffee-house; even, in a final despairing trope, to 'trees and stones ... the very soil itself' (p. 147, l. 353).

What keeps someone writing, when everything they have written for seems lost and nobody is even listening any longer? It is a stupid question, of course. 'Milton produced *Paradise Lost* for the same reason that a silkworm produces silk', wrote Marx. 'It was an activity of his nature.'[4] There is an obsessed quality in much of his work, a sense of the writer himself being written by compulsions outside his conscious control: Milton called it his 'heavenly muse', the inbreathing of the holy spirit. In any case, there are many reasons for writing, and worldly success, or fame, 'that last infirmity of noble mind', is only one of them. But it is true, too, that what sustains Milton's writings through personal disaster and the utter collapse of public hopes is his *idealism*. This word is often used loosely of people motivated by noble but perhaps impractical notions. With Milton it is more exact: like Plato, with whom he is always having a sort of private argument, he believed in the absolute priority of *ideas* over *things*, not just in people's minds but in the structure of society, indeed of reality. "Tis not the common law, nor the civil, but piety and justice that are our foundresses', he wrote in *Of Reformation*; and it is the abstractions like justice and piety that have substance and body in Milton's discourse (in the passage quoted, 'where ever they meet, [they] kiss each other') rather than their concrete embodiments like common or civil law. This deeply Platonic attitude – especially when it is combined with a kind of Christian stoicism, a providential theory of history and a strong sense of individual integrity – means that even when everything in the world is going against you, 'on evil days though fall'n and evil tongues,/In darkness, and with dangers compass'd round' (*Paradise Lost*, VII, 25–6), you can still sustain yourself with the unchanging power and purity of the Idea. Even an argument as topical and concrete in intention as *The Ready and Easy Way* reverts constantly to Platonic idealizations of justice and liberty, as his enemies were quick to point out:

> You trade altogether in universals, the region of deceits and fallacy, but never come so near particulars as to let us know which among diverse things of the same kind you would be at. For you admire commonwealths in general, and cry down kingship as much at large.
>
> (Shawcross 1970: p. 72)

This is the voice of English pragmatism, suspicious of theories and ideologies, preferring in its sensible, businesslike, slightly complacent way to deal with concrete 'particulars'. But pragmatism, for all its disclaimers, is a 'theory' too, rooted in history and imbued with ideology, the voice not of some immutable common sense but of identifiable interests and views of the world.

In 1660 it was the voice of the future, of the bourgeois politicians, financiers, and civil servants who constructed around the newly returned Charles II a framework of 'checks and balances' that ensured that he would never succumb to his father's delusions of absolutist grandeur, and who, when his stupider brother did succumb to them in 1688, promptly removed him and hired themselves a constitutional monarch closer to their style. And it is still to be heard, almost three centuries later, in Leavis's assertion that Milton's language 'calls pervasively for a kind of attention, compels an attitude towards itself, that is incompatible with sharp, concrete realisation'.

Of course Leavis's is not the last word on Milton, as we have seen; and his claim to have 'dislodged' him now looks rather silly, though it has to be admitted that the rediscovery of Milton's importance and originality in the last fifty years has been accompanied by a good deal of 'scholarship' of a kind that both he and Leavis would have had little time for. Nor do I mean to suggest that Milton's idealism must always be accepted at its own lofty valuation. On the contrary, as David Aers and Gunther Kress have shown, it closely reflects both the confident independence and the damaging ignorance of social and economic realities of a middle-class intellectual on a private income (Aers, Hodge, Kress 1981: pp. 152–83). But the relationship between theory and practice, universals and particulars, in poetry or in politics, remains a problem as it was when he wrote. My own view – for which I claim no originality at all – is that Milton was wrong: that it is not ideas that make revolutions in the life of nations or of individuals, but people's material needs and circumstances, Captain Poverty and his cousin Necessity; though ideas, like literature, may perform an important function in articulating those needs and circumstances. But he lived through the 'highest of times', and played a part in them; and his writings give us images and narratives and arguments with which to understand those times, as well, perhaps, as our own.

A NOTE ON THE TEXTS

The order of the texts in this selection follows the order of first publication, with the exception of half a dozen sonnets (pp. 125, 126, 136, and 137) not printed until 1673 or later, but which belong very clearly to an earlier date and would suffer by being taken out of sequence (I'm not assuming here a linear process of development in a writer's work – a questionable concept – but the importance of a particular historical and

21

contextual moment for certain highly topical poems). On the same principle, I have followed the first printed text, only adopting later revisions where they correct an obvious mistake. Other variant readings of any significance will be found in the notes.

Spelling and punctuation have been modernized. This is a hazardous undertaking, particularly since Milton, unlike most of his contemporaries, took a close interest in both and worked out his own practice, based on a rationalized, partly phonetic spelling system and a subtle and flexible use of punctuation marks, especially the colon and semicolon. But to retain either his spelling or his punctuation, in an edition not intended primarily for textual scholars, in the name of some supposed 'authenticity' would be quite misguided. Milton's spelling aims at rationality and modernity, in his own terms, not at the antiquarian quaintness it inevitably suggests to most readers nowadays; and his punctuation, even when it is not 'prosodic' (that is, pointing up the metrical structure and rhythm of the verse rather than articulating the sense), is based on rhetorical conventions entirely different from those underlying modern punctuation. On the other hand, punctuation, in particular, remains integral not only to the shape and rhythm of Milton's sentences but to their actual meaning as well; so I have tried to alter it as little as possible. (It is feasible, by the way, to talk about 'Milton's spelling and punctuation' in a way that would make little sense with Shakespeare or Donne, because it seems likely that he supervised the actual printing of his writings, even after he became blind, much more closely than most seventeenth-century authors did.)

In one instance only is a Miltonic convention retained, and that only in the poetry, where it matters for the metre: the elided 'e' in past participle endings where no extra syllable is to be voiced. *Comus*, 1. 47, is an example: 'Crush'd the sweet poison of misused wine', where 'crush'd' is one syllable, 'misused' (read *misuséd*) three. It follows that in the poems, wherever the '-ed' ending of a participle or participial adjective is written out, it should be voiced as a syllable.

The most accessible modern editions of all Milton's verse are those by Alistair Fowler (*Paradise Lost*) and John Carey (*Complete Shorter Poems*) published by Longmans (1971, two volumes in paperback, one in hardback), and by A. B. Wright and Gordon Campbell (Dent, 1980, one volume). The standard modern edition of the prose writings is the monumental Yale University Press *Complete Prose Works*, whose commentaries and notes are a major work of historical reference in their own right. This is beyond the reach of ordinary readers and students, in sheer bulk as well as cost; but Merritt Y. Hughes, one of the Yale editors, has produced a *Prose Selections* (1947), and there are selections from the prose works in the Everyman (Dent) and World's Classics (OUP) series.

NOTES TO THE INTRODUCTION

1 'Dialogical' is a word coined by Bakhtin (see Bakhtin (1973) *Problems of Dostoyevsky's Poetics*, translated by R. W. Rotsel, New York) to describe texts which present not a single consistent point of view but a plurality of 'voices' and perspectives. For him it specifically distinguishes the novel from other genres, from poetry in particular, so he probably would not have approved of its application to Milton's poetry.

2 I take the term 'intertextuality' from the French literary theorist Julia Kristeva (see Kristeva (1969) *Semiotike*, Paris). Developing Bakhtin's notion of 'dialogue', she argues that the meaning of literary texts is generated by their interrelationship with other texts: 'every text is constructed of a mosaic of citations, every text is an absorption and transformation of other texts'.

3 The two men, the last to be put to death for heresy in England, were Bartholomew Legate and Edward Wightman. 'Mortalism' is the belief that the soul is inseparable from the body and dies with it. 'Arianism' is the denial of the 'co-essentiality' or complete identity of the first two persons of the trinity, Father and Son.

4 Karl Marx (1975) *Theories of Surplus Value*, Moscow, p. 401.

JOHN MILTON

Selected Shorter Poems and Prose Writings

AN EPITAPH ON THE ADMIRABLE
DRAMATIC POET, W. SHAKESPEARE

What need my Shakespeare for his honour'd bones
The labour of an age in piled stones,
Or that his hallow'd relics should be hid
Under a star-ypointing pyramid?
Dear son of Memory, great heir of Fame,
What need'st thou such dull witness of thy name?
Thou in our wonder and astonishment
Hast built thyself a lasting monument.
For whilst to the shame of slow-endeavouring art
Thy easy numbers flow, and that each part   10
Hath from the leaves of thy unvalu'd book
Those Delphic lines with deep impression took,
Then thou, our fancy of herself bereaving,
Dost make us marble with too much conceiving,
And so sepulchred in such pomp dost lie
That kings for such a tomb would wish to die.

First published 1632

A MASQUE PRESENTED AT LUDLOW CASTLE, 1634

The Persons

The Attendant Spirit afterwards in the habit of Thyrsis.
Comus with his crew.
The Lady.
First Brother.
Second Brother.
Sabrina the Nymph.

The chief persons which presented were

The Lord Brackley,
Mr Thomas Egerton, his brother,
The Lady Alice Egerton.

★ *Numbers in square brackets refer to pages on which notes may be found.*

The first scene discovers a wild wood.
The Attendant Spirit descends or enters.

Before the starry threshold of Jove's court
My mansion is, where those immortal shapes
Of bright aërial Spirits live inspher'd
In regions mild of calm and serene air,
Above the smoke and stir of this dim spot
Which men call Earth, and with low-thoughted care
Confin'd and pester'd in this pinfold here,
Strive to keep up a frail and feverish being,
Unmindful of the crown that Virtue gives
After this mortal change to her true servants   10
Amongst th'enthroned gods on sainted seats.
Yet some there be that by due steps aspire
To lay their just hands on that golden key
That opes the Palace of Eternity.
To such my errand is, and but for such
I would not soil these pure ambrosial weeds
With the rank vapours of this sin-worn mould.
  But to my task. Neptune, besides the sway
Of every salt flood and each ebbing stream,
Took in by lot, 'twixt high and nether Jove,   20
Imperial rule of all the sea-girt isles
That like to rich and various gems inlay
The unadorned bosom of the deep,
Which he, to grace his tributary gods,
By course commits to several government,
And gives them leave to wear their sapphire crowns
And wield their little tridents; but this isle,
The greatest and the best of all the main,
He quarters to his blue-hair'd deities.
And all this tract that fronts the falling sun   30
A noble peer of mickle trust and power
Has in his charge, with temper'd awe to guide
An old and haughty nation proud in arms;
Where his fair offspring, nurs'd in princely lore,
Are coming to attend their father's state
And new-entrusted sceptre, but their way

28

Lies through the perplex'd paths of this drear wood,
The nodding horror of whose shady brows
Threats the forlorn and wandering passenger.
And here their tender age might suffer peril,   40
But that by quick command from sovereign Jove
I was despatch'd for their defence and guard;
And listen why, for I will tell ye now
What never yet was heard in tale or song
From old or modern bard in hall or bower.
   Bacchus, that first from out the purple grape
Crush'd the sweet poison of misused wine,
After the Tuscan mariners transform'd,
Coasting the Tyrrhene shore as the winds listed
On Circe's island fell (who knows not Circe,   50
The daughter of the Sun, whose charmed cup
Whoever tasted lost his upright shape,
And downward fell into a grovelling swine?).
This nymph, that gaz'd upon his clustering locks
With ivy berries wreath'd, and his blithe youth,
Had by him ere he parted thence a son,
Much like his father, but his mother more,
Whom therefore she brought up and Comus nam'd;
Who ripe, and frolic of his full-grown age,
Roving the Celtic and Iberian fields,   60
At last betakes him to this ominous wood,
And in thick shelter of black shades imbower'd
Excels his mother at her mighty art,
Offering to every weary traveller
His orient liquor in a crystal glass
To quench the drouth of Phoebus, which as they taste
(For most do taste through fond intemperate thirst)
Soon as the potion works, their human count'nance,
Th'express resemblance of the gods, is chang'd
Into some brutish form of wolf or bear,   70
Or ounce, or tiger, hog, or bearded goat,
All other parts remaining as they were;
And they, so perfect is their misery,
Not once perceive their foul disfigurement,
But boast themselves more comely than before,

29

And all their friends and native home forget,
To roll with pleasure in a sensual sty.
Therefore when any favour'd of high Jove
Chances to pass through this adventurous glade,
Swift as the sparkle of a glancing star   80
I shoot from Heav'n to give him safe convoy,
As now I do; but first I must put off
These my sky robes spun out of Iris' woof,
And take the weeds and likeness of a swain
That to the service of this house belongs,
Who with his soft pipe and smooth-dittied song
Well knows to still the wild winds when they roar,
And hush the waving woods, nor of less faith,
And in this office of his mountain watch
Likeliest and nearest to the present aid   90
Of this occasion. But I hear the tread
Of hateful steps. I must be viewless now.

> *Comus enters with a charming-rod in one
> hand, his glass in the other. With him a rout
> of monsters headed like sundry sorts of wild
> beasts, but otherwise like men and women,
> their apparel glistering; they come in making
> a riotous and unruly noise, with torches in
> their hands.*

Comus.   The star that bids the shepherd fold
          Now the top of Heav'n doth hold,
          And the gilded car of day
          His glowing axle doth allay
          In the steep Atlantic stream,
          And the slope sun his upward beam
          Shoots against the dusky pole,
          Pacing toward the other goal   100
          Of his chamber in the east.
          Meanwhile welcome joy, and feast,
          Midnight shout, and revelry,
          Tipsy dance, and jollity.
          Braid your locks with rosy twine,

30

Dropping odour, dropping wine.
Rigour now is gone to bed,
And Advice with scrupulous head,
Strict Age, and sour Severity,
With their grave saws, in slumber lie.   110
We that are of purer fire
Imitate the starry choir,
Who in their nightly watchful spheres
Lead in swift round the months and years.
The sounds and seas with all their finny drove
Now to the moon in wavering morris move,
And on the tawny sands and shelves
Trip the pert fairies and the dapper elves.
By dimpled brook and fountain brim
The wood-nymphs, deck'd with daisies trim,   120
Their merry wakes and pastimes keep.
What hath night to do with sleep?
Night hath better sweets to prove:
Venus now wakes, and wakens Love.
Come, let us our rites begin;
'Tis only daylight that makes sin,
Which these dun shades will ne'er report.
Hail Goddess of nocturnal sport,
Dark veil'd Cotytto, t'whom the secret flame
Of midnight torches burns; mysterious dame,   130
That ne'er art call'd but when the dragon womb
Of Stygian darkness spits her thickest gloom
And makes one blot of all the air,
Stay thy cloudy ebon chair
Wherein thou rid'st with Hecat, and befriend
Us, thy vow'd priests, till utmost end
Of all thy dues be done, and none left out,
Ere the blabbing eastern scout,
The nice Morn on th'Indian steep,
From her cabin'd loophole peep   140
And to the telltale Sun descry
Our conceal'd solemnity.
Come, knit hands and beat the ground
In a light fantastic round.

The Measure.

Break off, break off! I feel the different pace
Of some chaste footing near about this ground.
Run to your shrouds within these brakes and trees:
Our number may affright. Some virgin sure
(For so I can distinguish by mine art)
Benighted in these woods. Now to my charms   150
And to my wily trains; I shall ere long
Be well stock'd with as fair a herd as graz'd
About my mother Circe. Thus I hurl
My dazzling spells into the spongy air,
Of power to cheat the eye with blear illusion
And give it false presentments, lest the place
And my quaint habits breed astonishment
And put the damsel to suspicious flight,
Which must not be, for that's against my course.
I under fair pretence of friendly ends   160
And well-plac'd words of glozing courtesy
Baited with reasons not unplausible
Wind me into the easy-hearted man
And hug him into snares. When once her eye
Hath met the virtue of this magic dust,
I shall appear some harmless villager
Whom thrift keeps up about his country gear.
But here she comes: I fairly step aside
And hearken, if I may, her business here.

The Lady enters.

Lady.   This way the noise was, if mine ear be true,   170
My best guide now. Methought it was the sound
Of riot and ill-manag'd merriment,
Such as the jocund flute or gamesome pipe
Stirs up among the loose unletter'd hinds
When for their teeming flocks and granges full
In wanton dance they praise the bounteous Pan
And thank the gods amiss. I should be loth
To meet the rudeness and swill'd insolence
Of such late wassailers; yet O where else

Shall I inform my unacquainted feet   180
In the blind mazes of this tangled wood?
My brothers, when they saw me wearied out
With this long way resolving here to lodge
Under the spreading favour of these pines,
Stepp'd, as they said, to the next thicket side
To bring me berries, or such cooling fruit
As the kind hospitable woods provide.
They let me then, when the grey-hooded Ev'n
Like a sad votarist in palmer's weed
Rose from the hindmost wheels of Phoebus' wain.   190
But where they are, and why they came not back,
Is now the labour of my thoughts. 'Tis likeliest
They had engag'd their wandering steps too far,
And envious darkness, ere they could return,
Had stole them from me. Else, O thievish night,
Why shouldst thou, but for some felonious end,
In thy dark lantern thus close up the stars
That nature hung in Heav'n, and fill'd their lamps
With everlasting oil, to give due light
To the misled and lonely traveller?   200
This is the place, as well as I may guess,
Whence even now the tumult of loud mirth
Was rife and perfect in my listening ear,
Yet nought but single darkness do I find.
What might this be? A thousand fantasies
Begin to throng into my memory
Of calling shapes and beckoning shadows dire,
And airy tongues that syllable men's names
On sands and shores and desert wildernesses.
These thoughts may startle well, but not astound   210
The virtuous mind that ever walks attended
By a strong siding champion Conscience....
O welcome pure-eyed Faith, white-handed Hope,
Thou flittering Angel girt with golden wings,
And thou unblemish'd form of Chastity.
I see ye visibly, and now believe
That he, the Supreme Good, t'whom all things ill
Are but as slavish officers of vengeance,

Would send a glistering Guardian if need were
To keep my life and honour unassail'd.   220
Was I deceiv'd, or did a sable cloud
Turn forth her silver lining on the night?
I did not err, there does a sable cloud
Turn forth her silver lining on the night,
And casts a gleam over this tufted grove.
I cannot hallo to my brothers, but
Such noise as I can make to be heard farthest
I'll venture; for my new-enliven'd spirits
Prompt me, and they perhaps are not far off.

Song

Sweet Echo, sweetest nymph that liv'st unseen   230
  Within thy airy shell
  By slow Meander's margent green,
And in the violet-embroider'd vale
  Where the lovelorn nightingale
Nightly to thee her sad song mourneth well,
Canst thou not tell me of a gentle pair
  That likest thy Narcissus are?
  O if thou have
Hid them in some flowery cave,
  Tell me but where,   240
  Sweet queen of parley, daughter of the sphere.
  So may'st thou be translated to the skies,
And give resounding grace to all Heav'n's harmonies.

Comus. Can any mortal mixture of Earth's mould
Breathe such divine enchanting ravishment?
Sure something holy lodges in that breast,
And with these raptures moves the vocal air
To testify his hidden residence.
How sweetly did they float upon the wings
Of silence through the empty-vaulted night,   250
At every fall smoothing the raven down
Of Darkness till she smil'd. I oft have heard
My mother Circe with the Sirens three

Amidst the flowery-kirtl'd Naiades
Culling their potent herbs and baleful drugs,
Who as they sung would take the prison'd soul
And lap it in Elysium; Scylla wept,
And chid her barking waves into attention,
And fell Charybdis murmur'd soft applause.
Yet they in pleasing slumber lull'd the sense,   260
And in sweet madness robb'd it of its self;
But such a sacred and home-felt delight,
Such sober certainty of waking bliss,
I never heard till now. I'll speak to her,
And she shall be my Queen. Hail, foreign wonder,
Whom certain these rough shades did never breed,
Unless the Goddess that in rural shrine
Dwell'st here with Pan or Sylvan, by blest song
Forbidding every bleak unkindly fog
To touch the prosperous growth of this tall wood.   270
Lady.   Nay, gentle shepherd, ill is lost that praise
That is address'd to unattending ears.
Not any boast of skill, but extreme shift
How to regain my sever'd company,
Compell'd me to awake the courteous Echo
To give me answer from her mossy couch.
Comus.   What chance, good lady, hath bereft you thus?
Lady.   Dim darkness, and this heavy labyrinth.
Comus.   Could that divide you from near-ushering guides?
Lady.   They left me weary on a grassy turf.   280
Comus.   By falsehood, or discourtesy, or why?
Lady.   To seek i'the valley some cool friendly spring.
Comus.   And left your fair side all unguarded, lady?
Lady.   They were but twain, and purpos'd quick return.
Comus.   Perhaps forestalling night prevented them.
Lady.   How easy my misfortune is to hit!
Comus.   Imports their loss, beside the present need?
Lady.   No less than if I should my brothers lose.
Comus.   Were they of manly prime, or youthful bloom?
Lady.   As smooth as Hebe's their unrazor'd lips.   290
Comus.   Two such I saw, what time the labour'd ox
In his loose traces from the furrow came,

35

And the swink'd hedger at his supper sat.
I saw them under a green mantling vine
That crawls along the side of yon small hill,
Plucking ripe clusters from the tender shoots.
Their port was more than human as they stood;
I took it for a faery vision
Of some gay creatures of the element
That in the colours of the rainbow live   300
And play i'the plighted clouds. I was awe-struck,
And as I pass'd I worshipp'd. If those you seek,
It were a journey like the path to Heav'n
To help you find them.
Lady.   Gentle villager,
     What readiest way would bring me to that place?
Comus.   Due west it rises from this shrubby point.
Lady.   To find out that, good shepherd, I suppose,
     In such a scant allowance of starlight,
     Would overtask the best land-pilot's art,
     Without the sure guess of well-practis'd feet.   310
Comus.   I know each lane, and every alley green,
     Dingle or bushy dell of this wild wood,
     And every bosky bourn from side to side
     My daily walks and ancient neighbourhood;
     And if your stray attendance be yet lodg'd
     Or shroud within these limits, I shall know
     Ere morrow wake or the low roosted lark
     From her thatch'd pallet rouse. If otherwise,
     I can conduct you, lady, to a low
     But loyal cottage, where you may be safe   320
     Till further quest.
Lady.   Shepherd, I take thy word,
     And trust thy honest offer'd courtesy,
     Which oft is sooner found in lowly sheds
     With smoky rafters than in tap'stry halls
     And courts of Princes, where it first was nam'd
     And yet is most pretended. In a place
     Less warranted than this or less secure
     I cannot be, that I should fear to change it.
     Eye me, bless'd Providence, and square my trial
     To my proportion'd strength. Shepherd, lead on.   330

36

The two brothers.

Elder Brother.   Unmuffle, ye faint stars, and thou fair moon,
    That wont'st to love the traveller's benison,
    Stoop thy pale visage through an amber cloud
    And disinherit Chaos, that reigns here
    In double night of darkness and of shades.
    Or if your influence be quite damm'd up
    With black usurping mists, some gentle taper,
    Though a rush candle from the wicker hole
    Of some clay habitation, visit us
    With thy long levell'd rule of streaming light,   340
    And thou shall be our star of Arcady
    Or Tyrian Cynosure.
Second Brother.   Or if our eyes
    Be barr'd that happiness, might we but hear
    The folded flocks penn'd in their wattled cotes,
    Or sound of pastoral reed with oaten stops,
    Or whistle from the lodge, or village cock
    Count the night watches to his feathery dames,
    'Twould be some solace yet, some little cheering
    In this close dungeon of innumerous boughs.
    But O that hapless virgin, our lost sister,   350
    Where may she wander now, whither betake her
    From the chill dew, amongst rude burrs and thistles?
    Perhaps some cold bank is her bolster now,
    Or 'gainst the rugged bark of some broad elm
    Leans her unpillow'd head fraught with sad fears.
    What if in wild amazement and affright,
    Or while we speak within the direful grasp
    Of savage hunger or of savage heat?
Eld. Bro.   Peace, brother, be not over-exquisite
    To cast the fashion of uncertain evils;   360
    For grant they be so, while they rest unknown
    What need a man forestall his date of grief
    And run to meet what he would most avoid?
    Or if they be but false alarms of fear,
    How bitter is such self-delusion!
    I do not think my sister so to seek,
    Or so unprincipl'd in virtue's book

And the sweet peace that goodness bosoms ever,
As that the single want of light and noise
(Not being in danger, as I trust she is not)   370
Could stir the constant mood of her calm thoughts
And put them into misbecoming plight.
Virtue could see to do what virtue would
By her own radiant light, though sun and moon
Were in the flat sea sunk. And wisdom's self
Oft seeks to sweet retired solitude,
Where with her best nurse, contemplation,
She plumes her feathers, and lets grow her wings
That in the various bustle of resort
Were all to-ruffl'd and sometimes impair'd.   380
He that has light within his own clear breast
May sit i'the centre and enjoy bright day;
But he that hides a dark soul and foul thoughts
Benighted walks under the midday sun.
Himself is his own dungeon.
Sec. Bro.   'Tis most true
That musing meditation most affects
The pensive secrecy of desert cell,
Far from the cheerful haunt of men and herds,
And sits as safe as in a senate house.
For who would rob a hermit of his weeds,   390
His few books, or his beads or maple dish,
Or do his grey hairs any violence?
But beauty, like the fair Hesperian tree
Laden with blooming gold, had need the guard
Of dragon watch with unenchanted eye
To save her blossoms and defend her fruit
From the rash hand of bold incontinence.
You may as well spread out the unsunn'd heaps
Of miser's treasure by an outlaw's den,
And tell me it is safe, as bid me hope   400
Danger will wink on opportunity
And let a single helpless maiden pass
Uninjur'd in this wild surrounding waste.
Of night, or loneliness, it recks me not:
I fear the dread events that dog them both,

38

Lest some ill-greeting touch attempt the person
Of our unowned sister.

Eld. Bro.   I do not, brother,
Infer as if I thought my sister's state
Secure without all doubt or controversy;
Yet where an equal poise of hope and fear   410
Does arbitrate th'event, my nature is
That I incline to hope rather than fear,
And gladly banish squint suspicion.
My sister is not so defenceless left
As you imagine: she has a hidden strength
Which you remember not.

Sec. Bro.   What hidden strength,
Unless the strength of Heav'n, if you mean that?

Eld. Bro. I mean that too, but yet a hidden strength
Which, if Heav'n gave it, may be term'd her own.
'Tis chastity, my brother, chastity: 420
She that has that is clad in complete steel,
And like a quiver'd nymph with arrows keen
May trace huge forests and unharbour'd heaths,
Infamous hills and sandy perilous wilds,
Where through the sacred rays of chastity
No savage fierce, bandit or mountaineer
Will dare to soil her virgin purity.
Yea, there where very desolation dwells,
By grots and caverns shagg'd with horrid shades,
She may pass on with unblench'd majesty,   430
Be it not done in pride or in presumption.
Some say no evil thing that walks by night
In fog or fire, by lake or moorish fen,
Blue meagre hag, or stubborn unlaid ghost
That breaks his magic chains at curfew time,
No goblin, or swart fairy of the mine
Hath hurtful power o'er true virginity.
Do ye believe me yet, or shall I call
Antiquity from the old schools of Greece
To testify the arms of chastity?   440
Hence had the huntress Dian her dread bow,
Fair silver-shafted Queen for ever chaste,

Wherewith she tam'd the brinded lioness
And spotted mountain pard, but set at nought
The frivolous bolt of Cupid. Gods and men
Fear'd her stern frown, and she was Queen o'th'Woods.
What was that snaky-headed Gorgon shield
That wise Minerva wore, unconquer'd virgin,
Wherewith she freez'd her foes to congeal'd stone,
But rigid looks of chaste austerity,   450
And noble grace that dash'd brute violence
With sudden adoration and blank awe?
So dear to Heav'n is saintly chastity
That when a soul is found sincerely so
A thousand liveried Angels lackey her,
Driving far off each thing of sin and guilt,
And in clear dream and solemn vision
Tell her of things that no gross ear can hear,
Till oft converse with heav'nly habitants
Begin to cast a beam on th'outward shape,   460
The unpolluted temple of the mind,
And turns it by degrees to the soul's essence,
Till all be made immortal. But when lust
By unchaste looks, loose gestures and foul talk,
But most by lewd and lavish act of sin,
Lets in defilement to the inward parts,
The soul grows clotted by contagion,
Imbodies, and imbrutes, till she quite lose
The divine property of her first being.
Such are those thick and gloomy shadows damp   470
Oft seen in charnel vaults and sepulchers
Hovering and sitting by a new-made grave,
As loth to leave the body that it lov'd,
And link'd itself by carnal sensualty
To a degenerate and degraded state.
Sec. Bro.   How charming is divine philosophy!
Not harsh and crabbed, as dull fools suppose,
But musical as is Apollo's lute,
And a perpetual feast of nectar'd sweets
Where no crude surfeit reigns.
Eld. Bro.   List, list: I hear   480
Some far-off hallo break the silent air.

40

Sec. Bro. Me thought so too. What should it be?
Eld. Bro.   For certain

Either someone like us night-founder'd here
Or else some neighbour woodman, or at worst
Some roving robber calling to his fellows.

Sec. Bro. Heav'n keep my sister. Again, again, and near.
Best draw and stand upon your guard.

Eld. Bro.   I'll hallo.

If he be friendly he comes well; if not,
Defence is a good cause, and Heav'n be for us.

The Attendant Spirit, habited like a shepherd.

That hallo I should know. What are you? Speak.   490
Come not too near, you fall on iron stakes else.

Spirit. What voice is that? My young lord? Speak again.

Sec. Bro. O brother, 'tis my father's shepherd sure.

Eld. Bro. Thyrsis? Whose artful strains have oft delayed
The huddling brook to hear his madrigal
And sweeten'd every musk-rose of the dale?
How cam'st thou here, good swain? Hath any ram
Slipp'd from the fold, or young kid lost his dam,
Or straggling wether the penn'd flock forsook?
How couldst thou find this dark sequester'd nook?   500

Spirit. O my lov'd master's heir, and his next joy,
I came not here on such a trivial toy
As a stray'd ewe, or to pursue the stealth
Of pilfering wolf. Not all the fleecy wealth
That doth enrich these downs is worth a thought
To this my errand, and the care it brought.
But O my virgin lady, where is she?
How chance she is not in your company?

Eld. Bro. To tell thee sadly, shepherd, without blame
Or our neglect, we lost her as we came.   510

Spirit. Ay me unhappy then, my fears are true.

Eld. Bro. What fears, good Thyrsis? Prithee briefly show.

Spirit. I'll tell ye. 'Tis not vain or fabulous
(Though so esteem'd by shallow ignorance)
What the sage poets taught by th'heav'nly Muse
Storied of old in high immortal verse,
Of dire Chimeras and enchanted isles,

41

And rifted rocks whose entrance leads to Hell;
For such there be, but unbelief is blind.
Within the navel of this hideous wood,   520
Immur'd in cypress shades, a sorcerer dwells,
Of Bacchus and of Circe born, great Comus,
Deep-skill'd in all his mother's witcheries;
And here to every thirsty wanderer
By sly enticement gives his baneful cup
With many murmurs mix'd, whose pleasing poison
The visage quite transforms of him that drinks
And the inglorious likeness of a beast
Fixes instead, unmoulding reason's mintage
Character'd in the face. This I have learnt   530
Tending my flocks hard by i'the hilly crofts
That brow this bottom glade, whence night by night
He and his monstrous rout are heard to howl
Like stabled wolves or tigers at their prey,
Doing abhorred rites to Hecate
In their obscured haunts of inmost bowers.
Yet have they many baits and guileful spells
To inveigle and invite th'unwary sense
Of them that pass unweeting by the way.
This evening late, by then the chewing flocks   540
Had ta'n their supper on the savoury herb
Of knotgrass dew-besprent, and were in fold,
I sat me down to watch upon a bank
With ivy canopied and interwove
With flaunting honeysuckle, and began,
Wrapp'd in a pleasing fit of melancholy,
To meditate my rural minstrelsy,
Till fancy had her fill; but, ere a close,
The wonted roar was up amidst the woods
And fill'd the air with barbarous dissonance.   550
At which I ceas'd, and listen'd them a while,
Till an unusual stop of sudden silence
Gave respite to the drowsy-frighted steeds
That draw the litter of close-curtain'd sleep.
At last a soft and solemn breathing sound
Rose like a steam of rich distill'd perfumes,

And stole upon the air, that even silence
Was took ere she was ware, and wish'd she might
Deny her nature and be never more
Still to be so displac'd. I was all ear,   560
And took in strains that might create a soul
Under the ribs of Death; but O ere long
Too well I did perceive it was the voice
Of my most honour'd lady, your dear sister.
Amaz'd I stood, harrow'd with grief and fear,
And 'O poor hapless nightingale', thought I,
'How sweet thou sing'st, how near the deadly snare!'
Then down the lawns I ran with headlong haste,
Through paths and turnings often trod by day,
Till guided by mine ear I found the place   570
Where that damn'd wizard, hid in sly disguise,
(For so by certain signs I knew) had met
Already, ere my best speed could prevent,
The aidless innocent lady, his wish'd prey,
Who gently ask'd if he had seen such two,
Supposing him some neighbour villager.
Longer I durst not stay, but soon I guess'd
Ye were the two she meant. With that I sprung
Into swift flight, till I had found you here;
But further know I not.
Sec. Bro.   O night and shades,   580
How are ye join'd with Hell in triple knot
Against th'unarmed weakness of one virgin
Alone and helpless! Is this the confidence
You gave me, brother?
Eld. Bro.   Yes, and keep it still,
Lean on it safely: not a period
Shall be unsaid for me. Against the threats
Of malice or of sorcery, or that power
Which erring men call chance, this I hold firm.
Virtue may be assail'd, but never hurt,
Surpris'd by unjust force, but not enthrall'd.   590
Yea, even that which mischief meant most harm
Shall in the happy trial prove most glory.
But evil on itself shall back recoil,

43

And mix no more with goodness, when at last
Gather'd like scum, and settl'd to itself,
It shall be in eternal restless change
Self-fed, and self-consum'd. If this fail,
The pillar'd firmament is rottenness
And Earth's base built on stubble. But come, let's on.
Against th'opposing will and arm of Heaven   600
May never this just sword be lifted up;
But for that damn'd magician, let him be girt
With all the grisly legions that troop
Under the sooty flag of Acheron,
Harpies and Hydras, or all the monstrous bugs
Twixt Africa and Ind, I'll find him out
And force him to restore his purchase back,
Or drag him by the curls and cleave his scalp
Down to the hips.
Spirit.   Alas, good venturous youth,
I love thy courage yet and bold emprise,   610
But here thy sword can do thee little stead.
Far other arms and other weapons must
Be those that quell the might of hellish charms.
He with his bare wand can unthread thy joints,
And crumble all thy sinews.
Eld. Bro.   Why prithee, shepherd,
How durst thou then thyself approach so near
As to make this relation?
Spirit.   Care, and utmost shifts
How to secure the lady from surprisal,
Brought to my mind a certain shepherd lad,
Of small regard to see to, yet well-skill'd   620
In every virtuous plant and healing herb
That spreads her verdant leaf to th'morning ray.
He lov'd me well, and oft would beg me sing,
Which when I did, he on the tender grass
Would sit and hearken even to ecstasy,
And in requital ope his leathern scrip
And show me simples of a thousand names
Telling their strange and vigorous faculties.
Amongst the rest a small unsightly root,

44

But of divine effect, he cull'd me out.   630
The leaf was darkish, and had prickles on it,
But in another country, as he said,
Bore a bright golden flow'r, but not in this soil;
Unknown, and like esteem'd, and the dull swain
Treads on it daily with his clouted shoon,
And yet more med'cinal is it than that Moly
That Hermes once to wise Ulysses gave.
He call'd it Haemony, and gave it me
And bade me keep it as of sovereign use
Gainst all enchantments, mildew blast or damp   640
Or ghastly Furies' apparition.
I purs'd it up, but little reckoning made
Till now that this extremity compell'd.
But now I find it true, for by this means
I knew the foul enchanter though disguis'd,
Enter'd the very lime-twigs of his spells,
And yet came off. If you have this about you
(As I will give you when we go) you may
Boldly assault the necromancer's hall,
Where if he be, with dauntless hardihood   650
And brandish'd blade rush on him, break his glass,
And shed the luscious liquor on the ground.
But seize his wand; though he and his curs'd crew
Fierce sign of battle make and menace high,
Or like the sons of Vulcan vomit smoke,
Yet they will soon retire if he but shrink.

Eld. Bro. Thyrsis, lead on apace. I'll follow thee,
And some good Angel bear a shield before us.

> *The scene changes to a stately palace, set out
> with all manner of deliciousness: soft music,
> tables spread with all dainties. Comus
> appears with his rabble, and the Lady set in
> an enchanted chair, to whom he offers his
> glass, which she puts by, and goes about to
> rise.*

Comus. Nay, lady, sit; if I but wave this wand,
Your nerves are all chain'd up in alabaster,   660

And you a statue, or as Daphne was
Root-bound, that fled Apollo.
Lady.   Fool, do not boast.
  Thou canst not touch the freedom of my mind
  With all thy charms, although this corporal rind
  Thou hast immanacl'd, while Heaven sees good.
Comus.   Why are you vex'd, lady? Why do you frown?
  Here dwell no frowns nor anger; from these gates
  Sorrow flies far. See, here be all the pleasures
  That fancy can beget on youthful thoughts
  When the fresh blood grows lively and returns   670
  Brisk as the April buds in primrose-season.
  And first behold this cordial julep here
  That flames and dances in his crystal bounds,
  With spirits of balm and fragrant syrups mix'd.
  Not that Nepenthes which the wife of Thone
  In Egypt gave to Jove-born Helena
  Is of such power to stir up joy as this,
  To life so friendly, or so cool to thirst.
  Why should you be so cruel to yourself
  And to those dainty limbs which nature lent   680
  For gentle usage and soft delicacy?
  But you invert the covenants of her trust,
  And harshly deal like an ill borrower
  With that which you receiv'd on other terms,
  Scorning the unexempt condition
  By which all mortal frailty must subsist –
  Refreshment after toil, ease after pain,
  That have been tir'd all day without repast
  And timely rest have wanted. But, fair virgin,
  This will restore all soon.   690
Lady.   'Twill not, false traitor.
  'Twill not restore the truth and honesty
  Which thou hast banish'd from thy tongue with lies
  Was this the cottage and the safe abode
  Thou told'st me of? What grim aspects are these
  These ugly-headed monsters? Mercy guard me!
  Hence with thy brew'd enchantments, foul deceiver.
  Hast thou betray'd my credulous innocence

With visor'd falsehood and base forgery,
And would'st thou seek again to trap me here
With lickerish baits fit to ensnare a brute?   700
Were it a draught for Juno when she banquets,
I would not taste thy treasonous offer. None
But such as are good men can give good things,
And that which is not good is not delicious
To a well-govern'd and wise appetite.

Comus.   O foolishness of men! that lend their ears
To those budge doctors of the Stoic fur,
And fetch their precepts from the Cynic tub,
Praising the lean and sallow abstinence.
Wherefore did Nature pour her bounties forth   710
With such a full and unwithdrawing hand,
Covering the earth with odours, fruits and flocks,
Thronging the seas with spawn innumerable,
But all to please and sate the curious taste?
And set to work millions of spinning worms
That in their green shops weave the smooth-hair'd silk
To deck her sons; and that no corner might
Be vacant of her plenty, in her own loins
She hutch'd th'all-worshipp'd ore and precious gems
To store her children with. If all the world   720
Should in a fit of temperance feed on pulse,
Drink the clear stream, and nothing wear but frieze,
Th'all-giver would be unthank'd, would be unprais'd,
Not half his riches known, and yet despis'd,
And we should serve him as a grudging master,
As a penurious niggard of his wealth,
And live like Nature's bastards, not her sons,
Who would be quite surcharg'd with her own weight
And strangled with her waste fertility;
Th'earth cumber'd and the wing'd air dark'd with
    plumes,   730
The herds would over-multitude their lords,
The sea o'erfraught would swell, and th'unsought
    diamonds
Would so emblaze the forehead of the deep
And so bestud with stars that they below

Would grow inur'd to light, and come at last
To gaze upon the sun with shameless brows.
List, lady, be not coy, and be not cozen'd
With that same vaunted name Virginity.
Beauty is Nature's coin, must not be hoarded,
But must be current, and the good thereof   740
Consists in mutual and partaken bliss,
Unsavoury in the enjoyment of itself.
If you let slip time, like a neglected rose
It withers on the stalk with languish'd head.
Beauty is Nature's brag, and must be shown
In courts, at feasts, and high solemnities
Where most may wonder at the workmanship.
It is for homely creatures to keep home,
They had their name thence. Coarse complexions
And cheeks of sorry grain will serve to ply   750
The sampler and to tease the housewife's wool.
What need a vermeil-tinctur'd lip for that,
Love-darting eyes, or tresses like the morn?
There was another meaning in these gifts.
Think what, and be advis'd; you are but young yet.
Lady.   I had not thought to have unlock'd my lips
In this unhallow'd air, but that this juggler
Would think to charm my judgement as mine eyes,
Obtruding false rules prank'd in reason's garb.
I hate when vice can bolt her arguments,   760
And virtue has no tongue to check her pride.
Imposter, do not charge most innocent Nature,
As if she would her children should be riotous
With her abundance. She, good cateress,
Means her provision only to the good,
That live according to her sober laws
And holy dictate of spare temperance.
If every just man that now pines with want
Had but a moderate and beseeming share
Of that which lewdly pamper'd luxury   770
Now heaps upon some few with vast excess,
Nature's full blessings would be well dispens'd

48

In unsuperfluous even proportion,
And she no whit encumber'd with her store;
And then the giver would be better thank'd,
His praise due paid, for swinish gluttony
Ne'er looks to Heaven amidst his gorgeous feast,
But with besotted base ingratitude
Crams, and blasphemes his feeder. Shall I go on?
Or have I said enough? To him that dares   780
Arm his profane tongue with contemptuous words
Against the sun-clad power of chastity
Fain would I something say, yet to what end?
Thou hast nor ear nor soul to apprehend
The sublime notion and high mystery
That must be utter'd to unfold the sage
And serious doctrine of virginity;
And thou art worthy that thou shouldst not know
More happiness than this thy present lot.
Enjoy your dear wit and gay rhetoric,   790
That hath so well been taught her dazzling fence.
Thou art not fit to hear thyself convinc'd;
Yet should I try, the uncontrolled worth
Of this pure cause would kindle my rapt spirits
To such a flame of sacred vehemence
That dumb things would be mov'd to sympathize,
And the brute Earth would lend her nerves and shake
Till all thy magic structures, rear'd so high,
Were shatter'd into heaps o'er thy false head.

Comus.   She fables not; I feel that I do fear   800
Her words set off by some superior power,
And though not mortal, yet a cold shuddering dew
Dips me all o'er, as when the wrath of Jove
Speaks thunder and the chains of Erebus
To some of Saturn's crew. I must dissemble,
And try her yet more strongly. Come, no more.
This is mere moral babble, and direct
Against the canon laws of our foundation.
I must not suffer this; yet 'tis but the lees
And settlings of a melancholy blood.   810

49

But this will cure all straight, one sip of this
Will bathe the drooping spirits in delight
Beyond the bliss of dreams. Be wise, and taste....

> *The brothers rush in with swords drawn,*
> *wrest his glass out of his hand, and break it*
> *against the ground. His rout make sign of*
> *resistance, but are all driven in. The Atten-*
> *dant Spirit comes in.*

Spirit.   What, have you let the false enchanter scape?
O ye mistook, ye should have snatch'd his wand
And bound him fast. Without his rod revers'd
And backward mutters of dissevering power
We cannot free the Lady that sits here
In stony fetters fix'd and motionless.
Yet stay, be not disturb'd; now I bethink me,   820
Some other means I have which may be us'd
Which once of Meliboeus old I learnt,
The soothest shepherd that e'er pip'd on plains.
There is a gentle nymph not far from hence
That with moist curb sways the smooth Severn stream.
Sabrina is her name, a virgin pure;
Whilom she was the daughter of Locrine,
That had the sceptre from his father Brute.
She, guiltless damsel, flying the mad pursuit
Of her enraged stepdame Gwendolen,   830
Commended her fair innocence to the flood,
That stay'd her flight with his cross-flowing course.
The water nymphs that in the bottom play'd
Help up their pearled wrists and took her in,
Bearing her straight to aged Nereus' hall,
Who piteous of her woes rear'd her lank head
And gave her to his daughters to embathe
In nectar'd lavers strew'd with asphodel,
And through the porch and inlet of each sense
Dropp'd in ambrosial oils till she reviv'd   840
And underwent a quick immortal change,
Made goddess of the river. Still she retains
Her maiden gentleness, and oft at eve

Visits the herds along the twilight meadows,
Helping all urchin blasts and ill-luck signs
That the shrewd meddling elf delights to make,
Which she with precious vial'd liquors heals;
For which the shepherds at their festivals
Carol her goodness loud in rustic lays
And throw sweet garland wreaths into her stream   850
Of pansies, pinks and gaudy daffodils.
And, as the old swain said, she can unlock
The clasping charm and thaw the numbing spell,
If she be right invok'd in warbling song;
For maidenhood she loves, and will be swift
To aid a virgin, such as was herself,
In hard-besetting need. This will I try,
And add the power of some adjuring verse.

Song

Sabrina fair
    Listen where thou art sitting   860
Under the glassy, cool, translucent wave,
    In twisted braids of lilies knitting
The loose train of thy amber-dropping hair,
    Listen for dear honour's sake,
Goddess of the silver lake,
        Listen and save.

Listen and appear to us
In name of great Oceanus,
By th'earth-shaking Neptune's mace,
And Tethys' grave majestic pace,   870
By hoary Nereus' wrinkled look,
And the Carpathian wizard's hook,
By scaly Triton's winding shell,
And old soothsaying Glaucus' spell,
By Leucothea's lovely hands,
And her son that rules the strands,
By Thetis' tinsel-slipper'd feet,
And the songs of Sirens sweet,

By dead Parthenope's dear tomb,
And fair Ligea's golden comb   880
Wherewith she sits on diamond rocks
Sleeking her soft alluring locks,
By all the nymphs that nightly dance
Upon thy streams with wily glance,
Rise, rise, and heave thy rosy head
From thy coral-paven bed,
And bridle in thy headlong wave
Till thou our summons answer'd have.
     Listen and save.

    Sabrina rises, attended by water nymphs, and sings.

  By the rushy-fringed bank,   890
Where grows the willow and the osier dank,
   My sliding chariot stays,
Thick-set with agate, and the azurn sheen
Of turquoise blue, and emerald green
   That in the channel strays,
Whilst from off the waters fleet
Thus I set my printless feet
O'er the cowslip's velvet head,
   That bends not as I tread,
Gentle swain at thy request
    I am here.   900

Spirit.   Goddess dear,
  We implore thy powerful hand
  To undo the charmed band
  Of true virgin here distress'd
  Through the force and through the wile
  Of unbless'd enchanter vile.
Sabrina.   Shepherd, 'tis my office best
  To help ensnared chastity.
  Brightest lady, look on me,   910
  Thus I sprinkle on thy breast
  Drops that from my fountain pure
  I have kept of precious cure.
  Thrice upon thy finger's tip,

Thrice upon thy rubied lip,
Next this marble venom'd seat
Smear'd with gums of glutinous heat
I touch with chaste palms moist and cold.
Now the spell hath lost his hold,
And I must haste ere morning hour   920
To wait in Amphitrite's bower.

    Sabrina descends, and the Lady rises out of her seat.

Spirit.   Virgin daughter of Locrine,
Sprung of old Anchises' line,
May thy brimmed waves for this
Their full tribute never miss
From a thousand petty rills
That tumble down the snowy hills.
Summer drought or singed air
Never scorch thy tresses fair,
Nor wet October's torrent flood   930
Thy molten crystal fill with mud.
May thy billows roll ashore
The beryl and the golden ore.
May thy lofty head be crown'd
With many a tower and terrace round,
And here and there thy banks upon
With groves of myrrh and cinnamon.
Come, lady, while Heav'n lends us grace
Let us fly this cursed place,
Lest the sorcerer us entice   940
With some other new device.
Not a waste or needless sound
Till we come to holier ground.
I shall be your faithful guide
Through this gloomy covert wide,
And not many furlongs thence
Is your father's residence,
Where this night are met in state
Many a friend to gratulate
His wish'd presence; and beside,   950
All the swains that there abide

53

With jigs and rural dance resort.
We shall catch them at their sport,
And our sudden coming there
Will double all their mirth and cheer.
Come, let us haste; the stars are high,
But night sits monarch yet in the mid sky.

*The scene changes, presenting Ludlow town
and the President's castle. Then come in country dancers, after them the Attendant Spirit
with the two brothers and the Lady.*

Song

Spirit.   Back, shepherds, back, enough your play,
Till next sunshine holiday.
Here be, without duck or nod,   960
Other trippings to be trod
Of lighter toes, and such court guise
As Mercury did first devise
With the mincing Dryades
On the lawns and on the leas.

This second song presents them to their father and mother.

Noble Lord, and Lady bright,
I have brought ye new delight,
Here behold so goodly grown
Three fair branches of your own.
Heav'n hath timely tri'd their youth,   870
Their faith, their patience and their truth,
And sent them here through hard assays
With a crown of deathless praise,
To triumph in victorious dance
O'er sensual folly and intemperance.

The dances ended, the Spirit epiloguizes.

Spirit.   To the Ocean now I fly,
And those happy climes that lie
Where day never shuts his eye,

Up in the broad fields of the sky.
There I suck the liquid air   980
All amidst the gardens fair
Of Hesperus and his daughters three
That sing about the golden tree.
Along the crisped shades and bowers
Revels the spruce and jocund Spring;
The Graces and the rosy-bosom'd Hours
Thither all their bounties bring;
There eternal Summer dwells,
And west winds with musky wing
About the cedarn alleys fling   990
Nard, and cassia's balmy smells.
Iris there with humid bow
Waters the odorous banks that blow
Flowers of more mingled hue
Than her purfled scarf can show,
And drenches with Elysian dew
(List, mortals, if your ears be true)
Beds of hyacinth, and roses,
Where young Adonis oft reposes,
Waxing well of his deep wound   1000
In slumber soft, and on the ground
Sadly sits th'Assyrian queen;
But far above in spangled sheen
Celestial Cupid, her fam'd son, advanc'd
Holds his dear Psyche sweet entranc'd
After her wand'ring labours long,
Till free consent the gods among
Make her his eternal bride;
And from her fair unspotted side
Two blissful twins are to be born,   1010
Youth and Joy: so Jove hath sworn
    But now my task is smoothly done:
I can fly, or I can run
Quickly to the green Earth's end,
Where the bow'd welkin slow doth bend,
And from thence can soar as soon
To the corners of the Moon.

    Mortals that would follow me,
Love Virtue, she alone is free.
She can teach ye how to climb   1020
Higher than the sphery chime;
Or, if Virtue feeble were,
Heav'n itself would stoop to her.

First published 1637

LYCIDAS

Yet once more, O ye laurels, and once more,
Ye myrtles brown, with ivy never-sere,
I come to pluck your berries harsh and crude,
And with forc'd fingers rude
Shatter your leaves before the mellowing year.
Bitter constraint and sad occasion dear
Compels me to disturb your season due:
For Lycidas is dead, dead ere his prime
Young Lycidas, and hath not left his peer.
Who would not sing for Lycidas? he well knew   10
Himself to sing, and build the lofty rhyme.
He must not float upon his watery bier
Unwept, and welter to the parching wind
Without the meed of some melodious tear.
    Begin then, Sisters of the sacred well
That from beneath the seat of Jove doth spring;
Begin, and somewhat loudly sweep the string:
Hence with denial vain, and coy excuse.
So may some gentle Muse
With lucky words favour my destin'd urn,   20
And as he passes, turn
And bid fair peace be to my sable shroud.
For we were nurs'd upon the self-same hill,
Fed the same flock, by fountain, shade and rill.
    Together both, ere the high lawns appear'd
Under the glimmering eyelids of the morn,
We drove afield, and both together heard
What time the grey-fly winds her sultry horn,

Battening our flocks with the fresh dews of night,
Oft till the ev'n-star bright   30
Toward heav'n's descent had slop'd his burnish'd wheel.
Meanwhile the rural ditties were not mute
Temper'd to th'oaten flute:
Rough Satyrs danc'd, and Fauns with cloven heel
From the glad sound would not be absent long,
And old Dametas lov'd to hear our song.

　But O the heavy change, now thou art gone,
Now thou art gone, and never must return!
Thee shepherd, thee the woods and desert caves
With wild thyme and the gadding vine o'ergrown   40
And all their echoes mourn.
The willows and the hazel copses green
Shall now no more be seen
Fanning their joyous leaves to thy soft lays.
As killing as the canker to the rose,
Or taint-worm to the weanling herds that graze,
Or frost to flowers that their gay wardrobe wear
When first the whitethorn blows,
Such, Lycidas, thy loss to shepherd's ear.

　Where were ye Nymphs when the remorseless deep   50
Clos'd o'er the head of your lov'd Lycidas?
For neither were ye playing on the steep,
Where your old bards the famous Druids lie,
Nor on the shaggy top of Mona high,
Nor yet where Deva spreads her wizard stream.
Ay me, I fondly dream!
Had ye been there ... for what could that have done?
What could the Muse herself that Orpheus bore,
The Muse herself, for her enchanting son?
Whom universal nature did lament,   60
When by the rout that made the hideous roar
His gory visage down the stream was sent,
Down the swift Hebrus to the Lesbian shore.

　Alas! What boots it with uncessant care
To tend the homely slighted shepherd's trade,
And strictly meditate the thankless Muse?
Were it not better done as others use,

To sport with Amaryllis in the shade,
Hid in the tangles of Neaera's hair?
Fame is the spur that the clear spirit doth raise 70
(That last infirmity of noble mind)
To scorn delights and live laborious days;
But the fair guerdon where we hope to find,
And think to burst out into sudden blaze,
Comes the blind Fury with th'abhorred shears
And slits the thin-spun life. 'But not the praise',
Phoebus repli'd, and touch'd my trembling ears.
'Fame is no plant that grows on mortal soil,
Nor in the glistering foil
Set off to th'world, nor in broad rumour lies; 80
But lives, and spreads aloft by those pure eyes
And perfect witness of all-judging Jove:
As he pronounces lastly on each deed,
Of so much fame in Heav'n expect thy meed.'
    O fountain Arethuse, and thou honour'd flood,
Smooth-sliding Mincius, crown'd with vocal reeds,
That strain I heard was of a higher mood.
But now my oat proceeds,
And listens to the herald of the sea
That came in Neptune's plea. 90
He ask'd the waves, and ask'd the felon winds,
'What hard mishap hath doom'd this gentle swain?'
And question'd every gust of rugged wings
That blows from off each beaked promontory.
They knew not of his story,
And sage Hippotades their answer brings
That not a blast was from his dungeon stray'd;
The air was calm, and on the level brine
Sleek Panope with all her sisters play'd.
It was that fatal and perfidious bark, 100
Built in th'eclipse, and rigg'd with curses dark,
That sunk so low that sacred head of thine.
    Next Camus (reverend sire) went footing slow,
His mantle hairy and his bonnet sedge
Inwrought with figures dim, and on the edge
Like to that sanguine flower inscrib'd with woe.

'Ah! Who hath reft' (quoth he) 'my dearest pledge?'
Last came, and last did go,
The pilot of the Galilean lake.
Two massy keys he bore of metals twain   110
(The golden opes, the iron shuts amain).
He shook his mitr'd locks, and stern bespake:
'How well could I have spar'd for thee, young swain,
Enough of such as for their bellies' sake
Creep and intrude and climb into the fold?
Of other care they little reckoning make
Than how to scramble at the shearers' feast
And shove away the worthy bidden guest.
Blind mouths! that scarce themselves know how to hold
A sheephook, or have learn'd ought else the least   120
That to the faithful herdman's art belongs!
What recks it them? What need they? They are sped.
And when they list their lean and flashy songs
Grate on their scrannel pipes of wretched straw,
The hungry sheep look up, and are not fed,
But swoll'n with wind and the rank mist they draw,
Rot inwardly, and foul contagion spread:
Besides what the grim wolf with privy paw
Daily devours apace, and little said.
But that two-handed engine at the door   130
Stands ready to smite once, and smites no more.'
    Return, Alpheus, the dread voice is pass'd
That shrunk thy streams; return, Sicilian Muse,
And call the vales and bid them hither cast
Their bells and flowerets of a thousand hues.
Ye valleys low, where the mild whispers use
Of shades and wanton winds and gushing brooks,
On whose fresh lap the swart star sparely looks,
Throw hither all your quaint enamel'd eyes
That on the green turf suck the honey'd showers,   140
And purple all the ground with vernal flowers.
Bring the rathe primrose that forsaken dies,
The tufted crow-toe and pale jessamine,
The white pink, and the pansy freak'd with jet,
The glowing violet,

The musk-rose and the well-attir'd woodbine,
With cowslips wan that hang the pensive head,
And every flower that sad embroidery wears;
Bid amaranthus all his beauty shed,
And daffodillies fill their cups with tears   150
To strew the laureate hearse where Lycid lies.
For so, to interpose a little ease,
Let our frail thoughts dally with false surmise;
Ay me! whilst thee the shores and sounding seas
Wash far away, where e'er thy bones are hurl'd,
Whether beyond the stormy Hebrides,
Where thou perhaps under the humming tide
Visit'st the bottom of the monstrous world,
Or whether thou, to our moist vows deni'd,
Sleep'st by the fable of Bellerus old,   160
Where the great vision of the guarded Mount
Looks toward Namancos and Bayona's hold.
Look homeward Angel now, and melt with ruth,
And O ye dolphins, waft the hapless youth.
   Weep no more, woeful shepherds, weep no more;
For Lycidas your sorrow is not dead,
Sunk though he be beneath the watery floor:
So sinks the daystar in the ocean bed,
And yet anon repairs his drooping head
And tricks his beams and with new-spangl'd ore   170
Flames in the forehead of the morning sky;
So Lycidas sunk low, but mounted high
Through the dear might of him that walk'd the waves,
Where other groves and other streams along
With nectar pure his oozy locks he laves
And hears the unexpressive nuptial song
In the bless'd kingdoms meek of joy and love.
There entertain him all the saints above
In solemn troops and sweet societies,
That sing, and singing in their glory move,   180
And wipe the tears for ever from his eyes.
Now, Lycidas, the shepherds weep no more.
Henceforth thou art the genius of the shore
In thy large recompense, and shalt be good
To all that wander in that perilous flood.

60

Thus sang the uncouth swain to th'oaks and rills,
While the still morn went out with sandals grey;
He touch'd the tender stops of various quills,
With eager thought warbling his Doric lay.
And now the sun had stretch'd out all the hills,   190
And now was dropp'd into the western bay;
At last he rose, and twitch'd his mantle blue,
Tomorrow to fresh woods and pastures new.

First published 1638

from OF REFORMATION TOUCHING CHURCH-DISCIPLINE IN ENGLAND

Upon a time, the Body summoned all the Members to meet in the Guild for the common good (as Aesop's Chronicles aver many stranger accidents). The Head by right takes the first seat, and next to it a huge and monstrous Wen little less than the Head itself, growing to it by a narrower excrescency. The Members, amazed, began to ask one another what he was that took place next their chief. None could resolve; whereat the Wen, though unwieldy, with much ado gets up and bespeaks the assembly to this purpose: that as in place he was second to   10 the Head, so by due of merit; that he was to it an ornament and strength, and of special near relation; and that if the Head should fail, none were fitter than himself to step into his place. Therefore he thought it for the honour of the Body that such dignities and rich endowments should be decreed him as did adorn and set out the noblest Members. To this was answered that it should be consulted. Then was a wise and learned Philosopher sent for, that knew all the charters, laws and tenures of the Body. On him it is imposed by all as chief committee to examine   20 and discuss the claim and petition of right put in by the Wen; who soon perceiving the matter, and wondering at the boldness of such a swollen tumour, 'Wilt thou' quoth he 'that art but a bottle of vicious and hardened excrements contend with the lawful and free-born Mem-

bers, whose certain number is set by ancient and unre-
pealable statute? Head thou art none, though thou receive
this huge substance from it. What office bearest thou?
What good canst thou show by thee done to the Commonwealth?' The Wen, not easily dashed, replies that his   30
office was his glory, for so oft as the Soul would retire
out of the Head from over the steaming vapours of the
lower parts to divine contemplation, with him she found
the purest and quietest retreat, as being most remote from
soil and disturbance. 'Lourdan,' quoth the Philosopher,
'thy folly is as great as thy filth. Know that all the faculties of the Soul are confined of old to their several vessels
and ventricles, from which they cannot part without dissolution of the whole Body. And that thou containest no
good thing in thee, but art a heap of hard and loathsome   40
uncleanness, and art to the Head a foul disfigurement and
burden, when I have cut thee off and opened thee, as by
the help of these implements I will do, all men shall see.'

But to return, whence was digressed: seeing that the
throne of a king, as the wise King Solomon often remem-
bers us, 'is established in justice', which is the universal
justice that Aristotle so much praises, containing in it all
other virtues, it may assure us that the fall of prelacy,
whose actions are so far distant from justice, cannot shake
the least fringe that borders the royal canopy; but that   50
their standing doth continually oppose and lay battery to
regal safety shall by that which follows easily appear.
Among many secondary and accessory causes that support monarchy, these are not of least reckoning, though
common to all other states: the love of the subjects, the
multitude and valour of the people, and store of treasure.
In all these things hath the kingdom been of late sore
weakened, and chiefly by the prelates. First, let any man
consider that if any Prince shall suffer under him a commission of authority to be exercised till all the land groan   60
and cry out as against a whip of scorpions, whether this
be not likely to lessen and keel the affections of the
subject; next, what numbers of faithful and free-born
Englishmen and good Christians have been constrained to

62

forsake their dearest home, their friends and kindred, whom nothing but the wide ocean and the savage deserts of America could hide and shelter from the fury of the bishops. O sir, if we could but see the shape of our dear mother England, as poets are wont to give a personal form to what they please, how would she appear, think 70 ye, but in a mourning weed, with ashes upon her head and tears abundantly flowing from her eyes, to behold so many of her children exposed at once, and thrust from things of dearest necessity, because their conscience could not assent to things which the bishops thought 'indifferent'? What more binding than conscience? What more free than 'indifferency'? Cruel then must that 'indifferency' needs be that shall violate the strict necessity of conscience; merciless and inhumane that free choice and liberty that shall break asunder the bonds of religion. Let the 80 astrologer be dismayed at the portentous blaze of comets and impressions in the air, as foretelling troubles and changes to states; I shall believe there cannot be a more ill-boding sign to a nation (God turn the omen from us) than when the inhabitants, to avoid insufferable grievances at home, are enforced by heaps to forsake their native country.

Now whereas the only remedy and amends against the depopulation and thinness of a land within is the borrowed strength of firm alliance from without, these 90 priestly policies of theirs, having thus exhausted our domestic forces, have gone the way also to leave us as naked of our firmest and faithfullest neighbours abroad, by disparaging and alienating from us all Protestant princes and commonwealths, who are not ignorant that our prelates, and as many as they can infect, account them no better than a sort of sacrilegious and puritanical rebels, preferring the Spaniard our deadly enemy before them, and set all orthodox writers as nought in comparison of the Jesuits, who are indeed the only corrupters of youth 100 and good learning; and I have heard many wise and learned men in Italy say as much. It cannot be that the strongest knot of confederacy should not daily slacken when religion, which is the chief engagement of our league, shall be turned to their reproach. Hence it is that the prosperous and prudent states of the United Provinces (whom we ought to love, if not for themselves, yet for our own good work in them, they having been in a manner planted and erected by us, and having been since to us the faithful watchmen and discoverers of many a Popish and Austrian complotted treason, and with us the partners of many a bloody and victorious battle, whom the similitude of manners and language, the commodity of traffic which founded the old Burgundian league betwixt us, but chiefly religion should bind to us immortally), even such friends as these, out of some principles instilled into us by the prelates, have been often dismissed with distasteful answers, and sometimes unfriendly actions; nor is it to be considered to the breach of confederate nations whose mutual interest is of such high consequence though their merchants bicker in the East Indies, neither is it safe, or wary, or indeed Christianly, that the French king, of a different faith, should afford our nearest allies as good protection as we. Sir, I persuade myself, if our zeal to true religion and the brotherly usage of our truest friends were as notorious to the world as our prelatical schism and captivity to rochet apophthegms, we had ere this seen our old conquerors and afterward liege-men the Normans, together with the Bretons, our proper colony, and all the Gascons that are the rightful dowry of our ancient kings, come hither with cap and knee desiring the shadow of the English sceptre to defend them from the hot persecutions and taxes of the French. But when they come hither, and see a tympany of spaniolized bishops swaggering in the foretop of the state and meddling to turn and dandle the royal ball with unskilful and pedantic palms, no marvel though they think it as unsafe to commit religion and liberty to their arbitrating as to a synagogue of Jesuits.

But what do I stand reckoning upon advantages and gains lost by the misrule and turbulency of the prelates? What do I pick up so thriftily their scatterings and dimi-

nishings of the meaner subject, whilst they by their sedi-
tious practices have endangered to lose the King one third
of his main stock? What have they not done to banish
him from his own native country? But to speak of this
as it ought would ask a volume by itself. Thus as they
have unpeopled the kingdom by expulsion of so many
thousands, as they have endeavoured to lay the skirts of it
bare by disheartening and dishonouring our loyalest con-   150
federates abroad, so have they hamstrung the valour of
the subject by seeking to effeminate us all at home. Well
knows every wise nation that their liberty consists in
manly and honest labours, in sobriety, and rigorous honour to the marriage bed, which in both sexes should be
bred up from chaste hopes to loyal enjoyments; and when
the people slacken, and fall to looseness and riot, then do
they as much as if they laid down their necks for some
wily tyrant to get up and ride. Thus learnt Cyrus to tame
the Lydians, whom by arms he could not whilst they kept   160
themselves from luxury: with one easy proclamation to
set up stews, dancing, feasting and dicing, he made them
soon his slaves. I know not what drift the prelates had,
whose brokers they were, to prepare and supple us either
for a foreign invasion or domestic oppression; but this I
am sure, they took the ready way to despoil us both of
manhood and grace at once, and that in the shamefullest
and ungodliest manner upon that day which God's law
and even our own reason hath consecrated, that we might
have one day at least of seven set apart wherein to ex-   170
amine and increase our knowledge of God, to meditate
and commune of our faith, our hope, our eternal city in
Heaven, and to quicken withal the study and exercise of
charity: at such a time that men should be plucked from
their soberest and saddest thoughts, and by bishops, the
pretended Fathers of the Church, instigated by public
edict and with earnest endeavour pushed forward to gam-
ing, jigging, wassailing and mixed dancing, is a horror to
think. Thus did the reprobate hireling priest Balaam seek
to subdue the Israelites to Moab, if not by force, then by   180
this devilish policy, to draw them from the sanctuary of

65

God to the luxurious and ribald feasts of Baal-peor. Thus have they trespassed, not only against the monarchy of England, but of Heaven also; as others, I doubt not, can prosecute against them.

I proceed within my own bounds to show you next what good agents they are about the revenues and riches of the kingdom, which declares of what moment they are to monarchy, or what avail. Two leeches they have, that still suck and suck the kingdom: their ceremonies and 190 their courts. If any man will contend that ceremonies be lawful under the gospel, he may be answered otherwhere. This doubtless, that they ought to be many and over-costly, no true Protestant will affirm. Now I appeal to all wise men what an excessive waste of treasury there hath been within these few years in this land, not in the expedient, but in the idolatrous erection of temples beautified exquisitely to out-vie the papists, the costly and dear-bought scandals and snares of images, pictures, rich copes, gorgeous altar-cloths; and by the courses they took 200 and the opinions they held, it was not likely any stay would be or any end of their madness, where a pious pretext is so ready at hand to cover their insatiate desires. What can we suppose this will come to? What other materials than these have built up the spiritual Babel to the height of her abominations? Believe it, sir, right truly it may be said that Antichrist is Mammon's son. The sour leaven of human traditions, mixed in one putrefied mass with the poisonous dregs of hypocrisy in the hearts of prelates that lie basking in the sunny warmth of wealth 210 and promotion, is the serpent's egg that will hatch an Antichrist wheresoever, and engender the same monster as big or little, as the lump is which breeds him. If the splendour of gold and silver begin to lord it once again in the Church of England, we shall see Antichrist shortly wallow here, though his chief kennel be at Rome. If they had one thought upon God's glory and the advancement of Christian faith, they would be a means that with these expenses, thus profusely thrown away in trash, rather churches and schools might be built where they cry out 220

66

for want, and more added where too few are, a moderate maintenance distributed to every painful minister that now scarce sustains his family with bread, while the prelates revel like Belshazzar with their full carouses in goblets and vessels of gold snatched from God's temple; which I hope the worthy men of our land will consider.

Now then for their courts. What a mass of money is drawn from the veins into the ulcers of the kingdom this way their extortions, their open corruptions, the multitude of hungry and ravenous harpies that swarm about their offices declare sufficiently. And what though all this go not oversea? 'Twere better it did. Better a penurious kingdom, than where excessive wealth flows into the graceless and injurious hands of common sponges to the impoverishing of good and loyal men, and that by such execrable, such irreligious courses. If the sacred and dreadful works of holy discipline, censure, penance, excommunication and absolution, where no profane thing ought to have access, nothing to be assistant but sage and Christianly admonition, brotherly love, flaming charity and zeal, and then, according to the effects, paternal sorrow or paternal joy, mild severity, melting compassion; if such divine ministries as these, wherein the Angel of the Church represents the person of Christ Jesus, must lie prostitute to sordid fees, and not pass to and fro between our Saviour that of free grace redeemed us and the submissive penitent without the truckage of perishing coin and the butcherly execution of tormentors, rooks and rakeshames sold to lucre, then have the Babylonish merchants of souls just excuse. Hitherto, sir, you have heard how the prelates have weakened and withdrawn the external accomplishments of kingly prosperity, the love of the people, their multitude, their valour, their wealth; mining and sapping the outworks and redoubts of monarchy. Now hear how they strike at the very heart and vitals.

We know that monarchy is made up of two parts, the liberty of the subject and the supremacy of the king. I begin at the root. See what gentle and benign fathers they have been to our liberty. Their trade being, by the same alchemy that the Pope uses, to extract heaps of gold and silver out of the drossy bullion of the people's sins, and justly fearing that the quick-sighted Protestant's eye, cleared in great part from the mist of superstition, may at one time or other look with a good judgement into these their deceitful peddleries, to gain as many associates of guiltiness as they can and to infect the temporal magistrate with the like lawless (though not sacrilegious) extortion, see a while what they do: they engage themselves to preach and persuade an assertion for truth the most false, and to this monarchy the most pernicious and destructive, that could be chosen. What more baneful to monarchy than a popular commotion, for the dissolution of monarchy slides aptest into a democracy? And what stirs the Englishmen, as our wisest writers have observed, sooner to rebellion than violent and heavy hands upon their goods and purses? Yet these devout prelates, spite of our great Charter and the souls of our progenitors that wrested their liberties out of the Norman grip with their dearest blood and highest prowess, for these many years have not ceased in their pulpits wrenching and spraining the text, to set at nought and trample under foot all the most sacred and life-blood laws, statutes and Acts of Parliament that are the holy covenant of union and marriage between the King and his realm, by proscribing and confiscating from us all the right we have to our own bodies, goods and liberties. What is this but to blow a trumpet and proclaim a fire-cross to a hereditary and perpetual civil war? Thus much against the subject's liberty hath been assaulted by them. Now how they have spared supremacy, or likely are hereafter to submit to it, remains lastly to be considered.

The emulation that under the old Law was in the king toward the priest is now so come about in the gospel that all the danger is to be feared from the priest to the king. While the priest's office in the Law was set out with an exterior lustre of pomp and glory, kings were ambitious to be priests. Now priests, not perceiving the heavenly

68

brightness and inward splendour of their more glorious
evangelic ministry, with as great ambition affect to be   300
kings; as in all their courses is easy to be observed. Their
eyes ever imminent upon worldly matters, their desires
ever thirsting after worldly employments, instead of fervent and diligent study in the Bible they covet to be
expert in canons and decretals, which may enable them to
judge and interpose in temporal causes, however pretended ecclesiastical. Do they not hoard up pelf, seek to
be potent in secular strength, in state affairs, in lands,
lordships and demesnes, to sway and carry all before
them in high courts and privy councils, to bring into their   310
grasp the high and principal offices of the Kingdom?
Have they not been bold of late to check the common
law, to slight and brave the indiminishable majesty of our
highest court, the law-giving and sacred Parliament? Do
they not plainly labour to exempt churchmen from the
magistrate? Yea, so presumptuously as to question and
menace officers that represent the King's person for using
their authority against drunken priests? The cause of pro-
tecting murderous clergymen was the first heart-burning
that swelled up the audacious Becket to the pestilent and   320
odious vexation of Henry the second. Nay more, have
not some of their devoted scholars begun, I need not say
to nibble, but openly to argue against the King's supremacy? Is not the chief of them accused out of his own
book and his late canons to affect a certain, unquestion-
able Patriarchate, independent and unsubordinate to the
Crown? From whence, having first brought us to a servile estate of religion and manhood, and having predis-
posed his conditions with the Pope, that lays claim to this
land, or with some Pepin of his own creating, it were all   330
as likely for him to aspire to the monarchy among us as
that the Pope could find means so on the sudden both to
bereave the Emperor of the Roman territory with the
favour of Italy, and by an unexpected friend out of
France, while he was in danger to lose his new-got purchase, beyond hope to leap into the fair Exarchate of Raven-
na. A good while the Pope subtly acted the lamb, writing

to the Emperor 'my Lord Tiberius', 'my Lord Mauritius ;
but no sooner did this his Lord pluck at the images and
idols but he threw off his sheep's clothing and started up a   340
wolf, laying his paws upon the Emperor's right, as for-
feited to Peter. Why may not we as well, having been
forewarned at home by our renowned Chaucer and from
abroad by the great and learned Padre Paolo, from the
like beginnings (as we see they are) fear the like events?
Certainly a wise and provident king ought to suspect a
hierarchy in his realm, being ever attended as it is with
two such greedy purveyors, ambition and usurpation; I
say he ought to suspect a hierarchy to be as dangerous
and derogatory from his crown as a tetrarchy or a heptar-   350
chy. Yet now that the prelates had almost attained to
what their insolent and unbridled minds had hurried
them, to thrust the laity under the despotical rule of the
monarch that they themselves might confine the monarch
to a kind of pupilage under their hierarchy, observe but
how their own principles combat one another, and sup-
plant each one his fellow.

Having fitted us only for peace, and that a servile
peace, by lessening our numbers, draining our estates,
enfeebling our bodies, cowing our free spirits by those   360
ways as you have heard, their impotent actions cannot
sustain themselves the least moment unless they rouse us
up to a war fit for Cain to be the leader of: an abhorred, a
cursed, a fraternal war. England and Scotland, dearest
brothers both in nature and in Christ, must be set to wade
in one another's blood; and Ireland, our free denizen,
upon the back of us both, as occasion should serve – a
piece of service that the Pope and all his factors have been
compassing to do ever since the Reformation.

But ever blessed be he, and ever glorified, that from his   370
high watchtower in the heavens discerning the crooked
ways of perverse and cruel men hath hitherto maimed and
infatuated all their damnable inventions, and deluded their
great wizards with a delusion fit for fools and children.
Had God been so minded, he could have sent a spirit of
mutiny amongst us, as he did between Abimelech and the

Sechemites, to have made our funerals and slain heaps
more in number than the miserable surviving remnant.
But he, when we least deserved, sent out a gentle gale and
message of peace from the wings of those his Cherubims   380
that fan his mercy-seat. Nor shall the wisdom, the mod-
eration, the Christian piety, the constancy of our nobility
and commons of England be ever forgotten, whose calm
and temperate connivance could sit still and smile out the
stormy bluster of men more audacious and precipitant
than of solid and deep reach, till their own fury had run
itself out of breath, assailing by rash and heady
approaches the impregnable situation of our liberty and
safety; that laughed such weak enginery to scorne, such
poor drifts, to make a national war of a surplice-brabble,   390
a tippet-scuffle, and engage the unattainted honour of
English knighthood to unfurl the streaming red cross or
to rear the horrid standard of those fatal guly dragons for
so unworthy a purpose as to force upon their fellow-
subjects that which themselves are weary of, the skeleton
of a mass-book. Nor must the patience, the fortitude, the
firm obedience of the nobles and people of Scotland striving against manifold provocations, nor must their sincere
and moderate proceedings hitherto be unremembered, to
the shameful conviction of all their detractors.   400

Go on both hand in hand, O nations, never to be
disunited; be the praise and the heroic song of all posterity. Merit this, but seek only virtue, not to extend your
limits; for what needs to win a fading triumphant laurel
out of the tears of wretched men? But to settle the pure
worship of God in his Church, and justice in the state:
then shall the hardest difficulties smooth out themselves
before ye; envy shall sink to hell, craft and malice be
confounded, whether it be home-bred mischief or outlandish cunning. Yea, other nations will then covet to   410
serve ye, for lordship and victory are but the pages of
justice and virtue. Commit securely to true wisdom the
vanquishing and uncasing of craft and subtlety, which are
but her two runagates. Join your invincible might to do
worthy and godlike deeds, and then he that seeks to break

71

your union, a cleaving curse be his inheritance to all generations.

Sir, you have now at length this question for the time, and as my memory would best serve me in such a copious and vast theme, fully handled, and you yourself may judge whether prelacy be the only church-government agreeable to monarchy. Seeing therefore the perilous and confused estate into which we are fallen, and that, to the certain knowledge of all men, through the irreligious pride and hateful tyranny of prelates (as the innumerable and grievous complaints of every shire cry out), if we will now resolve to settle affairs either according to pure religion or sound policy, we must first of all begin roundly to cashier and cut away from the public body the noisome and diseased tumour of prelacy, and come from schism to unity with our neighbour reformed sister churches, which with the blessing of peace and pure doctrine have now long time flourished, and doubtless with all hearty joy and gratulation will meet and welcome our Christian union with them, as they have been all this while grieved at our strangeness and little better than separation from them. And for the discipline propounded, seeing that it hath been inevitably proved that the natural and fundamental causes of political happiness in all governments are the same, and that this church-discipline is taught in the Word of God and, as we see, agrees according to wish with all such states as have received it, we may infallibly assure ourselves that it will as well agree with monarchy, though all the tribe of aphorismers and politicasters would persuade us there be secret and mysterious reasons against it. For upon the settling hereof, mark what nourishing and cordial restorements to the state will follow. The ministers of the gospel attending only to the work of salvation every one within his limited charge, besides the diffusive blessings of God upon all our actions, the King shall sit without an old disturber, a daily encroacher and intruder; shall rid his kingdom of a strong sequestered and collateral power, a confronting mitre, whose potent wealth and wakeful ambition he had just cause to hold in jealousy; not to repeat the other present evils which only their removal will remove. And because things simply pure are inconsistent in the mass of nature, nor are the elements or humours in man's body exactly homogeneal, and hence the best-founded commonwealths and least barbarous have aimed at a certain mixture and temperament, partaking the several virtues of each other state, that each part drawing to itself may keep up a steady and even uprightness in common, there is no civil government that hath been known, no not the Spartan, not the Roman (though both for this respect so much praised by the wise Polybius), more divinely and harmoniously tuned, more equally balanced as it were by the hand and scale of Justice, than is the commonwealth of England, where under a free and untutored monarch the noblest, worthiest and most prudent men, with full approbation and suffrage of the people, have in their power the supreme and final determination of highest affairs.

Now if conformity of church discipline to the civil be so desired, there can be nothing more parallel, more uniform, than when under the sovereign prince, Christ's viceregent, using the sceptre of David according to God's law, the godliest, the wisest, the learnedest ministers in their several charges have the instructing and disciplining of God's people by whose free and full election they are consecrated to that holy and equal aristocracy. And why should not the piety and conscience of Englishmen as members of the Church be trusted in the election of pastors to functions that nothing concern a monarch, as well as their worldly wisdoms are privileged as members of the state in suffraging their knights and burgesses to matters that concern him nearly? And if, in weighing these several offices, their difference in time and quality be cast in, I know they will not turn the beam of equal judgement the moiety of a scruple. We therefore having already a kind of apostolical and ancient church-election in our state, what a perverseness would it be, in us of all others, to retain forcibly a kind of imperious and stately

73

election in our Church? And what a blindness to think that what is already evangelical, as it were, by a happy chance in our polity should be repugnant to that which is the same by divine command in the ministry? Thus then we see that our ecclesial and political choices may consent and sort as well together, without any rupture in the state, as Christians and freeholders. But as for honour, that ought indeed to be different and distinct as either office looks a several way. The minister, whose calling and end is spiritual, ought to be honoured as a father and physician to the soul, if he be found to be so, with a son-like and disciple-like reverence, which is indeed the dearest and most affectionate honour, most to be desired by a wise man, and such as will easily command a free and plentiful provision of outward necessaries, without his further care of this world. The magistrate, whose charge is to see to our persons and estates, is to be honoured with a more elaborate and personal courtship, with large salaries and stipends, that he himself may abound in those things whereof his legal justice and watchful care give us the quiet enjoyment. And this distinction of honour will bring forth a seemly and graceful uniformity over all the kingdom.

Then shall the nobles possess all the dignities and offices of temporal honour to themselves, sole lords without the improper mixture of scholastic and pusillanimous upstarts. The Parliament shall void her upper house of the same annoyances. The common and civil laws shall be both set free, the former from the control, the other from the mere vassalage and copyhold of the clergy. And whereas temporal laws rather punish men when they have transgressed than form them to be such as should transgress seldomest, we may conceive great hopes, through the showers of divine benediction watering the unmolested and watchful pains of the ministry, that the whole inheritance of God will grow up so straight and blameless that the civil magistrate may with far less toil and difficulty, and far more ease and delight, steer the tall and goodly vessel of the commonwealth through all the gusts and tides of the world's mutability.

74

Here I might have ended, but that some objections which I have heard commonly flying about press me to the endeavour of an answer. We must not run, they say, into sudden extremes. This is a fallacious rule, unless understood only of the actions of virtue about things indifferent; for if it be found that those two extremes be vice and virtue, falsehood and truth, the greater extremity of virtue and superlative truth we run into, the more virtuous and the more wise we become. And he that, flying from degenerate and traditional corruption, fears to shoot himself too far into the meeting embraces of a divinely-warranted reformation had better not have run at all. And for the suddenness, it cannot be feared. Who should oppose it? The papists? They dare not. The Protestants otherwise affected? They were mad: there is nothing will be removed but what to them is professedly indifferent. The long affection which the people have borne to it, what for itself, what for the odiousness of the prelates, is evident. From the first year of Queen Elizabeth it hath still been more and more propounded, desired and beseeched, yea sometimes favourably forwarded by the Parliaments themselves. Yet if it were sudden and swift, provided still it be from worse to better, certainly we ought to hie us from evil like a torrent, and rid ourselves of corrupt discipline as we would shake fire out of our bosoms.

Speedy and vehement were the reformations of all the good kings of Judah, though the people had been nuzzled in idolatry never so long before. They feared not the bugbear danger, nor the lion in the way that the sluggish and timorous politician thinks he sees. No more did our brethren of the Reformed Churches abroad; they ventured (God being their guide) out of rigid Popery into that which we in mockery call precise Puritanism, and yet we see no inconvenience befell them. Let us not dally with God when he offers us a full blessing, to take as much of it as we think will serve our ends and turn him back the rest upon his hands, lest in his anger he snatch all from us again.

Next they allege the antiquity of episcopacy through all

540

550

560

570

75

ages. What it was in the Apostles' time, that questionless it must be still; and therein I trust the ministers will be able to satisfy the Parliament. But if episcopacy be taken for prelacy, all the ages they can deduce it through will make it no more venerable than papacy. Most certain it is, as all our stories bear witness, that ever since their coming to the See of Canterbury, for near twelve hun- 580
dred years (to speak of them in general) they have been in England to our souls a sad and doleful succession of illiterate and blind guides; to our purses and goods a wasteful band of robbers, a perpetual havoc and rapine; to our state a continual Hydra of mischief and molestation, the forge of discord and rebellion. This is the trophy of their antiquity and boasted succession through so many ages. And for those prelate-martyrs they glory of, they are to be judged what they were by the gospel, and not the gospel to be tried by them. 590

And it is to be noted that if they were for bishoprics and ceremonies, it was in their prosperity and fullness of bread; but in their persecution which purified them, and near their death which was their garland, they plainly disliked and condemned the ceremonies, and threw away those episcopal ornaments wherein they were installed as foolish and detestable, for so the words of Ridley at his degradement, and his letter to Hooper, expressly show. Neither doth the author of our church history spare to record sadly the fall (for so he terms it) and infirmities of 600
these martyrs, though we would deify them. And why should their martyrdom more countenance corrupt doc- trine or discipline than their subscriptions justify their treason to the royal blood of this realm, by diverting and entailing the right of the Crown from the true heirs to the houses of Northumberland and Suffolk, which had it took effect this present King had in all likelihood never sat on this throne, and the happy union of this island had been frustrated?

Lastly, whereas they add that some of the learnedest of 610
the reformed abroad admire our episcopacy, it had been more for the strength of the argument to tell us that some

76

of the wisest statesmen admire it, for thereby we might guess them weary of the present discipline as offensive to their state, which is the bug we fear; but being they are churchmen, we may rather suspect them for some prelatizing spirits that admire our bishoprics, not episcopacy.

The next objection vanishes of itself, propounding a doubt whether a greater inconvenience would not grow from the corruption of any other discipline than from that 620 of episcopacy. This seems an unseasonable foresight, and out of order to defer and put off the most needful constitution of one right discipline while we stand balancing the discommodities of two corrupt ones. First constitute that which is right, and of itself it will discover and rectify that which swerves, and easily remedy the pretended fear of having a Pope in every parish; unless we call the zealous and meek censure of the Church a Popedom, which who so does let him advise how he can reject the pastorly rod and sheep-hook of Christ, and those 630 cords of love, and not fear to fall under the iron sceptre of his anger, that will dash him to pieces like a potsherd.

At another doubt of theirs I wonder: whether this discipline which we desire be such as can be put in practice within this kingdom. They say it cannot stand with the common law, nor with the King's safety; the government of episcopacy is now so weaved into the common law. In God's name let it weave out again; let not human quillets keep back divine authority. 'Tis not the common law, nor the civil, but piety and justice that are our found- 640 resses. They stoop not, neither change colour for aristocracy, democracy or monarchy, nor yet at all interrupt their just courses; but far above the taking notice of these inferior niceties, with perfect sympathy wherever they meet kiss each other. Lastly, they are fearful that the discipline which will succeed cannot stand with the King's safety. Wherefore? It is but episcopacy reduced to what it should be. Were it not that the tyranny of prelates under the name of bishops hath made our ears tender and startling, we might call every good minister a bishop, as 650 every bishop, yea the Apostles themselves, are called

ministers, and the angels ministering spirits, and the
ministers again angels. But wherein is this propounded
government so shrewd? Because the government of
assemblies will succeed. Did not the Apostles govern the
Church by assemblies? How should it else be catholic?
How should it have communion? We count it sacrilege to
take from the rich prelates their lands and revenues which
is sacrilege in them to keep, using them as they do; and
can we think it safe to defraud the living Church of God   660
of that right which God has given her in assemblies?
Oh, but the consequence: assemblies draw to them the
supremacy of ecclesiastical jurisdiction. No, surely, they
draw no supremacy but that authority which Christ, and
Saint Paul in his name, confers upon them. The King may
still retain the same supremacy in the assemblies as in the
Parliament: here he can do nothing alone against the common law, and there neither alone nor with consent against
the scriptures. But is this all? No, this ecclesiastical supremacy draws to it the power to excommunicate kings;   670
and then follows the worst that can be imagined. Do they
hope to avoid this by keeping prelates, that have so often
done it? Not to exemplify the malapert insolence of our
own bishops in this kind towards our kings, I shall turn
back to the 'primitive and pure times' which the objectors
would have the rule of reformation to us.

Not an assembly, but one Bishop alone, Saint Ambrose
of Milan, held Theodosius the most Christian Emperor
under excommunication above eight months together,
drove him from the church in the presence of his nobles;   680
which the good Emperor bore with heroic humility, and
never ceased by prayers and tears till he was absolved. For
which, coming to the Bishop with supplication into the
Salutatory (some out-porch of the church), he was
charged by him of tyrannical madness against God for
coming into holy ground. At last, upon conditions
absolved, and after great humiliation approaching to the
altar to offer (as those thrice pure times then thought
meet), he had scarce withdrawn his hand and stood
awhile when a bold Archdeacon comes in the Bishop's   690

78

name and chases him from within the rails, telling him
peremptorily that the place wherein he stood was for
none but the priests to enter or to touch: and this is
another piece of pure primitive divinity. Think ye then
our bishops will forgo the power of excommunication on
whomsoever? No, certainly, unless to compass sinister
ends, and then revoke when they see their time. And yet
this most mild (though withal dreadful) and inviolable
prerogative of Christ's diadem, excommunication, serves
for nothing with them but to prog and pander for fees, or   700
to display their pride and sharpen their revenge, debarring
men the protection of the law; and I remember not
whether in some cases it bereave not men all right to their
worldly goods and inheritances, besides the denial of
Christian burial. But in the evangelical and reformed use
of this sacred censure no such prostitution, no such Iscariotical drifts are to be doubted, as that spiritual doom and
sentence should invade worldly possession, which is the
rightful lot and portion even of the wickedest men, as
frankly bestowed upon them by the all-dispensing bounty   710
as rain and sunshine. No, no, it seeks not to bereave or
destroy the body; it seeks to save the soul by humbling
the body, not by imprisonment or pecuniary mulct,
much less by stripes or bonds or disinheritance, but by
fatherly admonishment and Christian rebuke, to cast it
into godly sorrow, whose end is joy and ingenuous bash-
fulness to sin. If that cannot be wrought, then as a tender
mother takes her child and holds it over the pit with
scaring words that it may learn to fear where danger is, so
doth excommunication as dearly and as freely, without   720
money, use her wholesome and saving terrors. She is
instant; she beseeches; by all the dear and sweet promises
of salvation she entices and woos; by all the threatenings
and thunders of the Law and rejected gospel she charges
and adjures. This is all her armoury, her munition, her
artillery; then she awaits with long-sufferance and yet
ardent zeal. In brief, there is no act in all the errand of
God's ministers to mankind wherein passes more lover-
like contestation between Christ and the soul of a re-

79

generate man lapsing than before, and in, and after the   730
sentence of excommunication. As for the fogging proctorage of money, with such an eye as struck Gehezi with
leprosy and Simon Magus with a curse, so does she look,
and so threaten her fiery whip against that banking den of
thieves that dare thus baffle and buy and sell the awful
and majestic wrinkles of her brow. He that is rightly and
apostolically sped with her invisible arrow, if he can be at
peace with his soul, and not smell within him the brim-
stone of hell, may have fair leave to tell all his bags over
undiminished of the least farthing, may eat his dainties,   740
drink his wine, use his delights, enjoy his lands and liberties, not the least skin raised, not the least hair misplaced
for all that excommunication has done. Much more may
a king enjoy his rights and prerogatives undeflowered,
untouched, and be as absolute and complete a king as all
his royalties and revenues can make him. And therefore
little did Theodosius fear a plot upon his Empire when he
stood excommunicate by Saint Ambrose, though it were
done either with much haughty pride or ignorant zeal.

But let us rather look upon the Reformed Churches   750
beyond the seas, the Grizons, the Swiss, the Hollanders,
the French, that have a supremacy to live under as well as
we. Where do the churches in all these places strive for
supremacy? Where do they clash and jostle supremacies
with the civil magistrate? In France, a more severe
monarchy than ours, the Protestants under this church
government carry the name of the best subjects the King
has; and yet Presbytery, if it must be so called, does there
all that it desires to do. How easy were it, if there be such
great suspicion, to give no more scope to it in England.   760
But let us not, for fear of a scarecrow, or else through
hatred to be reformed, stand hankering and politizing,
when God with spread hands testifies to us and points us
out the way to our peace.

Let us not be so over-credulous, unless God hath
blinded us, as to trust our souls into the hands of men
that beg so devoutly for the pride and gluttony of their
own backs and bellies, that sue and solicit so eagerly, not

for the saving of souls (the consideration of which can
have here no place at all) but for their bishoprics, deaner-   770
ies, prebends and canonries. How can these men not be
corrupt, whose very cause is the bribe of their own pleading? Whose mouths cannot open without the strong
breath and loud stench of avarice, simony and sacrilege,
embezzling the treasury of the Church on painted and
gilded walls of temples wherein God hath testified to have
no delight, warming their palace kitchens, and from
thence their unctuous and epicurean paunches, with the
alms of the blind, the lame, the impotent, the aged, the
orphan, the widow? For with these the treasury of Christ   780
ought to be; here must be his jewels bestowed; his rich
cabinet must be emptied here; as the constant martyr
Saint Lawrence taught the Roman Praetor. Sir, would
you know what the remonstrance of these men would
have, what their Petition implies? They entreat us that we
would not be weary of those insupportable grievances
that our shoulders have hitherto cracked under. They
beseech us that we would think 'em fit to be our Justices
of Peace, our Lords, our highest Officers of State, though
they come furnished with no more experience than they   790
learnt between the cook and the manciple, or more pro-
foundly, at the College audit or the Regent House, or, to
come to their deepest insight, at their patron's table. They
would request us to endure still the rustling of their silken
cassocks, and that we would burst our midriffs rather
than laugh to see them under sail in all their lawn and
sarsnet, their shrouds and tackle, with a geometrical
rhomboides upon their heads. They would bear us in
hand that we must of duty still appear before them once a
year in Jerusalem like good circumcised males, and   800
females, to be taxed by the poll, to be sconced our head-
money, our tuppences, in their chandlerly shop-book of
Easter. They pray us that it would please us to let them
still hale us and worry us with their band-dogs and pursuivants, and that it would please the Parliament that they
may yet have the whipping, fleecing and flaying of us in
their diabolical courts, to tear the flesh from our bones

81

and into our wide wounds instead of balm to pour in tne
oil of tartar, vitriol and mercury: surely a right reasonable, innocent and soft-hearted petition. O the relenting   810
bowels of the Fathers! Can this be granted them unless
God have smitten us with frenzy from above, and with a
dazzling giddiness at noonday? Should not those men
rather be heard that come to plead against their own
preferments, their worldly advantages, their own abundance, for honour and obedience to God's word, the conversion of souls, the Christian peace of the land and union
of the reformed Catholic Church, the unappropriating
and unmonopolizing the rewards of learning and industry
from the greasy clutch of ignorance and high feeding? We   820
have tried already and miserably felt what ambition,
worldly glory and immoderate wealth can do, what the
boisterous and contradictional hand of a temporal, earthly
and corporeal spirituality can avail to the edifying of
Christ's holy Church. Were it such a desperate hazard to
put to the venture the universal votes of Christ's congregation, the fellowly and friendly yoke of a teaching
and laborious ministry, the pastor-like and apostolic im-
itation of meek and unlordly discipline, the gentle and
benevolent mediocrity of church-maintenance without   830
the ignoble hucksterage of piddling tithes? Were it such
an incurable mischief to make a little trial what all this
would do to the flourishing and growing up of Christ's
mystical body, as rather to use every poor shift, and if
that serve not, to threaten uproar and combustion, and
shake the brand of civil discord?

O sir, I do now feel myself enwrapped on the sudden
into those mazes and labyrinths of dreadful and hideous
thoughts, that which way to get out or which way to end
I know not, unless I turn mine eyes and with your help   840
lift up my hands to that eternal and propitious throne
where nothing is readier than grace and refuge to the
distresses of mortal suppliants; and it were a shame to
leave these serious thoughts less piously than the heathen
were wont to conclude their graver discourses.

Thou therefore that sitst in light and glory unapproach-

82

able, Parent of angels and men! Next thee I implore, omnipotent King, redeemer of that lost remnant whose nature thou didst assume, ineffable and everlasting Love! And thou, the third subsistence of divine infinitude, illuminating Spirit, the joy and solace of created things! One tri-personal Godhead! Look upon this thy poor and almost spent and expiring Church; leave her not thus a prey to these importunate wolves, that wait and think long before they devour thy tender flock, these wild boars that have broke into thy vineyard and left the print of their polluting hooves on the souls of thy servants. O let them not bring about their damned designs, that stand now at the entrance of the bottomless pit, expecting the watchword to open and let out those dreadful locusts and scorpions, to reinvolve us in that pitchy cloud of infernal darkness where we shall never more see the sun of thy truth again, never hope for the cheerful dawn, never more hear the bird of morning sing. Be moved with pity at the afflicted state of this our shaken monarchy, that now lies labouring under her throes and struggling against the grudges of more dreadful calamities.

O thou that after the impetuous rage of five bloody inundations, and the succeeding sword of intestine war soaking the land in her own gore, didst pity the sad and ceaseless revolution of our swift and thick-coming sorrows when we were quite breathless, of thy free grace didst motion peace and terms of covenant with us, and having first well-nigh freed us from antichristian thralldom didst build up this Britannic empire to a glorious and enviable height with all her daughter islands about her, stay us in this felicity; let not the obstinacy of our half-obedience and will-worship bring forth that viper of sedition that for these fourscore years hath been breeding to eat through the entrails of our peace, but let her cast her abortive spawn without the danger of this travailing and throbbing kingdom, that we may still remember in our solemn thanksgivings how for us the northern ocean, even to the frozen Thule, was scattered with the proud shipwrecks of the Spanish Armada, and the very maw of

Hell ransacked and made to give up her concealed destruction ere she could vent it in that horrible and damned blast.

O how much more glorious will those former deliverances appear when we shall know them not only to have saved us from greatest miseries past but to have reserved us for greatest happiness to come. Hitherto thou hast but freed us, and that not fully, from the unjust and tyrannous claim of thy foes; now unite us entirely and appropriate us to thyself, tie us everlastingly in willing homage to thy eternal throne.

And now we know, O thou our most certain hope and defence, that thine enemies have been consulting all the sorceries of the Great Whore, and have joined their plots with that sad intelligencing tyrant that mischiefs the world with his mines of Ophir and lies thirsting to revenge his naval ruins that have larded our seas. But let them all take counsel together, and let it come to nought; let them decree, and do thou cancel it; let them gather themselves and be scattered; let them embattle themselves and be broken; for thou art with us.

Then, amidst the hymns and halleluiahs of saints, some one may perhaps be heard offering at high strains in new and lofty measures to sing and celebrate thy divine mercies and marvellous judgements in this land throughout all ages, whereby this great and warlike nation, instructed and inured to the fervent and continual practice of truth and righteousness, and casting far from her the rags of her old vices, may press on hard to that high and happy emulation to be found the soberest, wisest and most Christian people at that day when thou, the eternal and shortly-expected King, shalt open the clouds to judge the several kingdoms of the world, and distributing national honours and rewards to religious and just commonwealths, shalt put an end to all earthly tyrannies, proclaiming thy universal and mild monarchy through Heaven and Earth; where they undoubtedly that by their labours, counsels and prayers have been earnest for the common good of religion and their country shall receive,

890

900

910

920

above the inferior orders of the blessed, the regal addition
of Principalities, Legions and Thrones into their glorious
titles, and in supereminence of beatific vision progressing
the dateless and irrevoluble circle of eternity shall clasp
inseparable hands with joy and bliss in over-measure for
ever.   930

But they, contrary, that by the impairing and diminu-
tion of the true faith, the distresses and servitude of their
country, aspire to high dignity, rule and promotion here,
after a shameful end in this life (which God grant them)
shall be thrown down eternally into the darkest and
deepest gulf of Hell, where under the despiteful control,
the trample and spurn of all the other damned, that in the
anguish of their torture shall have no other ease than to
exercise a raving and bestial tyranny over them as their
slaves and negroes, they shall remain in that plight for   940
ever, the basest, the lowermost, the most dejected, most
underfoot and downtrodden vassals of perdition.

First published 1641

from AREOPAGITICA

Dionysius Alexandrinus was, about the year 240, a person
of great name in the Church for piety and learning, who
had wont to avail himself much against heretics by being
conversant in their books; until a certain Presbyter laid it
scrupulously to his conscience, how he durst venture
himself among those defiling volumes. The worthy man,
loth to give offence, fell into a new debate with himself
what was to be thought; when suddenly a vision sent
from God (it is his own Epistle that so avers it) confirmed
him, in these words: 'Read any books whatever come to   10
thy hands, for thou art sufficient both to judge aright and
to examine each matter.' To this revelation he assented
the sooner, as he confesses, because it was answerable to
that of the Apostle to the Thessalonians: 'Prove all things,
hold fast that which is good'; and he might have added
another remarkable saying of the same author: 'To the

pure all things are pure' – not only meats and drinks, but all kind of knowledge, whether of good or evil. The knowledge cannot defile, nor consequently the books, if the will and conscience be not defiled. For books are as meats and viands are, some of good, some of evil sub- stance; and yet God, in that unapocryphal vision, said with- out exception 'Rise, Peter, kill and eat', leaving the choice to each man's discretion. Wholesome meats to a vitiated stomach differ little or nothing from unwholesome, and best books to a naughty mind are not unappliable to occasions of evil. Bad meats will scarce breed good nourishment in the healthiest concoction; but herein the difference is of bad books, that they to a discreet and judicious reader serve in many respects to discover, to confute, to forewarn and to illustrate. Whereof what bet- ter witness can ye expect I should produce than one of your own now sitting in Parliament, the chief of learned men reputed in this land, Mr Selden, whose volume of natural and national laws proves, not only by great au- thorities brought together but by exquisite reasons and theorems almost mathematically demonstrative, that all opinions, yea errors, known, read and collated are of main service and assistance toward the speedy attainment of what is truest. I conceive therefore that when God did enlarge the universal diet of man's body, saving ever the rules of temperance, he then also, as before, left arbitrary the dieting and repasting of our minds, as wherein every mature man might have to exercise his own leading capacity.

How great a virtue is temperance, how much of mo- ment through the whole life of man; yet God commits the managing so great a trust, without particular law or prescription, wholly to the demeanour of every grown man. And therefore when he himself tabled the Jews from heaven, that 'omer' which was every man's daily portion of manna is computed to have been more than might have sufficed the heartiest feeder thrice as many meals; for those actions which enter into a man rather than issue out of him, and therefore defile not, God uses not to captivate

86

under a perpetual childhood of prescription, but trusts
him with the gift of reason to be his own chooser. There
were but little work left for preaching, if law and compulsion should grow so fast upon those things which
heretofore were governed only by exhortation. Solomon   60
informs us that much reading is a weariness of the flesh;
but neither he nor other inspired author tells us that such
or such reading is unlawful. Yet certainly, had God
thought good to limit us herein, it had been much more
expedient to have told us what was unlawful than what
was wearisome. As for the burning of those Ephesian
books by Saint Paul's converts, 'tis replied the books
were magic: the Syriac so renders them. It was a private
act, a voluntary act, and leaves us to a voluntary imita-
tion. The men in remorse burnt those books which were   70
their own; the magistrate by this example is not
appointed. These men practised the books; another might
perhaps have read them in some sort usefully.

Good and evil, we know, in the field of this world
grow up together almost inseparably, and the knowledge
of good is so involved and interwoven with the knowledge of evil, and in so many cunning resemblances hardly to be discerned, that those confused seeds which were
imposed on Psyche as an incessant labour to cull out and
sort asunder were not more intermixed. It was from out   80
the rind of one apple tasted that the knowledge of good
and evil, as two twins cleaving together, leapt forth into
the world; and perhaps this is that doom which Adam fell
into of knowing good and evil, that is to say of knowing
good by evil. As therefore the state of man now is, what
wisdom can there be to choose, what continence to forbear, without the knowledge of evil? He that can
apprehend and consider vice with all her baits and seem-
ing pleasures, and yet abstain, and yet distinguish, and yet
prefer that which is truly better, he is the true warfaring 90
Christian. I cannot praise a fugitive and cloistered virtue,
unexercised and unbreathed, that never sallies out and
sees her adversary, but slinks out of the race where that
immortal garland is to be run for, not without dust and

heat. Assuredly we bring not innocence into the world, we bring impurity much rather; that which purifies us is trial, and trial is by what is contrary. That virtue therefore which is but a youngling in the contemplation of evil, and knows not the utmost that vice promises to her followers, and rejects it, is but a blank virtue, not a pure: her whiteness is but an excremental whiteness. Which was the reason why our sage and serious poet Spenser, whom I dare be known to think a better teacher than Scotus or Aquinas, describing true temperance under the person of Guyon, brings him in with his Palmer through the Cave of Mammon and the Bower of Earthly Bliss, that he might see and know, and yet abstain.

Since therefore the knowledge and survey of vice is in this world so necessary to the constituting of human virtue, and the scanning of error to the confirmation of truth, how can we more safely and with less danger scout into the regions of sin and falsity than by reading all manner of tractates and hearing all manner of reason? And this is the benefit that may be had of books promiscuously read. But of the harm that may result thence, three kinds are usually reckoned. First is feared the infection that may spread. But then all human learning and controversy in religious points must remove out of the world, yea the Bible itself; for that ofttimes relates blasphemy not nicely, it describes the carnal sense of wicked men not unelegantly, it brings in holiest men passionately murmuring against providence through all the arguments of Epicurus. In other great disputes it answers dubiously and darkly to the common reader. And ask a Talmudist what ails the modesty of his marginal *keri*, that Moses and all the prophets cannot persuade him to pronounce the textual *chetiv*. For these causes we all know the Bible itself put by the papist into the first rank of prohibited books. The ancientest Fathers must be next removed, as Clement of Alexandria, and that Eusebian book of evangelic preparation, transmitting our ears through a hoard of heathenish obscenities to receive the gospel. Who finds not that Irenaeus, Epiphanius, Jerome and others discover more heresies than they well confute, and that oft for heresy which is the truer opinion? Nor boots it to say for these, and all the heathen writers of greatest infection (if it must be thought so) with whom is bound up the life of human learning, that they writ in an unknown tongue, so long as we are sure those languages are known as well to the worst of men, who are both most able and most diligent 140 to instil the poison they suck first into the courts of princes, acquainting them with the choicest delights and criticisms of sin; as perhaps did that Petronius whom Nero called his *arbiter*, the master of his revels, and that notorious ribald of Arezzo, dreaded and yet dear to the Italian courtiers. (I name not him, for posterity's sake, whom Harry the eighth named in merriment his Vicar of Hell.) By which compendious way all the contagion that foreign books can infuse will find a passage to the people far easier and shorter than an Indian voyage, though it 150 could be sailed either by the north of Cataio or of Canada westward, while our Spanish licensing gags the English press never so severely.

But on the other side, that infection which is from books of controversy in religion is more doubtful and dangerous to the learned than to the ignorant; and yet those books must be permitted untouched by the licenser. It will be hard to instance where any ignorant man hath been ever seduced by papistical book in English, unless it were commended and expounded to him by some of that 160 clergy; and indeed all such tractates, whether false or true, are as the prophecy of Isaiah was to the eunuch, not to be understood without a guide. But of our priests and doctors how many have been corrupted by studying the comments of Jesuits and Sorbonnists, and how fast they could infuse that corruption into the people, our experience is both late and sad. It is not forgot since the acute and distinct Arminius was perverted merely by the perusing of a nameless discourse written at Delft, which at first he took in hand to confute. Seeing therefore that those 170 books, and those in great abundance, which are likeliest to taint both life and doctrine cannot be suppressed with-

out the fall of learning and of all ability in disputation,
and that these books of either sort are most and soonest
catching to the learned, from whom to the common
people whatever is heretical or dissolute may quickly be
conveyed, and that evil manners are as perfectly learnt
without books a thousand other ways which cannot be
stopped, and evil doctrine not with books can propagate
except a teacher guide, which he might also do without   180
writing and so beyond prohibiting, I am not able to
unfold how this cautelous enterprise of licensing can be
exempted from the number of vain and impossible
attempts; and he who were pleasantly disposed could not
well avoid to liken it to the exploit of that gallant man
who thought to pound up the crows by shutting his
park-gate. Besides another inconvenience: if learned men
be the first receivers out of books and dispreaders both of
vice and error, how shall the licensers themselves be con-
fided in, unless we can confer upon them, or they assume   190
to themselves above all others in the land, the grace of
infallibility and uncorruptedness? And again, if it be true
that a wise man like a good refiner can gather gold out of
the drossiest volume, and that a fool will be a fool with
the best book, there is no reason that we should deprive a
wise man of any advantage to his wisdom while we seek
to restrain from a fool that which, being restrained, will
be no hindrance to his folly. For if there should be so
much exactness always used to keep that from him which
is unfit for his reading, we should, in the judgement of   200
Aristotle not only but of Solomon and of our Saviour,
not vouchsafe him good precepts, and by consequence
not willingly admit him to good books, as being certain
that a wise man will make better use of an idle pamphlet
than a fool will do of sacred scripture.

'Tis next alleged we must not expose ourselves to
temptations without necessity; and next to that, not employ our time in vain things. To both these objections
one answer will serve, out of the grounds already laid:
that to all men such books are not temptations nor vani-   210
ties, but useful drugs and materials wherewith to temper

and compose effective and strong medicines, which man's life cannot want. The rest, as children and childish men who have not the art to qualify and prepare these working minerals, well may be exhorted to forbear, but hindered forcibly they cannot be by all the licensing that Sainted Inquisition could ever yet contrive. Which is what I promised to deliver next, that this order of licensing conduces nothing to the end for which it was framed, and hath almost prevented me by being clear already while thus much hath been explaining. 220

See the ingenuity of truth, who when she gets a free and willing hand opens herself faster than the pace of method and discourse can overtake her. It was the task which I began with: to show that no nation or well-instituted state, if they valued books at all, did ever use this way of licensing. And it might be answered that this is a piece of prudence lately discovered; to which I return that as it was a thing slight and obvious to think on, so if it had been difficult to find out, there wanted not among 230 them long since who suggested such a course, which they not following leave us a pattern of their judgement, that it was not the not knowing but the not approving that was the cause of their not using it. Plato, a man of high authority indeed, but least of all for his commonwealth in the book of his *Laws*, which no city ever yet received, fed his fancy with making many edicts to his airy burgomasters, which they who otherwise admire him wish had been rather buried and excused in the genial cups of an academic night-sitting; by which laws he seems to toler- 240 ate no kind of learning but by unalterable decree, consisting most of practical traditions, to the attainment whereof a library of smaller bulk than his own dialogues would be abundant; and there also enacts that no poet should so much as read to any private man what he had written until the judges and law-keepers had seen it and allowed it. But that Plato meant this law peculiarly to that commonwealth which he had imagined, and to no other, is apparent. Why was he not else a lawgiver to himself, but a transgressor, and to be expelled by his own magistrates, 250

both for the wanton epigrams and dialogues which he
made and his perpetual reading of Sophron Mimus and
Aristophanes, books of grossest infamy, and also for
commending the latter of them, though he were the malicious libeller of his chief friends, to be read by the tyrant
Dionysius, who had little need of such trash to spend his
time on? but that he knew this licensing of poems had
reference and dependence to many other provisos there
set down in his fancied republic, which in this world
would have no place; and so neither he himself nor any   260
magistrate or city ever imitated that course, which taken
apart from those other collateral injunctions must needs
be vain and fruitless. For if they fell upon one kind of
strictness, unless their care were equal to regulate all other
things of like aptness to corrupt the mind, that single
endeavour, they knew, would be but a fond labour: to
shut and fortify one gate against corruption, and be
necessitated to leave others round about wide open.

If we think to regulate printing, thereby to rectify manners, we must regulate all recreations and pastimes, all   270
that is delightful to man. No music must be heard, no
song be set or sung, but what is grave and Doric. There
must be licensing dancers, that no gesture, motion or
deportment be taught our youth but what by their
allowance shall be thought honest; for such Plato was
provided of. It will ask more than the work of twenty
licensers to examine all the lutes, the violins and the
guitars in every house. They must not be suffered to
prattle as they do, but must be licensed what they may
say. And who shall silence all the airs and madrigals that   280
whisper softness in chambers? The windows also and the
balconies must be thought on: there are shrewd books
with dangerous frontispieces set to sale. Who shall prohi-
bit them, shall twenty licensers? The villages also must
have their visitors to enquire what lectures the bagpipe
and the rebeck reads, even to the balladry and the gamut
of every municipal fiddler; for these are the countryman's
Arcadias and his Montemayors. Next, what more national
corruption, for which England hears ill abroad, than

household gluttony? Who shall be the rectors of our daily 290
riotıng? And what shall be done to inhibit the multitudes
that frequent those houses where drunkenness is sold and
harboured? Our garments also should be referred to the
licensing of some more sober work-masters to see them
cut into a less wanton garb. Who shall regulate all the
mixed conversation of our youth, male and female
together, as is the fashion of this country? Who shall still
appoint what shall be discoursed, what presumed, and no
further? Lastly, who shall forbid and separate all idle
resort, all evil company? 300

These things will be, and must be; but how they shall
be least hurtful, how least enticing: herein consists the
grave and governing wisdom of a state. To sequester out
of the world into Atlantic and Utopian polities, which
never can be drawn into use, will not mend our condition, but to ordain wisely as in this world of evil, in the
midst whereof God hath placed us unavoidably. Nor is it
Plato's licensing of books will do this, which necessarily
pulls along with it so many other kinds of licensing as
will make us all both ridiculous and weary, and yet 310
frustrate. But those unwritten or at least unconstraining
laws of virtuous education, religious and civil nurture,
which Plato there mentions as the bonds and ligaments of
the commonwealth, the pillars and the sustainers of every
written statute, these they be which will bear chief sway
in such matters as these, when all licensing will be easily
eluded. Impunity and remissness for certain are the bane
of a commonwealth; but here the great art lies to discern
in what the law is to bid restraint and punishment, and in
what things persuasion only is to work. If every action 320
which is good or evil in man at ripe years were to be
under pittance and prescription and compulsion, what
were virtue but a name? What praise could then be due to
well-doing, what grammercy to be sober, just or conti-
nent? Many there be that complain of divine providence
for suffering Adam to trangress. Foolish tongues! When
God gave him reason, he gave him freedom to choose,
for reason is but choosing. He had been else a mere

93

artificial Adam, such an Adam as he is in the motions. We
ourselves esteem not of that obedience or love or gift   330
which is of force. God therefore left him free, set before
him a provoking object ever almost in his eyes: herein
consisted his merit, herein the right of his reward, the
praise of his abstinence. Wherefore did he create passions
within us, pleasures round about us, but that these, rightly tempered, are the very ingredients of virtue? They are
not skilful considerers of human things who imagine to
remove sin by removing the matter of sin; for besides that
it is a huge heap increasing under the very act of dimi-
nishing, though some part of it may for a time be with-   340
drawn from some persons, it cannot from all, in such a
universal thing as books are; and when this is done, yet
the sin remains entire. Though ye take from a covetous
man all his treasure, he has yet one jewel left: ye cannot
bereave him of his covetousness. Banish all objects of
lust, shut up all youth into the severest discipline that can
be exercised in any hermitage, ye cannot make them
chaste that came not thither so.

Such great care and wisdom is required to the right
managing of this point. Suppose we could expel sin by   350
this means; look, how much we thus expel of sin, so
much we expel of virtue. For the matter of them both is
the same: remove that and ye remove them both alike.
This justifies the high providence of God, who though he
command us temperance, justice, continence, yet pours
out before us even to a profuseness all desirable things,
and gives us minds that can wander beyond all limit and
satiety. Why should we then affect a rigour contrary to
the manner of God and of nature by abridging or scanting
those means, which books freely permitted are, both to   360
the trial of virtue and the exercise of truth? It would be
better done to learn that the law must needs be frivolous
which goes to restrain things uncertainly and yet equally
working to good and to evil. And were I the chooser, a
dram of well-doing should be preferred before many
times as much the forcible hindrance of evil-doing. For
God sure esteems the growth and completing of one
virtuous person more than the restraint of ten vicious.

. . .

Well knows he who uses to consider that our faith and
knowledge thrives by exercise as well as our limbs and   370
complexion. Truth is compared in scripture to a streaming fountain. If her waters flow not in a perpetual progression, they sicken into a muddy pool of conformity and
tradition. A man may be a heretic in the truth; and if he
believe things only because his Pastor says so or the
Assembly so determines, without knowing other reason,
though his belief be true, yet the very truth he holds
becomes his heresy. There is not any burden that some
would gladlier post off to another than the charge and
care of their religion. There be, who knows not that there   380
be of Protestants and professors who live and die in as
arrant an implicit faith as any lay papist of Loreto. A
wealthy man addicted to his pleasure and to his profits
finds religion to be a traffic so entangled and of so many
piddling accounts that of all mysteries he cannot skill to
keep a stock going upon that trade. What should he do?
Fain he would have the name to be religious; fain he
would bear up with his neighbours in that. What does he
therefore but resolves to give over toiling, and to find
himself out some factor to whose care and credit he may   390
commit the whole managing of his religious affairs: some
divine of note and estimation that must be. To him he
adheres, resigns the whole warehouse of his religion with
all the locks and keys into his custody, and indeed makes
the very person of that man his religion, esteems his
associating with him a sufficient evidence and commenda-
tory of his own piety. So that a man may say his religion
is now no more within himself, but is become a dividual
movable, and goes and comes near him according as that
good man frequents the house. He entertains him, gives   400
him gifts, feasts him, lodges him. His religion comes
home at night, prays, is liberally supped and sumptuously
laid to sleep, rises, is saluted, and after the malmsey or
some well-spiced brewage, and better breakfasted than he
whose morning appetite would have gladly fed on green
figs between Bethany and Jerusalem, his religion walks
abroad at eight, and leaves his kind entertainer in the shop
trading all day without his religion.

Another sort there be, who when they hear that all things shall be ordered, all things regulated and settled, nothing written but what passes through the custom-house of certain publicans that have the tonnaging and poundaging of all free-spoken truth, will straight give themselves up into your hands, make 'em and cut 'em out what religion ye please. There be delights, there be recreations and jolly pastimes that will fetch the day about from sun to sun and rock the tedious year as in a delightful dream. What need they torture their heads with that which others have taken so strictly and so unalterably into their own purveying? These are the fruits which a dull ease and cessation of our knowledge will bring forth among the people. How goodly, and how to be wished, were such an obedient unanimity as this; what a fine conformity would it starch us all into, doubtless a staunch and solid piece of framework as any January could freeze together.

Nor much better will be the consequence even among the clergy themselves. It is no new thing, never heard of before, for a parochial minister who has his reward and is at his Hercules' pillars in a warm benefice to be easily inclinable, if he have nothing else that may rouse up his studies, to finish his circuit in an English concordance and a topic folio, the gatherings and savings of a sober graduateship, a *Harmony* and a *Catena*, treading the constant round of certain common doctrinal heads, attended with their uses, motives, marks and means, out of which, as out of an alphabet or sol-fa, by forming and transforming, joining and disjoining variously, a little bookcraft and two hours meditation might furnish him unspeakably to the performance of more than a weekly charge of sermoning – not to reckon up the infinite helps of interlinearies, breviaries, synopses and other loitering gear. But as for the multitude of sermons ready printed and piled up on every text that is not difficult, our London-trading St Thomas in his vestry, and add to boot St Martin and St Hugh, have not within their hallowed limits more vendible ware of all sorts ready-made; so that

penury he never need fear of pulpit-provision, having
where so plenteously to refresh his magazine. But if his
rear and flanks be not impaled, if his back door be not   450
secured by the rigid licenser but that a bold book may
now and then issue forth and give the assault to some of
his old collections in their trenches, it will concern him
then to keep waking, to stand in watch, to set good
guards and sentinels about his received opinions, to walk
the round and counter-round with his fellow-inspectors,
fearing lest any of his flock be seduced, who also then
would be better instructed, better exercised and disci-
plined. And God send that the fear of this diligence which
must then be used do not make us affect the laziness of a   460
licensing church. For if we be sure we are in the right,
and do not hold the truth guiltily, which becomes not; if
we ourselves condemn not our own weak and frivolous
teaching, and the people for an untaught and irreligious
gadding rout, what can be more fair than when a man
judicious, learned and of a conscience, for aught we
know, as good as theirs that taught us what we know,
shall, not privily from house to house (which is more
dangerous) but openly by writing, publish to the world
what his opinion is, what his reasons, and wherefore that   470
which is now thought cannot be sound? Christ urged it as
wherewith to justify himself that he preached in public;
yet writing is more public than preaching, and more easy
to refutation if need be, there being so many whose
business and profession merely it is to be the champions
of truth, which if they neglect, what can be imputed but
their sloth or unability?

Thus much we are hindered and disinured by this
course of licensing toward the true knowledge of what
we seem to know. For how much it hurts and hinders the   480
licensers themselves in the calling of their ministry, more
than any secular employment if they will discharge that
office as they ought, so that of necessity they must neglect either the one duty or the other, I insist not, because
it is a particular, but leave it to their own conscience how
they will decide it there.

There is yet behind of what I purposed to lay open: the incredible loss and detriment that this plot of licensing puts us to. More than if some enemy at sea should stop up all our havens and ports and creeks, it hinders and   490 retards the importation of our richest merchandise, truth. Nay, it was first established and put in practice by anti-christian malice and mystery, on set purpose to extinguish, if it were possible, the light of reformation, and to settle falsehood; little differing from that policy wherewith the Turk upholds his *Alcoran* by the prohibition of printing. 'Tis not denied, but gladly confessed, we are to send our thanks and vows to Heaven louder than most nations for that great measure of truth which we enjoy, especially in those main points between us and the Pope,   500 with his appurtenances the prelates. But he who thinks we are to pitch our tent here, and have attained the utmost prospect of reformation that the mortal glass wherein we contemplate can show us till we come to beatific vision, that man by this very opinion declares that he is yet far short of truth.

Truth indeed came once into the world with her divine Master, and was a perfect shape most glorious to look upon. But when he ascended, and his Apostles after him were laid asleep, then straight arose a wicked race of   510 deceivers who (as that story goes of the Egyptian Typhon with his conspirators, how they dealt with the god Osiris) took the virgin Truth, hewed her lovely form into a thousand pieces and scattered them to the four winds. From that time ever since, the sad friends of Truth, such as durst appear, imitating the careful search that Isis made for the mangled body of Osiris, went up and down gathering up limb by limb still as they could find them. We have not yet found them all, Lords and Commons, nor ever shall do, till her Master's second coming. He   520 shall bring together every joint and member, and shall mould them into an immortal feature of loveliness and perfection. Suffer not these licensing prohibitions to stand at every place of opportunity, forbidding and disturbing them that continue seeking, that continue to do our obse-

quies to the torn body of our martyred saint. We boast
our light, but if we look not wisely on the sun itself it
smites us into darkness. Who can discern those planets
that are oft combust, and those stars of brightest magni-
tude that rise and set with the sun, until the opposite   530
motion of their orbs bring them to such a place in the
firmament where they may be seen evening or morning?
The light which we have gained was given us, not to be
ever staring on, but by it to discover onward things more
remote from our knowledge. It is not the unfrocking of a
priest, the unmitring of a bishop and the removing him
from off the Presbyterian shoulders that will make us a
happy nation; no, if other things as great in the Church
and in the rule of life both economical and political be not
looked into and reformed, we have looked so long upon   540
the blaze that Zwinglius and Calvin hath beaconed up to
us that we are stark blind. There be who perpetually
complain of schisms and sects, and make it such a calam-
ity that any man dissents from their maxims. 'Tis their
own pride and ignorance which causes the disturbing,
who neither will hear with meekness nor can convince;
yet all must be suppressed which is not found in their
syntagma. They are the troublers, they are the dividers of
unity who neglect and permit not others to unite those
dissevered pieces which are yet wanting to the body of   550
Truth. To be still searching what we know not by what
we know, still closing up truth to truth as we find it (for
all her body is homogeneal and proportional): this is the
golden rule in theology as well as in arithmetic, and
makes up the best harmony in a church; not the forced
and outward union of cold and neutral and inwardly
divided minds.

Lords and Commons of England, consider what nation
it is whereof ye are, and whereof ye are the governors: a
nation not slow and dull, but of a quick, ingenious and   560
piercing spirit, acute to invent, subtle and sinewy to discourse, not beneath the reach of any point the highest that
human capacity can soar to. Therefore the studies of
learning in her deepest sciences have been so ancient and

so eminent among us that writers of good antiquity and ablest judgement have been persuaded that even the school of Pythagoras and the Persian wisdom took beginning from the old philosophy of this island. And that wise and civil Roman Julius Agricola, who governed once here for Caesar, preferred the natural wits of Britain before the laboured studies of the French. Nor is it for nothing that the grave and frugal Transylvanian sends out yearly from as far as the mountainous borders of Russia and beyond the Hercynian wilderness not their youth, but their staid men, to learn our language and our theologic arts. Yet that which is above all this, the favour and the love of Heaven, we have great argument to think in a peculiar manner propitious and propending towards us. Why else was this nation chosen before any other, that out of her as out of Sion should be proclaimed and sounded forth the first tidings and trumpet of reformation to all Europe? And had it not been the obstinate perverseness of our prelates against the divine and admirable spirit of Wyclif, to suppress him as a schismatic and innovator, perhaps neither the Bohemian Huss and Jerome, no nor the name of Luther or of Calvin had been ever known; the glory of reforming all our neighbours had been completely ours. But now, as our obdurate clergy have with violence demeaned the matter, we are become hitherto the latest and the backwardest scholars of whom God offered to have made us the teachers. Now once again by all concurrence of signs, and by the general instinct of holy and devout men as they daily and solemnly express their thoughts, God is decreeing to begin some new and great period in his Church, even to the reforming of reformation itself. What does he then but reveal himself to his servants, and as his manner is, first to his Englishmen: I say, as his manner is, first to us, though we mark not the method of his counsels, and are unworthy.

Behold now this vast city: a city of refuge, the mansion house of liberty, encompassed and surrounded with his protection. The shop of war hath not there more anvils and hammers waking, to fashion out the plates and in-

struments of armed Justice in defence of beleaguered
Truth, than there be pens and heads there sitting by their
studious lamps, musing, searching, revolving new notions and ideas wherewith to present as with their homage and their fealty the approaching reformation; others
as fast reading, trying all things, assenting to the force of
reason and convincement. What could a man require   610
more from a nation so pliant and so prone to seek after
knowledge? What wants there to such a towardly and
pregnant soil but wise and faithful labourers, to make a
knowing people, a nation of prophets, of sages and of
worthies? We reckon more than five months yet to harvest. There need not be five weeks, had we but eyes to
lift up: the fields are white already. Where there is much
desire to learn, there of necessity will be much arguing,
much writing, many opinions; for opinion in good men is
but knowledge in the making. Under these fantastic ter-   620
rors of sect and schism we wrong the earnest and zealous
thirst after knowledge and understanding which God hath
stirred up in this city. What some lament of, we should
rather rejoice at, should rather praise this pious forward-
ness among men to reassume the ill-deputed care of their
religion into their own hands again. A little generous
prudence, a little forbearance of one another and some
grain of charity might win all these differences to join and
unite into one general and brotherly search after truth,
could we but forgo this prelatical tradition of crowding   630
free consciences and Christian liberties into canons and
precepts of men. I doubt not, if some great and worthy
stranger should come among us, wise to discern the
mould and temper of a people and how to govern it,
observing the high hopes and aims, the diligent alacrity of
our extended thoughts and reasonings in the pursuance of
truth and freedom, but that he would cry out, as Pyrrhus
did admiring the Roman docility and courage, if such
were my Epirots I would not despair the greatest design
that could be attempted to make a church or kingdom   640
happy.

Yet these are the men cried out against for schismatics

101

and sectaries; as if, while the temple of the Lord was building, some cutting, some squaring the marble, others hewing the cedars, there should be a sort of irrational men who could not consider there must be many schisms and many dissections made in the quarry and in the timber ere the house of God can be built. And when every stone is laid artfully together, it cannot be united into a continuity, it can but be contiguous in this world; neither can every piece of the building be of one form. Nay, rather, the perfection consists in this, that out of many moderate varieties and brotherly dissimilitudes that are not vastly disproportional arises the goodly and the graceful symmetry that commends the whole pile and structure. Let us therefore be more considerate builders, more wise in spiritual architecture, when great reformation is expected. For now the time seems come wherein Moses the great prophet may sit in Heaven rejoicing to see that memorable and glorious wish of his fulfilled, when not only our seventy Elders but all the Lord's people are become prophets. No marvel then though some men, and some good men too perhaps, but young in goodness as Joshua then was, envy them. They fret, and out of their own weakness are in agony lest these divisions and subdivisions will undo us. The adversary again applauds, and waits the hour. When they have branched themselves out, saith he, small enough into parties and partitions, then will be our time. Fool! He sees not the firm root out of which we all grow, though into branches, nor will beware until he see our small divided maniples cutting through at every angle of his ill-united and unwieldy brigade. And that we are to hope better of all these supposed sects and schisms, and that we shall not need that solicitude, honest perhaps though over-timorous, of them that vex in this behalf, but shall laugh in the end at those malicious applauders of our differences, I have these reasons to persuade me.

First, when a city shall be as it were besieged and blocked about, her navigable river infested, inroads and incursions round, defiance and battle oft rumoured to be marching up even to her walls and suburb trenches, that

650

660

670

680

then the people (or the greater part, more than at other times), wholly taken up with the study of highest and most important matters to be reformed, should be disputing, reasoning, reading, inventing, discoursing even to a rarity and admiration things not before discoursed or written of, argues first a singular good will, contentedness and confidence in your prudent foresight and safe government, Lords and Commons; and from thence derives itself to a gallant bravery and well-grounded contempt of their enemies, as if there were no small number of as great spirits among us as his was who, when Rome was nigh besieged by Hannibal, being in the city bought that piece of ground at no cheap rate whereon Hannibal himself encamped his own regiment.   690

Next, it is a lively and cheerful presage of our happy success and victory. For as in a body, when the blood is fresh, the spirits pure and vigorous not only to vital but to rational faculties, and those in the acutest and pertest   700 operations of wit and subtlety, it argues in what good plight and constitution the body is, so when the cheerfulness of the people is so sprightly up as that it has not only wherewith to guard well its own freedom and safety but to spare and to bestow upon the solidest and sublimest points of controversy and new invention, it betokens us not degenerated, nor drooping to a fatal decay, but casting off the old and wrinkled skin of corruption to outlive these pangs and wax young again, entering the glorious ways of truth and prosperous virtue destined to   710 become great and honourable in these latter ages. Methinks I see in my mind a noble and puissant nation rousing herself like a strong man after sleep, and shaking her invincible locks. Methinks I see her as an eagle, mewing her mighty youth and kindling her undazzled eyes at the full midday beam, purging and unscaling her longabused sight at the fountain itself of heavenly radiance, while the whole noise of timorous and flocking birds, with those also that love the twilight, flutter about amazed at what she means, and in their envious gabble   720 would prognosticate a year of sects and schisms.

What should ye do then? Should ye suppress all this

103

flowery crop of knowledge and new light sprung up and yet springing daily in this city? Should ye set an oligarchy of twenty engrossers over it, to bring a famine upon our minds again, when we shall know nothing but what is measured to us by their bushel? Believe it, Lords and Commons, they who counsel ye to such a suppressing do as good as bid ye suppress yourselves; and I will soon show how. If it be desired to know the immediate cause 730 of all this free writing and free speaking, there cannot be assigned a truer than your own mild and free and humane government. It is the liberty, Lords and Commons, which your own valorous and happy counsels have purchased us, liberty which is the nurse of all great wits. This is that which hath rarefied and enlightened our spirits like the influence of heaven; this is that which hath enfranchised, enlarged and lifted up our apprehensions degrees above themselves. Ye cannot make us now less capable, less knowing, less eagerly pursuing of the truth 740 unless ye first make yourselves, that made us so, less the lovers, less the founders of our true liberty. We can grow ignorant again, brutal, formal and slavish, as ye found us; but you then must first become that which ye cannot be, oppressive, arbitrary and tyrannous, as they were from whom ye have freed us. That our hearts are now more capacious, our thoughts more erected to the search and expectation of greatest and exactest things, is the issue of your own virtue propagated in us. Ye cannot suppress that unless ye reinforce an abrogated and merciless law, 750 that fathers may despatch at will their own children. And who shall then stick closest to ye, and excite others? Not he who takes up arms for cote and conduct, and his four nobles of Danegelt. Although I dispraise not the defence of just immunities, yet I love my peace better, if that were all. Give me the liberty to know, to utter and to argue freely according to conscience, above all liberties.

First published 1644

ON THE MORNING OF CHRIST'S NATIVITY

I

This is the month, and this the happy morn
Wherein the son of Heav'n's eternal King,
Of wedded maid and virgin mother born,
Our great redemption from above did bring;
For so the holy sages once did sing,
   That he our deadly forfeit should release,
And with his Father work us a perpetual peace.

II

That glorious form, that light unsufferable
And that far-beaming blaze of majesty
Wherewith he wont at Heav'n's high council-table   10
To sit the midst of trinal unity
He laid aside; and here with us to be
   Forsook the courts of everlasting day,
And chose with us a darksome house of mortal clay.

III

Say, heavenly Muse, shall not thy sacred vein
Afford a present to the infant God?
Hast thou no verse, no hymn or solemn strain
To welcome him to this his new abode,
Now while the heaven, by the sun's team untrod,
   Hath took no print of the approaching light,   20
And all the spangled host keep watch in squadrons bright?

IV

See how from far upon the eastern road
The star-led wizards haste with odours sweet:
O run, prevent them with thy humble ode,
And lay it lowly at his blessed feet;
Have thou the honour first thy Lord to greet,
   And join thy voice unto the Angel choir,
From out his secret altar touch'd with hallow'd fire.

The Hymn

I

It was the winter wild,
While the Heav'n-born child   30
   All meanly wrapp'd in the rude manger lies;
Nature, in awe to him,
Had doff'd her gaudy trim,
   With her great Master so to sympathize:
It was no season then for her
To wanton with the sun her lusty paramour.

II

Only with speeches fair
She woos the gentle air
   To hide her guilty front with innocent snow,
And on her naked shame,   40
Pollute with sinful blame,
   The saintly veil of maiden white to throw,
Confounded that her Maker's eyes
Should look so near upon her foul deformities.

III

But he, her fears to cease,
Sent down the meek-eyed Peace;
   She, crown'd with olive green, came softly sliding
Down through the turning sphere,
His ready harbinger,
   With turtle wing the amorous clouds dividing,   50
And waving wide her myrtle wand
She strikes a universal peace through sea and land.

IV

No war or battle's sound
Was heard the world around:
   The idle spear and shield were high up-hung;
The hooked chariot stood
Unstain'd with hostile blood,

The trumpet spake not to the armed throng,
And kings sat still with awe-full eye,
As if they surely knew their sovereign Lord was by.   60

V

But peaceful was the night
Wherein the Prince of Light
   His reign of peace upon the earth began:
The winds, with wonder whist,
Smoothly the waters kiss'd,
   Whispering new joys to the mild ocean,
Who now hath quite forgot to rave
While birds of calm sit brooding on the charmed wave.

VI

The stars with deep amaze
Stand fix'd in steadfast gaze,   70
   Bending one way their precious influence,
And will not take their flight
For all the morning light,
   Or Lucifer that often warn'd them thence,
But in their glimmering orbs did glow
Until their Lord himself bespake, and bid them go.

VII

And though the shady gloom
Had given day her room,
   The sun himself withheld his wonted speed,
And hid his head for shame,   80
As his inferior flame
   The new-enlighten'd world no more should need;
He saw a greater sun appear
Than his bright throne or burning axletree could bear.

VIII

The shepherds on the lawn
Or ere the point of dawn
   Sat simply chatting in a rustic row;
Full little thought they then
That the mighty Pan

Was kindly come to live with them below.   90
Perhaps their loves, or else their sheep,
Was all that did their silly thoughts so busy keep;

IX

When such music sweet
Their hearts and ears did greet
   As never was by mortal finger struck,
Divinely-warbled voice
Answering the stringed noise,
   As all their souls in blissful rapture took:
The air, such pleasure loth to lose,
With thousand echoes still prolongs each heavenly close.   100

X

Nature, that heard such sound
Beneath the hollow round
   Of Cynthia's seat the airy region thrilling,
Now was almost won
To think her part was done,
   And that her reign here had its last fulfilling;
She knew such harmony alone
Could hold all heaven and earth in happier union.

XI

At last surrounds their sight
A globe of circular light,   110
   That with long beams the shame-fac'd night array'd;
The helmed Cherubim
And sworded Seraphim
   Are seen in glittering ranks with wings display'd,
Harping in loud and solemn choir
With unexpressive notes to Heaven's newborn heir.

XII

Such music (as 'tis said)
Before was never made

But when of old the sons of morning sung,
While the Creator great   120
His constellations set,
   And the well-balanc'd world on hinges hung,
And cast the dark foundations deep,
And bid the weltering waves their oozy channel keep.

XIII

Ring out, ye crystal spheres,
Once bless our human ears
   (If ye have power to touch our senses so),
And let your silver chime
Move in melodious time,
   And let the base of Heav'n's deep organ blow,   130
And with your ninefold harmony
Make up full consort to th'angelic symphony.

XIV

For if such holy song
Enwrap our fancy long,
   Time will run back and fetch the age of gold,
And speckled vanity
Will sicken soon and die,
   And leprous sin will melt from earthly mould,
And Hell itself will pass away
And leave her dolorous mansions to the peering day.   140

XV

Yea, Truth and Justice then
Will down return to men
   Th'enamell'd arras of the rainbow wearing,
And Mercy set between,
Thron'd in celestial sheen,
   With radiant feet the tissu'd clouds down steering,
And Heav'n as at some festival
Will open wide the gates of her high palace hall.

XVI

But wisest Fate says no,
This must not yet be so;   150
   The babe lies yet in smiling infancy
That on the bitter cross
Must redeem our loss,
   So both himself and us to glorify.
Yet first to those ychain'd in sleep
The wakeful trump of doom must thunder through the deep

XVII

With such a horrid clang
As on Mount Sinai rang
   While the red fire and smouldering clouds outbrake.
The aged Earth, aghast   160
With terror of that blast,
   Shall from the surface to the centre shake,
When at the world's last session
The dreadful Judge in middle air shall spread his throne.

XVIII

And then at last our bliss
Full and perfect is,
   But now begins, for from this happy day
Th'old dragon, under ground
In straiter limits bound,
   Not half so far casts his usurped sway,   170
And, wroth to see his kingdom fail,
Swinges the scaly horror of his folded tail.

XIX

The oracles are dumb;
No voice or hideous hum
   Runs through the arched roofs in words deceiving.
Apollo from his shrine
Can no more divine,
   With hollow shriek the steep of Delphos leaving.

110

No nightly trance or breathed spell
Inspires the pale-ey'd priest from the prophetic cell.   180

XX

The lonely mountains o'er
And the resounding shore
   A voice of weeping heard and loud lament;
From haunted spring, and dale
Edg'd with poplar pale,
   The parting genius is with sighing sent.
With flower-inwoven tresses torn
The nymphs in twilight shade or tangled thickets mourn.

XXI

In consecrated earth
And on the holy hearth   190
   The lars and lemures moan with midnight plaint;
In urns, and altars round,
A drear and dying sound
   Affrights the flamens at their service quaint;
And the chill marble seems to sweat
While each peculiar power forgoes his wonted seat.

XXII

Peor and Baalim
Forsake their temples dim
   With that twice-batter'd god of Palestine,
And mooned Ashtaroth,   200
Heav'n's queen and mother both,
   Now sits not girt with taper's holy shine;
The Libyc Hammon shrinks his horn;
In vain the Tyrian maids their wounded Thammuz mourn.

XXIII

And sullen Moloch fled
Hath left in shadows dread
   His burning idol all of blackest hue;

In vain with cymbals' ring
They call the grisly king,
    In dismal dance about the furnace blue;   210
The brutish gods of Nile as fast,
Isis and Orus and the dog Anubis haste.

XXIV

Nor is Osiris seen
In Memphian grove or green,
    Trampling the unshower'd grass with lowings loud;
Nor can he be at rest
Within his sacred chest,
    Naught but profoundest Hell can be his shroud;
In vain with timbrel'd anthems dark
The sable-stoled sorcerers bear his worshipp'd ark.   220

XXV

He feels from Judah's land
The dreaded infant's hand,
    The rays of Bethlehem blind his dusky ey'n;
Nor all the gods beside
Longer dare abide,
    Not Typhon huge ending in snaky twine:
Our babe, to show his godhead true,
Can in his swaddling-bands control the damned crew.

XXVI

So when the sun in bed,
Curtain'd with cloudy red,   230
    Pillows his chin upon an orient wave,
The flocking shadows pale
Troop to th'infernal jail;
    Each fetter'd ghost slips to his several grave,
And the yellow-skirted fays
Fly after the night-steeds, leaving their moon-lov'd maze.

112

XXVII

But see, the virgin bless'd
Hath laid her babe to rest.
   Time is our tedious song should here have ending:
Heav'n's youngest-teemed star   240
Hath fix'd her polish'd car,
   Her sleeping Lord with handmaid lamp attending;
And all about the courtly stable
Bright-harness'd Angels sit in order serviceable.

First published 1645

ON TIME

Fly, envious Time, till thou run out thy race;
Call on the lazy leaden-stepping hours
Whose speed is but the heavy plummet's pace,
And glut thyself with what thy womb devours,
Which is no more than what is false and vain
And merely mortal dross:
So little is our loss,
So little is thy gain.
For when as each thing bad thou hast entomb'd,
And last of all thy greedy self consum'd,   10
Then long Eternity shall greet our bliss
With an individual kiss,
And Joy shall overtake us as a flood,
When every thing that is sincerely good
And perfectly divine
With Truth and Peace and Love shall ever shine
About the supreme throne
Of him t'whose happy-making sight alone,
When once our heav'nly-guided soul shall climb,
Then all this earthy grossness quit,   20
Attir'd with stars we shall for ever sit,
   Triumphing over Death, and Chance, and thee O Time.

First published 1645

UPON THE CIRCUMCISION

Ye flaming Powers and winged Warriors bright
That erst with music and triumphant song,
First heard by happy watchful shepherds' ear,
So sweetly sung your joy the clouds along
Through the soft silence of the listening night,
Now mourn, and if sad share with us to bear
Your fiery essence can distil no tear,
Burn in your sighs, and borrow
Seas wept from our deep sorrow:
He who with all Heav'n's heraldry whilere   10
Enter'd the world now bleeds to give us ease.
Alas, how soon our sin
  Sore doth begin
    His infancy to seize!
O more exceeding love, or law more just?
Just law indeed, but more exceeding love!
For we by rightful doom remediless
Were lost in death, till he that dwelt above,
High thron'd in secret bliss, for us frail dust
Empti'd his glory ev'n to nakedness,   20
And that great covenant which we still transgress
Entirely satisfi'd,
And the full wrath beside
Of vengeful justice bore for our excess,
And seals obedience first with wounding smart
This day; but O, ere long
Huge pangs and strong
  Will pierce more near his heart.

First published 1645

AT A SOLEMN MUSIC

Bless'd pair of Sirens, pledges of Heav'n's joy,
Sphere-born harmonious sisters, Voice and Verse,
Wed your divine sounds, and mix'd power employ
Dead things with inbreath'd sense able to pierce,
And to our high-rais'd fantasy present

114

That undisturbed song of pure concent
Ay sung before the sapphire-colour'd throne
To him that sits thereon
With saintly shout and solemn jubilee,
Where the bright Seraphim in burning row   10
Their loud uplifted angel trumpets blow,
And the cherubic host in thousand choirs
Touch their immortal harps of golden wires,
With those just spirits that wear victorious palms
Hymns devout and holy psalms
Singing everlastingly,
That we on Earth with undiscording voice
May rightly answer that melodious noise;
As once we did, till disproportion'd sin
Jarr'd against nature's chime, and with harsh din   20
Broke the fair music that all creatures made
To their great Lord, whose love their motion sway'd
In perfect diapason, whilst they stood
In first obedience and their state of good.
O may we soon again renew that song,
And keep in tune with Heav'n till God ere long
To his celestial consort us unite
To live with him, and sing in endless morn of light.

First published 1645

L'ALLEGRO

Hence, loathed Melancholy,
    Of Cerberus and blackest Midnight born
In Stygian cave forlorn,
    'Mongst horrid shapes and shrieks and sights unholy.
Find out some uncouth cell
    Where brooding Darkness spreads his jealous wings
And the night-raven sings;
    There, under ebon shades and low-brow'd rocks
As ragged as thy locks,
    In dark Cimmerian desert ever dwell.   10

115

But come, thou goddess fair and free,
In heav'n yclept Euphrosyne
And by men heart-easing Mirth,
Whom lovely Venus at a birth
With two sister Graces more
To ivy-crowned Bacchus bore;
Or whether (as some sager sing)
The frolic wind that breathes the spring,
Zephyr, with Aurora playing
As he met her once a-maying,   20
There, on beds of violets blue
And fresh-blown roses wash'd in dew,
Fill'd her with thee, a daughter fair,
So buxom, blithe and debonair.
Haste thee, nymph, and bring with thee
Jest and youthful jollity,
Quips and cranks and wanton wiles,
Nods and becks and wreathed smiles
Such as hang on Hebe's cheek
And love to live in dimple sleek,   30
Sport, that wrinkled care derides,
And laughter holding both his sides.
Come, and trip it as ye go
On the light fantastic toe,
And in thy right hand lead with thee
The mountain nymph, sweet Liberty;
And if I give thee honour due,
Mirth, admit me of thy crew
To live with her and live with thee
In unreproved pleasures free: 40
To hear the lark begin his flight,
And singing startle the dull night
From his watchtower in the skies,
Till the dappled dawn doth rise,
Then to come in spite of sorrow
And at my window bid good morrow
Through the sweet-briar or the vine
Or the twisted eglantine,
While the cock with lively din
Scatters the rear of darkness thin,   50

116

And to the stack or the barn door
Stoutly struts his dames before;
Oft listening how the hounds and horn
Cheerly rouse the slumbering morn
From the side of some hoar hill,
Through the high wood echoing shrill;
Some time walking, not unseen,
By hedgerow elms on hillocks green,
Right against the eastern gate
Where the great sun begins his state   60
Rob'd in flames and amber light,
The clouds in thousand liveries dight,
While the ploughman near at hand
Whistles o'er the furrow'd land,
And the milkmaid singeth blithe,
And the mower whets his scythe,
And every shepherd tells his tale
Under the hawthorn in the dale.
Straight mine eye hath caught new pleasures
While the landscape round it measures: 70
Russet lawns, and fallows gray
Where the nibbling flocks do stray,
Mountains on whose barren breast
The labouring clouds do often rest,
Meadows trim with daisies pied,
Shallow brooks, and rivers wide.
Towers and battlements it sees
Bosom'd high in tufted trees,
Where perhaps some beauty lies,
The cynosure of neighbouring eyes.   80
Hard by a cottage chimney smokes
From betwixt two aged oaks,
Where Corydon and Thyrsis met
Are at their savoury dinner set
Of herbs and other country messes
Which the neat-handed Phyllis dresses;
And then in haste her bower she leaves,
With Thestylis to bind the sheaves,
Or if the earlier season lead,
To the tann'd haycock in the mead.   90

117

Sometimes with secure delight
The upland hamlets will invite,
When the merry bells ring round,
And the jocund rebecks sound
To many a youth and many a maid
Dancing in the chequer'd shade,
And young and old come forth to play
On a sunshine holiday
Till the livelong daylight fail.
Then to the spicy, nut-brown ale,   100
With stories told of many a feat:
How fairy Mab the junkets ate –
She was pinch'd and pull'd, she said;
And he, by Friar's lantern led,
Tells how the drudging goblin sweat
To earn his cream-bowl duly set,
When in one night, ere glimpse of morn,
His shadowy flail hath thresh'd the corn
That ten day-labourers could not end,
Then lies him down the lubber fiend,   110
And stretch'd out all the chimney's length
Basks at the fire his hairy strength,
And crop-full out of doors he flings
Ere the first cock his matin rings.
Thus done the tales, to bed they creep,
By whispering winds soon lull'd asleep.
Tower'd cities please us then,
And the busy hum of men,
Where throngs of knights and barons bold
In weeds of peace high triumphs hold,   120
With store of ladies, whose bright eyes
Rain influence and judge the prize
Of wit or arms, while both contend
To win her grace, whom all commend.
There let Hymen oft appear
In saffron robe with taper clear,
And pomp, and feast, and revelry,
With masque and antique pageantry,
Such sights as youthful poets dream

On summer eves by haunted stream.   130
Then to the well-trod stage anon
If Jonson's learned sock be on,
Or sweetest Shakespeare, fancy's child,
Warble his native wood-notes wild.
And ever against eating cares
Lap me in soft Lydian airs
Married to immortal verse,
Such as the meeting soul may pierce
In notes, with many a winding bout
Of linked sweetness long drawn out,   140
With wanton heed and giddy cunning,
The melting voice through mazes running,
Untwisting all the chains that tie
The hidden soul of harmony,
That Orpheus' self may heave his head
From golden slumber on a bed
Of heap'd Elysian flowers, and hear
Such strains as would have won the ear
Of Pluto to have quite set free
His half-regain'd Euridice.   150
These delights if thou canst give,
Mirth, with thee I mean to live.

First published 1645

IL PENSEROSO

Hence, vain deluding joys,
    The brood of Folly, without father bred;
How little you bestead,
    Or fill the fixed mind with all your toys.
Dwell in some idle brain,
    And fancies fond with gaudy shapes possess
As thick and numberless
    As the gay motes that people the sunbeams,
Or likest hovering dreams,
    The fickle pensioners of Morpheus' train.   10
But hail, thou Goddess sage and holy,

Hail, divinest Melancholy,
Whose saintly visage is too bright
To hit the sense of human sight,
And therefore to our weaker view
O'erlaid with black, staid wisdom's hue;
Black, but such as in esteem
Prince Memnon's sister might beseem,
Or that starr'd Ethiop queen that strove
To set her beauty's praise above   20
The sea-nymphs, and their powers offended.
Yet thou art higher far descended:
Thee bright-hair'd Vesta long of yore
To solitary Saturn bore;
His daughter she (in Saturn's reign
Such mixture was not held a stain);
Oft in glimmering bowers and glades
He met her, and in secret shades
Of woody Ida's inmost grove,
While yet there was no fear of Jove.   30
Come, pensive nun, devout and pure,
Sober, steadfast and demure,
All in a robe of darkest grain
Flowing with majestic train,
And sable stole of Cypress lawn
Over thy decent shoulders drawn;
Come, but keep thy wonted state,
With even step and musing gait
And looks commercing with the skies,
Thy rapt soul sitting in thine eyes.   40
There held in holy passion still
Forget thyself to marble, till
With a sad leaden downward cast
Thou fix them on the earth as fast;
And join with thee calm Peace, and Quiet,
Spare Fast that oft with gods doth diet,
And hears the Muses in a ring
Ay round about Jove's altar sing,
And add to these retired Leisure,
That in trim gardens takes his pleasure;   50

120

But first, and chiefest, with thee bring
Him that yon soars on golden wing
Guiding the fiery-wheeled throne,
The Cherub Contemplation.
And the mute silence whist along,
'Less Philomel will deign a song
In her sweetest, saddest plight,
Smoothing the rugged brow of night
While Cynthia checks her dragon yoke
Gently o'er th'accustom'd oak.   60
Sweet bird, that shunn'st the noise of folly,
Most musical, most melancholy!
Thee, chauntress, oft the woods among
I woo to hear thy even-song;
And missing thee, I walk unseen
On the dry smooth-shaven green,
To behold the wand'ring moon
Riding near her highest noon
Like one that hath been led astray
Through the heav'n's wide pathless way,   70
And oft, as if her head she bow'd,
Stooping through a fleecy cloud.
Oft, on a plat of rising ground,
I hear the far-off curfew sound
Over some wide-water'd shore,
Swinging low with sullen roar.
Or if the air will not permit,
Some still, removed place will fit,
Where glowing embers through the room
Teach light to counterfeit a gloom,   80
Far from all resort of mirth
Save the cricket on the hearth,
Or the bellman's drowsy charm
To bless the doors from nightly harm.
Or let my lamp at midnight hour
Be seen in some high lonely tower,
Where I may oft outwatch the Bear
With thrice-great Hermes, or unsphere
The spirit of Plato to unfold

121

What worlds or what vast regions hold   90
The immortal mind that hath forsook
Her mansion in this fleshly nook,
And of those daemons that are found
In fire, air, flood or under ground,
Whose power hath a true consent
With planet or with element.
Sometime let gorgeous Tragedy
In scepter'd pall come sweeping by,
Presenting Thebes' or Pelops' line
Or the tale of Troy divine,   100
Or what (though rare) of later age
Ennobled hath the buskin'd stage.
But O, sad virgin, that thy power
Might raise Musaeus from his bower,
Or bid the soul of Orpheus sing
Such notes as, warbled to the string,
Drew iron tears down Pluto's cheek,
And made Hell grant what love did seek;
Or call up him that left half-told
The story of Cambuscan bold,   110
Of Camball and of Algarsife,
And who had Canace to wife
That own'd the virtuous ring and glass,
And of the wondrous horse of brass
On which the Tartar king did ride;
And if aught else great bards beside
In sage and solemn tunes have sung
Of tourneys and of trophies hung,
Of forests, and enchantments drear,
Where more is meant than meets the ear.   120
Thus, Night, oft see me in thy pale career,
Till civil-suited Morn appear,
Not trick'd and frounc'd as she was wont
With the Attic boy to hunt,
But kerchief'd in a comely cloud
While rocking winds are piping loud,
Or usher'd with a shower still
When the gust hath blown his fill,

122

Ending on the rustling leaves,
With minute drops from off the eaves.   130
And when the sun begins to fling
His flaring beams, me, Goddess, bring
To arched walks of twilight groves
And shadows brown that Sylvan loves
Of pine or monumental oak,
Where the rude axe with heaved stroke
Was never heard the nymphs to daunt
Or fright them from their hallow'd haunt.
There in close covert by some brook
Where no profaner eye may look   140
Hide me from day's garish eye,
While the bee with honey'd thigh
That at her flowery work doth sing
And the waters murmuring
With such consort as they keep
Entice the dewy-feather'd sleep;
And let some strange mysterious dream
Wave at his wings in airy stream
Of lively portraiture display'd,
Softly on my eyelids laid.   150
And as I wake, sweet music breathe
Above, about or underneath,
Sent by some spirit to mortals good,
Or th'unseen Genius of the wood.
But let my due feet never fail
To walk the studious cloister's pale,
And love the high-embowed roof
With antique pillars' massy proof,
And storied windows richly dight
Casting a dim religious light.   160
There let the pealing organ blow
To the full-voic'd choir below
In service high and anthems clear,
As may with sweetness through mine ear
Dissolve me into ecstasies,
And bring all Heav'n before mine eyes.
And may at last my weary age

Find out the peaceful hermitage,
The hairy gown and mossy cell,
Where I may sit and rightly spell   170
Of every star that heav'n doth show
And every herb that sips the dew,
Till old experience do attain
To something like prophetic strain.
These pleasures, Melancholy, give
And I with thee will choose to live.

First published 1645

'HOW SOON HATH TIME, THE SUBTLE THIEF OF YOUTH'

How soon hath Time, the subtle thief of youth,
    Stol'n on his wing my three and twentieth year!
    My hasting days fly on with full career,
    But my late spring no bud or blossom show'th.
Perhaps my semblance might deceive the truth
    That I to manhood am arriv'd so near,
    And inward ripeness doth much less appear
    That some more timely-happy spirits indu'th.
Yet be it less or more, or soon or slow,
    It shall be still in strictest measure ev'n   10
    To that same lot, however mean or high,
Toward which Time leads me, and the will of Heav'n.
    All is, if I have grace to use it so,
    As ever in my great Taskmaster's eye.

First published 1645

'CAPTAIN OR COLONEL OR KNIGHT IN ARMS'

Captain or colonel or knight in arms,
    Whose chance on these defenceless doors may seize,
    If ever deed of honour did thee please,
    Guard them, and him within protect from harms.
He can requite thee, for he knows the charms
    That call fame on such gentle acts as these,

124

And he can spread thy name o'er lands and seas
　Whatever clime the sun's bright circle warms.
Lift not thy spear against the Muse's bower;
　The great Emathian conqueror bid spare　　　　　　　10
　The house of Pindarus when temple and tower
Went to the ground, and the repeated air
　Of sad Electra's poet had the power
　To save th'Athenian walls from ruin bare.

First published 1645

'A BOOK WAS WRIT OF LATE CALL'D TETRACHORDON'

A book was writ of late call'd *Tetrachordon*,
　And woven close, both matter, form and style,
　The subject new. It walk'd the town a while
　Numb'ring good intellects; now seldom por'd on.
Cries the stall-reader, 'Bless us! What a word on
　A title-page is this!' And some in file
　Stand spelling false, while one might walk to Mile-
　End Green. Why is it harder, sirs, than Gordon,
Colkitto, or Macdonnel, or Galasp?
　Those rugged names to our like mouths grow sleek　　　　10
　That would have made Quintilian stare and gasp.
Thy age, like ours, O soul of Sir John Cheke,
　Hated not learning worse than toad or asp,
　When thou taught'st Cambridge and King Edward Greek.

Composed 1645–72　　　　*First published 1673*

'HARRY, WHOSE TUNEFUL AND WELL-MEASUR'D SONG'

Harry, whose tuneful and well-measur'd song
　First taught our English music how to span
　Words with just note and accent, not to scan
　With Midas' ears, committing short and long,
Thy worth and skill exempts thee from the throng
　With praise enough for envy to look wan;
　To after age thou shalt be writ the man

That with smooth air couldst humour best our tongue.
Thou honour'st verse, and verse must lend her wing
  To honour thee, the priest of Phoebus' choir,   10
  That tun'st their happiest lines in hymn or story.
Dante shall give Fame leave to set thee higher
  Than his Casella, whom he woo'd to sing,
  Met in the milder shades of Purgatory.

First published 1648

'FAIRFAX, WHOSE NAME IN ARMS THROUGH EUROPE RINGS'

Fairfax, whose name in arms through Europe rings,
  Filling each mouth with envy or with praise,
  And all her jealous monarchs with amaze
  And rumours loud, that daunt remotest kings,
Thy firm unshaken virtue ever brings
  Victory home, though new rebellions raise
  Their Hydra-heads, and the false North displays
  Her broken league to imp their serpent wings;
O yet a nobler task awaits thy hand,
  For what can war but endless war still breed   10
  Till truth and right from violence be freed,
And public faith clear'd from the shameful brand
  Of public fraud. In vain doth valour bleed
  While avarice and rapine share the land.

Composed 1648?

from THE TENURE OF KINGS AND MAGISTRATES

No man who knows aught can be so stupid to deny that
all men naturally were born free, being the image and
resemblance of God himself, and were by privilege above
all the creatures born to command and not to obey; and
that they lived so, till from the root of Adam's transgres-
sion falling among themselves to do wrong and violence,
and foreseeing that such courses must needs tend to the

destruction of them all, they agreed by common league to
bind each other from mutual injury and jointly to defend
themselves against any that gave disturbance or opposi-   10
tion to such agreement. Hence came cities, towns and
commonwealths. And because no faith in all was found
sufficiently binding, they saw it needful to ordain some
authority that might restrain by force and punishment
what was violated against peace and common right. This
authority and power of self-defence and preservation,
being originally and naturally in every one of them and
unitedly in them all, for ease, for order and lest each man
should be his own partial judge they communicated and
derived either to one, whom for the eminence of his   20
wisdom and integrity they chose above the rest, or to
more than one whom they thought of equal deserving.
The first was called a king, the others magistrates; not to
be their lords and masters (though afterward those names,
in some places, were given voluntarily to such as had
been authors of inestimable good to the people) but to be
their deputies and commissioners, to execute by virtue of
their entrusted power that justice which else every man
by the bond of nature and of covenant must have executed for himself and for one another. And to him that   30
shall consider well why among free persons one man by
authority and right should bear authority and jurisdiction
over another, no other end or reason can be imaginable.

These for a while governed well, and with much equity
decided all things at their own arbitrement, till the temptation of such a power left absolute in their hands perverted them at length to injustice and partiality. Then did
they, who now by trial had found the danger and incon-
veniences of committing arbitrary power to any, invent
laws either framed or consented to by all that should   40
confine and limit the authority of whom they chose to
govern them, that so man, of whose failing they had
proof, might no more rule over them, but law and
reason, abstracted as much as might be from personal
errors and frailties; while as the magistrate was set above
the people, so the law was set above the magistrate.

127

When this would not serve, but that the law was either
not executed or misapplied, they were constrained from
that time – the only remedy left them – to put conditions
and take oaths from all kings and magistrates at their first   50
installment to do impartial justice by law; who upon
those terms, and no other, received allegiance from the
people, that is to say, bond or covenant to obey them in
execution of those laws which they, the people, had
themselves made or assented to; and this oft-times with
express warning that if the king or magistrate proved
unfaithful to his trust, the people would be disengaged.
They added also councillors and parliaments, not to be
only at his beck, but with him or without him at set
times, or at all times when any danger threatened, to have   60
care of public safety. Therefore saith Claudius Sesell, a
French statesman, 'the Parliament was set as a bridle to
the King' – which I instance rather not because our English lawyers have not said the same long before but
because that French monarchy is granted by all to be a far
more absolute than ours.

That this, and the rest of what hath hitherto been
spoken, is most true might be copiously made appear
throughout all stories, heathen and Christian, even of
those nations where kings and emperors have sought   70
means to abolish all ancient memory of the people's right
by their encroachments and usurpations. But I spare long
insertions, appealing to the known constitutions of both
the latest Christian empires in Europe, the Greek and
German, besides the French, Italian, Aragonian, English
and not least the Scottish histories; not forgetting this
only by the way, that William the Norman, though a
conqueror, and not unsworn at his coronation, was com-
pelled the second time to take oath at St Albans ere the
people would be brought to yield obedience.   80

It being thus manifest that the power of kings and
magistrates is nothing else but what is only derivative,
transferred and committed to them in trust from the
people to the common good of them all, in whom the
power yet remains fundamentally and cannot be taken

128

from them without a violation of their natural birthright, and seeing that from hence Aristotle and the best of political writers have defined a king him who governs to the good and profit of his people and not for his own ends, it follows from necessary causes that the titles of 'sovereign lord', 'natural lord' and the like are either arrogancies or flatteries, not admitted by emperors and kings of best note, and disliked by the church both of the Jews (Isaiah 26.13) and ancient Christians (as appears by Tertullian and others); although generally the people of Asia, and with them the Jews also (especially since the time they chose a king against the advice and counsel of God), are noted by wise authors much inclinable to slavery.

Secondly, that to say (as is usual) the king hath as good right to his crown and dignity as any man to his inheritance is to make the subject no better than the king's slave, his chattel or his possession, that may be bought and sold; and doubtless, if hereditary title were sufficiently enquired, the best foundation of it would be found either but in courtesy or convenience. But suppose it to be of right hereditary: what can be more just and legal, if a subject, for certain crimes, be to forfeit by law from himself and posterity all his inheritance to the king, than that a king, for crimes proportional, should forfeit all his title and inheritance to the people; unless the people must be thought created all for him, he not for them, and they all in one body inferior to him single, which were a kind of treason against the dignity of mankind to affirm.

Thirdly, it follows that to say kings are accountable to none but God is the overturning of all law and government; for if they may refuse to give account, then all covenants made with them at coronation, all oaths, are in vain and mere mockeries, all laws which they swear to keep, made to no purpose. For if the king fear not God (as how many of them do not?), we hold then our lives and estates by the tenure of his mere grace and mercy, as from a god not a mortal magistrate, a position that none but court parasites or men besotted would maintain. Aristotle therefore, whom we commonly allow for one of

129

the best interpreters of nature and morality, writes in the
fourth of his *Politics*, chapter ten, that monarchy un-
accountable is the worst sort of tyranny, and least of all to
be endured by free-born men. And surely no Christian
prince, not drunk with high mind and prouder than those
pagan Caesars that deified themselves, would arrogate so   130
unreasonably above human condition or derogate so base-
ly from a whole nation of men his brethren, as if for him
only subsisting and to serve his glory, valuing them in
comparison of his own brute will and pleasure no more
than so many beasts or vermin under his feet, not to be
reasoned with but to be trod on; among whom there
might be found so many thousand men for wisdom,
virtue, nobleness of mind, and all other respects but the
fortune of his dignity, far above him.

Yet some would persuade us that this absurd opinion   140
was King David's, because in the fifty-first Psalm he cries
out to God 'Against thee only have I sinned'; as if David
had imagined that to murder Uriah and adulterate his
wife had been no sin against his neighbour, whenas that
Law of Moses was to the king expressly (Deuteronomy
17) not to think so highly of himself above his brethren.
David therefore, by those words, could mean no other
than either that the depth of his guiltiness was known to
God only or to so few as had not the will or power to
question him, or that the sin against God was greater   150
beyond compare than against Uriah. Whatever his meaning were, any wise man can see that the pathetical words
of a Psalm can be no certain decision to a point that hath
abundantly more certain rules to go by. How much more
rationally spake the heathen king Demophoon in a
tragedy of Euripides than these interpreters would put
upon King David: 'I rule not my people by tyranny, as if
they were barbarians, but am myself liable, if I do unjust-
ly, to suffer justly.' Not unlike was the speech of Trajan,
the worthy Emperor, to one whom he made general of   160
his praetorian forces: 'Take this drawn sword', saith he,
'to use for me if I reign well, if not, to use against me.'
Thus Dio relates. And not Trajan only; but Theodosius

the younger, a Christian Emperor and one of the best, caused it to be enacted as a rule undeniable and fit to be acknowledged by all kings and emperors, that a prince is bound to the laws, that on the authority of law the authority of a prince depends and to the laws ought to submit; which edict of his remains yet unrepealed in the Code of Justinian (Book 1, title 24) as a sacred constitution to all the succeeding emperors. How then can any king in Europe maintain and write himself accountable to none but God, when emperors in their own imperial statutes have written and decreed themselves accountable to law? And indeed, where such an account is not feared, he that bids a man reign over him above law may bid as well a savage beast.

It follows lastly that since the king or magistrate holds his authority of the people both originally and naturally, for their good in the first place and not his own, then may the people as oft as they shall judge it for the best either choose him or reject him, retain him or depose him, though no tyrant, merely by the liberty and right of free-born men to be governed as seems to them best.

For as to this question in hand, what the people by their just right may do in change of government or of governor, we see it cleared sufficiently, besides other ample authority, even from the mouths of princes themselves. And surely they that shall boast, as we do, to be a free nation, and not have in themselves the power to remove or to abolish any governor, supreme or subordinate, with the government itself upon urgent causes, may please their fancy with a ridiculous and painted freedom fit to cozen babies, but are indeed under tyranny and servitude, as wanting that power, which is the root and source of all liberty, to dispose and economize in the land which God hath given them, as masters of family in their own house and free inheritance; without which natural and essential power of a free nation, though bearing high their heads, they can in due esteem be thought no better than slaves and vassals born in the tenure and occupation of another

131

inheriting lord, whose government, though not illegal or intolerable, hangs over them as a lordly scourge, not as a free government, and therefore to be abrogated. How much more justly then may they fling off tyranny or tyrants, who being once deposed can be no more than private men, as subject to the reach of justice and arraignment as any other transgressors? And certainly if men (not to speak of heathen) both wise and religious have done justice upon tyrants what way they could soonest, how much more mild and human then is it to give them fair and open trial, to teach lawless kings, and all who so much adore them, that not mortal man or his imperious will but Justice is the only true sovereign and supreme majesty upon earth? Let men cease therefore out of faction and hypocrisy to make outcries and horrid things of things so just and honourable. Though perhaps till now no Protestant state or kingdom can be alleged to have openly put to death their king, which lately some have written and imputed to their great glory, much mistaking the matter, it is not neither ought to be the glory of a Protestant state never to have put their king to death; it is the glory of a Protestant king never to have deserved death. And if the Parliament and military Council do what they do without precedent, if it appear their duty, it argues the more wisdom, virtue and magnanimity that they know themselves able to be a precedent to others, who perhaps in future ages, if they prove not too degenerate, will look up with honour and aspire toward these exemplary and matchless deeds of their ancestors as to the highest top of their civil glory and emulation; which heretofore in the pursuance of fame and foreign dominion spent itself vaingloriously abroad, but henceforth may learn a better fortitude, to dare execute highest justice on them that shall by force of arms endeavour the oppressing and bereaving of religion and their liberty at home, that no unbridled potentate or tyrant, but to his sorrow for the future, may presume such high and irresponsible licence over mankind to havoc and turn upside down whole kingdoms of men as though they were no

132

more in respect of his perverse will than a nation of pismires.

As for the party called Presbyterians, of whom I believe very many to be good and faithful Christians, though misled by some of turbulent spirit, I wish them earnestly and calmly not to fall off from their first principles, nor to affect rigour and superiority over men not under them; not to compel unforcible things, in religion especially, which if not voluntary becomes a sin; nor to assist the 250 clamour and malicious drifts of men whom they themselves have judged to be the worst of men, the obdurate enemies of God and his Church; nor to dart against the actions of their brethren, for want of other argument, those wrested laws and scriptures thrown by prelates and malignants against their own sides, which, though they hurt not otherwise, yet taken up by them to the condemnation of their own doings give scandal to all men and discover in themselves either extreme passion or apostasy. Let them not oppose their best friends and associates, 260 who molest them not at all, infringe not the least of their liberties, unless they call it their liberty to bind other men's consciences, but are still seeking to live at peace with them and brotherly accord. Let them beware an old and perfect enemy, who though he hope by sowing discord to make them his instruments yet cannot forbear a minute the open threatening of his destined revenge upon them, when they have served his purposes. Let them fear therefore, if they be wise, rather what they have done already than what remains to do, and be warned in time 270 they put no confidence in princes whom they have provoked, lest they be added to the examples of those that miserably have tasted the event. Stories can inform them how Christian the second, King of Denmark not much above a hundred years past, driven out by his subjects and received again upon new oaths and conditions, broke through them all to his most bloody revenge, slaying his chief opposers when he saw his time, both them and their children, invited to a feast for that purpose; how Maximilian dealt with those of Bruges, though by mediation of 280

133

the German princes reconciled to them by solemn and
public writings drawn and sealed; how the massacre at
Paris was the effect of that credulous peace which the
French Protestants made with Charles the ninth their
king; and that the main visible cause which to this day
hath saved the Netherlands from utter ruin was their final
not believing the perfidious cruelty which as a constant
maxim of state hath been used by the Spanish kings on
their subjects that have taken arms and after trusted them,
as no later age but can testify, heretofore in Belgia itself,   290
and this very year in Naples. And to conclude with one
past exception, though far more ancient: David (whose
sanctified prudence might be alone sufficient not to war-
rant us only but to instruct us), when once he had taken
arms, never after that trusted Saul, though with tears and
much relenting he twice promised not to hurt him. These
instances, few of many, might admonish them, both English and Scotch, not to let their own ends and the driving on of a faction betray them blindly into the snare of
those enemies whose revenge looks on them as the men   300
who first begun, fomented and carried on beyond the
cure of any sound or safe accommodation all the evil
which hath since unavoidably befallen them and their
King.

I have something also to the divines, though brief to
what were needful: not to be disturbers of the civil affairs,
being in hands better able and more belonging to manage
them, but to study harder and to attend the office of good
pastors, knowing that he whose flock is least among them
hath a dreadful charge, not performed by mounting twice   310
into the chair with a formal preachment huddled up at the
odd hours of a whole lazy week, but by incessant pains
and watching in season and out of season, from house to
house, over the souls of whom they have to feed; which if
they ever well considered, how little leisure would they
find to be the most pragmatical sidesmen of every popular tumult and sedition? And all this while are to learn
what the true end and reason is of the gospel which they
teach, and what a world it differs from their censorious

134

and supercilious lording over conscience. It would be 320
good also they lived so as they might persuade the people
they hated covetousness, which worse than heresy is
idolatry; hated pluralities and all kind of simony; left rambling from benefice to benefice like ravenous wolves
seeking where they may devour the biggest. Of which if
some, well and warmly seated from the beginning, be not
guilty, 'twere good they held not conversation with such
as are. Let them be sorry that, being called to assemble
about reforming the Church, they fell to progging and
soliciting the Parliament, though they had renounced the 330
name of priests, for a new settling of their tithes and
oblations, and double-lined themselves with spiritual
places of commodity beyond the possible discharge of
their duty. Let them assemble in Consistory with their
Elders and Deacons, according to ancient ecclesiastical
rule, to the preserving of church-discipline, each in his
several charge, and not a pack of clergymen by themselves to belly-cheer in their presumptuous Sion or to
promote designs, abuse and gull the simple laity, and stir
up tumult as the prelates did for the maintenance of their 340
pride and avarice.

These things if they observe, and wait with patience,
no doubt but all things will go well without their impor-
tunities or exclamations, and the printed letters which
they send subscribed with the ostentation of great characters and little moment would be more considerable than
now they are. But if they be the ministers of Mammon
instead of Christ, and scandalize his Church with the
filthy love of gain, aspiring also to sit, the closest and
heaviest of all tyrants, upon the conscience, and fall 350
notoriously into the same sins whereof so lately and so
loud they accused the prelates, as God rooted out those
wicked ones immediately before, so will he root out them
their imitators, and to vindicate his own glory and religion will uncover their hypocrisy to the open world and
visit upon their own heads that 'curse ye, Meroz', the
very motto of their pulpits, wherewith so frequently, not
as Meroz but more like atheists, they have blasphemed

135

the vengeance of God and traduced the zeal of his people.
And that they be not what they go for, true ministers of 360
the Protestant doctrine, taught by those abroad famous
and religious men who first reformed the Church or by
those no less zealous who withstood corruption and the
bishops here at home, branded with the name of Puritans
and Nonconformists, we shall abound with testimonies to
make appear, that men may yet more fully know the
difference between Protestant divines and these pulpit-
firebrands.

First published 1649

'CROMWELL, OUR CHIEF OF MEN,
WHO THROUGH A CLOUD'

Cromwell, our chief of men, who through a cloud
  Not of war only but detractions rude
  Guided by faith and matchless fortitude
  To peace and truth thy glorious way hast plough'd,
And on the neck of crowned fortune proud
  Hast rear'd God's trophies and his work pursu'd,
  While Darwen stream with blood of Scots imbru'd
  And Dunbar field resounds thy praises loud
And Worcester's laureate wreath, yet much remains
  To conquer still: peace hath her victories 10
  No less renown'd than war, new foes arise
Threatening to bind our souls with secular chains.
  Help us to save free conscience from the paw
  Of hireling wolves whose gospel is their maw.

Composed 1652

'WHEN I CONSIDER HOW MY LIGHT IS SPENT'

When I consider how my light is spent
  Ere half my days in this dark world and wide,
  And that one talent which is death to hide
  Lodg'd with me useless, though my soul more bent
To serve therewith my Maker and present
  My true account, lest he returning chide,

'Doth God exact day-labour, light deni'd?'
I fondly ask; but Patience, to prevent
That murmur, soon replies, 'God doth not need
   Either man's work or his own gifts. Who best   10
   Bear his mild yoke, they serve him best. His state
Is kingly. Thousands at his bidding speed
   And post o'er land and ocean without rest;
   They also serve who only stand and wait.'

Composed 1652–3?

ON THE LATE MASSACRE IN PIEDMONT

Avenge O Lord thy slaughter'd saints, whose bones
   Lie scatter'd on the Alpine mountains cold;
   Ev'n them who kept thy truth so pure of old
   When all our fathers worshipp'd stocks and stones
Forget not: in thy book record their groans
   Who were thy sheep and in their ancient fold
   Slain by the bloody Piedmontese that roll'd
   Mother with infant down the rocks. Their moans
The vales redoubl'd to the hills, and they
   To heav'n. Their martyr'd blood and ashes sow   10
   O'er all th'Italian fields where still doth sway
The triple tyrant, that from these may grow
   A hundred-fold, who having learnt thy way
   Early may fly the Babylonian woe.

Composed 1655

'METHOUGHT I SAW MY LATE ESPOUSED SAINT'

Methought I saw my late espoused saint
   Brought to me like Alcestis from the grave,
   Whom Jove's great son to her glad husband gave
   Rescu'd from death by force, though pale and faint.
Mine, as whom wash'd from spot of childbed taint
   Purification in th'old Law did save,

And such as yet once more I trust to have
  Full sight of her in Heav'n without restraint,
Came vested all in white, pure as her mind.
  Her face was veil'd, yet to my fanci'd sight   10
  Love, sweetness, goodness in her person shin'd
So clear as in no face with more delight.
  But O, as to embrace me she inclin'd,
  I wak'd, she fled, and day brought back my night.

Composed 1658?

from THE READY AND EASY WAY TO
ESTABLISH A FREE COMMONWEALTH

I doubt not but all ingenuous and knowing men will
easily agree with me that a free Commonwealth, without
single person or house of lords, is by far the best government, if it can be had. 'But we have all this while', say
they, 'been expecting it, and cannot yet attain it.' 'Tis true
indeed; when monarchy was dissolved, the form of a
Commonwealth should have forthwith been framed and
the practice thereof immediately begun, that the people
might have soon been satisfied and delighted with the
decent order, ease and benefit thereof. We had been then   10
by this time firmly rooted past fear of commotions or
mutations, and now flourishing. This care of timely settling a new government in stead of the old, too much
neglected, hath been our mischief.

    Yet the cause thereof may be ascribed with most reason
to the frequent disturbances, interruptions and dissolu-
tions which the Parliament hath had, partly from the
impatient or disaffected people, partly from some ambitious leaders in the army, much contrary, I believe, to the
mind and approbation of the army itself and their other   20
commanders, once undeceived or in their own power.
Now is the opportunity, now the very season wherein we
may obtain a free Commonwealth and establish it for
ever in the land without difficulty or much delay. Writs
are sent out for elections (and which is worth observing,

in the name not of any king but of the keepers of our
liberty) to summon a free Parliament, which then only
will indeed be free and deserve the true honour of that
supreme title if they preserve us a free people; which
never Parliament was more free to do, being now called   30
not, as heretofore, by the summons of a king but by the
voice of liberty. And if the people, laying aside prejudice
and impatience, will seriously and calmly now consider
their own good both religious and civil, their own liberty
and the only means thereof, as shall be here laid before
them, and will elect their knights and burgesses able men,
and (according to the just and necessary qualifications,
which for aught I hear remain yet in force unrepealed, as
they were formerly decreed in Parliament) men not
addicted to a single person or house of lords, the work is   40
done; at least, the foundation firmly laid of a free Commonwealth, and good part also erected of the main structure. For the ground and basis of every just and free
government (since men have smarted so oft for committing all to one person) is a general council of ablest men,
chosen by the people to consult of public affairs from
time to time for the common good. In this Grand Council must the sovereignty, not transferred but delegated
only and as it were deposited, reside. With this caution,
they must have the forces by sea and land committed to   50
them for preservation of the common peace and liberty;
must raise and manage the public revenue, at least with
some inspectors deputed for satisfaction of the people
how it is employed; must make or propose – as more
expressly shall be said anon – civil laws; treat of com-
merce, peace or war with foreign nations; and for the
carrying on some particular affairs with more secrecy and
expedition must elect, as they have already out of their
own number and others, a Council of State.

And, although it may seem strange at first hearing, by   60
reason that men's minds are prepossessed with the notion
of successive parliaments, I affirm that the Grand or
General Council, being well chosen, should be perpetual;
for so their business is or may be, and ofttimes urgent,

the opportunity of affairs gained or lost in a moment. The day of Council cannot be set, as the day of a festival, but must be ready always to prevent or answer all occasions. By this continuance they will become every way skilfullest, best provided of intelligence from abroad, best acquainted with the people at home, and the people with 70 them. The ship of the Commonwealth is always under sail. They sit at the stern, and if they steer well, what need is there to change them, it being rather dangerous? Add to this that the Grand Council is both foundation and pillar of the whole state, and to move pillars and foundations, not faulty, cannot be safe for the building. I see not therefore how we can be advantaged by successive and transitory Parliaments, but that they are much likelier continually to unsettle rather than to settle a free government, to breed commotions, changes, novelties and un- 80 certainties, to bring neglect upon present affairs and opportunities while all minds are suspense with expectation of a new assembly, and the assembly for a good space taken up with the new settling of itself; after which, if they find no great work to do, they will make it by altering or repealing former acts or making and multiplying new, that they may seem to see what their predecessors saw not, and not to have assembled for nothing; till all law be lost in the multitude of clashing statutes.

But if the ambition of such as think themselves injured 90 that they also partake not of the government and are impatient till they be chosen cannot brook the perpetuity of others chosen before them, or if it be feared that long continuance of power may corrupt sincerest men, the known expedient is (and by some lately propounded) that annually – or if the space be longer, so much perhaps the better – the third part of Senators may go out according to the precedence of their election and the like number be chosen in their places, to prevent the settling of too absolute a power if it should be perpetual; and this they call 100 'partial rotation'. But I could wish that this wheel or partial wheel in state, if it be possible, might be avoided, as having too much affinity with the wheel of fortune; for

140

it appears not how this can be done without danger and mischance of putting out a great number of the best and ablest, in whose stead new elections may bring in as many raw, unexperienced and otherwise affected, to the weakening and much altering for the worse of public transactions. Neither do I think a perpetual Senate, especially chosen and entrusted by the people, much in this land to be feared, where the well-affected either in a standing army or in a settled militia have their arms in their own hands. Safest therefore to me it seems, and of least hazard or interruption to affairs, that none of the Grand Council be moved, unless by death or just conviction of some crime; for what can be expected firm or steadfast from a floating foundation? However, I forejudge not any probable expedient, any temperament that can be found in things of this nature, so disputable on either side.

Yet, lest this which I affirm be thought my single opinion, I shall add sufficient testimony. Kingship itself is therefore counted the more safe and durable because the king, and for the most part his council, is not changed during life; but a commonwealth is held immortal, and therein firmest, safest and most above fortune. For the death of a king causeth oft-times many dangerous alterations, but the death now and then of a senator is not felt, the main body of them still continuing permanent in greatest and noblest commonwealths, and as it were eternal. Therefore among the Jews the supreme council of seventy, called the Sanhedrim, founded by Moses, in Athens that of Areopagus, in Sparta that of the Ancients, in Rome the Senate, consisted of members chosen for term of life, and by that means remained as it were still the same to generations. In Venice they change indeed ofter than every year some particular councils of state, as that of six or such other; but the true Senate, which upholds and sustains the government, is the whole aristocracy immovable. So in the United Provinces the States General, which are indeed but a council of state deputed by the whole union, are not usually the same persons for

141

above three or six years; but the States of every city, in
whom the sovereignty hath been placed time out of
mind, are a standing senate without succession, and
accounted chiefly in that regard the main prop of their
liberty. And why they should be so in every well-ordered
commonwealth, they who write of policy give these
reasons: that 'to make the senate successive not only im
pairs the dignity and lustre of the senate, but weakens the   150
whole commonwealth and brings it into manifest danger;
while by this means the secrets of state are frequently
divulged and matters of greatest consequence committed
to inexpert and novice counsellors, utterly to seek in the
full and intimate knowledge of affairs past'.

I know not therefore what should be peculiar in England, to make successive Parliaments thought safest or
convenient here more than in other nations, unless it be
the fickleness which is attributed to us as we are islanders;
but good education and acquisite wisdom ought to cor-   160
rect the fluxible fault, if any such be, of our watery
situation. It will be objected that in those places where
they had perpetual senates they had also popular remedies
against their growing too imperious, as in Athens, besides
Areopagus, another senate of four or five hundred, in
Sparta the Ephori, in Rome the Tribunes of the people.
But the event tells us that these remedies either little
availed the people or brought them to such a licentious
and unbridled democracy as in fine ruined themselves
with their own excessive power; so that the main reason   170
urged why popular assemblies are to be entrusted with
the people's liberty rather than a senate of principal men,
because great men will be still endeavouring to enlarge
their power but the common sort will be contented to
maintain their own liberty, is by experience found false,
none being more immoderate and ambitious to amplify
their power than such popularities; which was seen in the
people of Rome who, at first contented to have their
Tribunes, at length contended with the Senate that one
Consul, then both, soon after that the Censors and   180
Praetors also should be created plebeian and the whole

142

empire put into their hands, adoring lastly those who
were most adverse to the Senate, till Marius, by fulfilling
their inordinate desires, quite lost them all the power for
which they had so long been striving and left them under
the tyranny of Sulla. The balance therefore must be exactly so set as to preserve and keep up due authority on
either side, as well in the senate as in the people; and this
annual rotation of a senate to consist of three hundred,
as is lately propounded, requires also another popular   190
assembly upward of a thousand, with an answerable rotation, which, besides that it will be liable to all those
inconveniencies found in the foresaid remedies, cannot
but be troublesome and chargeable, both in their motion
and their session, to the whole land: unwieldy with their
own bulk, unable in so great a number to mature their
consultations as they ought (if any be allotted them), and
that they meet not from so many parts remote to sit a
whole year lieger in one place, only now and then to hold
up a forest of fingers or to convey each man his bean or   200
ballot into the box without reason shown or common
deliberation, incontinent of secrets, if any be imparted to
them, emulous and always jarring with the other senate.

The much better way doubtless will be, in this wavering condition of our affairs, to defer the changing or
circumscribing of our Senate, more than may be done
ease, till the Commonwealth be thoroughly settled in
peace and safety, and they themselves give us the occasion. Military men hold it dangerous to change the form
of battle in view of an enemy; neither did the people of   210
Rome bandy with their Senate while any of the Tarquins
lived, the enemies of their liberty, nor sought by creating
Tribunes to defend themselves against the fear of their
patricians till, sixteen years after the expulsion of their
kings and in full security of their state, they had or
thought they had just cause given them by the Senate.
Another way will be to well-qualify and refine elections,
not committing all to the noise and shouting of a rude
multitude, but permitting only those of them who are
rightly qualified to nominate as many as they will, and   220

out of that number others of a better breeding to choose a less number more judiciously, till after a third or fourth sitting and refining of exactest choice they only be left chosen who are the due number and seem by most voices the worthiest. To make the people fittest to choose, and the chosen fittest to govern, will be to mend our corrupt and faulty education: to teach the people faith not without virtue, temperance, modesty, sobriety, parsimony, justice; not to admire wealth or honour; to hate turbulence and ambition; to place everyone his private welfare and happiness in the public peace, liberty and safety. They shall not then need to be much mistrustful of their chosen patriots in the Grand Council, who will be then rightly called the true keepers of our liberty, though the most of their business will be in foreign affairs. But to prevent all mistrust, the people then will have their several ordinary assemblies (which will henceforth quite annihilate the odious power and name of Committees) in the chief towns of every county, without the trouble, charge or time lost of summoning and assembling from far in so great a number and so long residing from their own houses or removing from their families, to do as much at home in their several shires, entire or subdivided, toward the securing of their liberty as a numerous assembly of them all, formed and convened on purpose with the wariest rotation; whereof I shall speak more ere the end of this discourse, for it may be referred to time, so we be still going on by degrees to perfection.

The people, well weighing and performing these things, I suppose would have no cause to fear though the Parliament, abolishing that name (as originally signifying but the 'parley' of our Lords and Commons with their Norman king, when he pleased to call them), should with certain limitations of their power sit perpetual, if their ends be faithful and for a free Commonwealth, under the name of a Grand or General Council. Till this be done, I am in doubt whether our state will be ever certainly and thoroughly settled, never likely till then to see an end of our troubles and continual changes, or at least never the

230

240

250

true settlement and assurance of our liberty. The Grand 260
Council being thus firmly constituted to perpetuity and
still, upon the death or default of any member, supplied
and kept in full number, there can be no cause alleged
why peace, justice, plentiful trade and all prosperity
should not thereupon ensue throughout the whole land,
with as much assurance as can be of human things that
they shall so continue, if God favour us and our wilful
sins provoke him not, even to the coming of our true and
rightful and only to be expected King, only worthy as he
is our only Saviour, the Messiah, the Christ, the only heir 270
of his eternal Father, the only by him anointed, and
ordained, since the work of our redemption finished,
universal Lord of all mankind.

The way propounded is plain, easy and open before us,
without intricacies, without the introducement of new or
obsolete forms or terms or exotic models, ideas that
would effect nothing but with a number of new injunctions to manacle the native liberty of mankind, turning all
virtue into prescription, servitude and necessity, to the
great impairing and frustrating of Christian liberty. I say 280
again, this way lies free and smooth before us, is not
tangled with inconveniencies, invents no new encumb-
rances, requires no perilous, no injurious alteration or cir-
cumscription of men's lands and proprieties; secure that in
this Commonwealth, temporal and spiritual lords removed, no man or number of men can attain to such
wealth or vast possession as will need the hedge of an
agrarian law (never successful, but the cause rather of
sedition, save only where it began seasonably with first
possession) to confine them from endangering our public 290
liberty. To conclude, it can have no considerable objection made against it that it is not practicable, lest it be said
hereafter that we gave up our liberty for want of a ready
way or distinct form proposed of a free Commonwealth.
And this facility we shall have above our next neighbouring commonwealth (if we can keep us from the fond
conceit of something like a Duke of Venice, put lately
into many men's heads by someone or other subtly driv-

ing on under that notion his own ambitious ends to lurch
a crown), that our liberty shall not be hampered or ho-   300
vered over by any engagement to such a potent family as
the house of Nassau of whom to stand in perpetual doubt
and suspicion, but we shall live the clearest and absolutest
free nation in the world.

I have no more to say at present. Few words will save us,
well considered; few and easy things, now seasonably
done. But if the people be so affected as to prostitute
religion and liberty to the vain and groundless
apprehension that nothing but kingship can restore trade,
not remembering the frequent plagues and pestilences that   310
then wasted this city such as through God's mercy we
never have felt since, and that trade flourishes nowhere
more than in the free commonwealths of Italy, Germany
and the Low Countries before their eyes at this day, yet if
trade be grown so craving and importunate through the
profuse living of tradesmen that nothing can support it
but the luxurious expenses of a nation upon trifles or
superfluities, so as if the people generally should betake
themselves to frugality it might prove a dangerous matter, lest tradesmen should mutiny for want of trading,   320
and that therefore we must forgo and set to sale religion,
liberty, honour, safety, all concernments divine or human
to keep up trading, if lastly after all this light among us
the same reason shall pass for current to put our necks
again under kingship as was made use of by the Jews to
return back to Egypt and to the worship of their idol
queen, because they falsely imagined that they then lived
in more plenty and prosperity, our condition is not sound
but rotten, both in religion and all civil prudence, and
will bring us soon, the way we are marching, to those   330
calamities which attend always and unavoidably on luxury, all national judgements under foreign or domestic
slavery: so far we shall be from mending our condition by
monarchizing our government, whatever new conceit
now possesses us.
    However with all hazard I have ventured what I

thought my duty to speak in season and to forewarn my
country in time, wherein I doubt not but there be many
wise men in all places and degrees, but am sorry the
effects of wisdom are so little seen among us. Many   340
circumstances and particulars I could have added in those
things whereof I have spoken; but a few main matters,
now put speedily in execution, will suffice to recover us
and set all right. And there will want at no time who are
good at circumstances, but men who set their minds on
main matters and sufficiently urge them in these most
difficult times I find not many. What I have spoken is the
language of that which is not called amiss 'the Good Old
Cause'. If it seem strange to any, it will not seem more
strange, I hope, than convincing to backsliders. Thus   350
much I should perhaps have said though I were sure I
should have spoken only to trees and stones, and had
none to cry to but, with the Prophet, 'O earth, earth,
earth!', to tell the very soil itself what her perverse inhabitants are deaf to; nay, though what I have spoke should
happen (which Thou suffer not, who didst create mankind free, nor Thou next, who didst redeem us from
being servants of men!) to be the last words of our expiring liberty. But I trust I shall have spoken persuasion to
abundance of sensible and ingenuous men; to some,   360
perhaps, whom God may raise of these stones to become
children of reviving liberty, and may reclaim, though
they seem now choosing them a captain back for Egypt,
to bethink themselves a little and consider whither they
are rushing, to exhort this torrent also of the people not
to be so impetuous, but to keep their due channel, and at
length recovering and uniting their better resolutions,
now that they see already how open and unbounded the
insolence and rage is of our common enemies, to stay
these ruinous proceedings, justly and timely fearing to   370
what a precipice of destruction the deluge of this epidemic
madness would hurry us through the general defection of
a misguided and abused multitude.

First published 1660

'CYRIACK, WHOSE GRANDSIRE ON THE ROYAL BENCH'

Cyriack, whose grandsire on the royal bench
  Of British Themis with no mean applause
  Pronounc'd and in his volumes taught our laws
  Which others at their bar so often wrench,
Today deep thoughts resolve with me to drench
  In mirth, that after no repenting draws;
  Let Euclid rest, and Archimedes pause,
  And what the Swede intend, and what the French.
To measure life learn thou betimes, and know
  Toward solid good what leads the nearest way.   10
  For other things mild heaven a time ordains,
And disapproves that care, though wise in show,
  That with superfluous burden loads the day
  And, when God sends a cheerful hour, refrains.

First published 1673

'CYRIACK, THIS THREE YEARS' DAY THESE EYES, THOUGH CLEAR'

Cyriack, this three years' day these eyes, though clear
  To outward view of blemish or of spot,
  Bereft of sight their seeing have forgot,
  Nor to their idle orbs doth day appear
Or sun or moon or star throughout the year,
  Or man or woman. Yet I argue not
  Against Heaven's hand or will, nor bate one jot
  Of heart or hope, but still bear up and steer
Right onward. What supports me dost thou ask?
  The conscience, friend, to have lost them overpli'd   10
  In Liberty's defence, my noble task
Of which all Europe talks from side to side.
  This thought might lead me through the world's vain mask
Content, though blind, had I no better guide.

First published 1694

148

Critical commentary

In 1634 Milton was 25, and still living with his parents in Hammersmith. His father was a well-known amateur musician, and it may have been through him that Milton came to know the composer Henry Lawes. But the scrivener had also done business with the Egerton family, and at some point in the previous two or three years Milton had contributed three songs and a speech (*Arcades*, Carey, *CSP*: pp. 155–61) to a dramatic entertainment for the old Countess of Derby, widow of Sir Thomas Egerton, Keeper of the Seal and Lord Chancellor under Elizabeth. Egerton had been a friend of Francis Bacon and employer of the poet Donne. The countess was herself related to Edmund Spenser, who dedicated his *Tears of the Muses* (1591) to her; and she had performed in at least one of Ben Jonson's masques.

These connections, which link the Egertons with two of the three English writers, Spenser and Jonson (the third being Shakespeare), who had the strongest influence on Milton as a young poet, all point to the importance in the period of literary patronage. In the absence of copyright protection and royalty payments, and given the small size of the reading public and the problems of distribution outside London, very few writers of any kind could hope to survive simply on the sales of books. Many had another occupation (Spenser was a civil servant, Jonson and Shakespeare were actors), but most relied also on the financial support and prestige of wealthy patrons. The most prominent of these, like the Dudleys, Howards, Sidneys, and Herberts, were often the centre of political groupings as well, and patronage had an ideological as well as an economic significance, for patron and client alike. Reflecting the courtly idea – however ill-founded in reality – of a literate, cultivated, and munificent ruling class, it placed writers in a position of dependency on wealth and power that had direct consequences for their writing. It also encouraged the development of genres specifically suited to the characteristics of an aristocratic literary culture.

Of these, the one most obviously shaped by the values and rituals of that culture is the masque. Originally no more than a sequence of songs and dances, usually performed in private houses or small indoor theatres, masques (so-called because the performers were often disguised) combined music, dance, scenic spectacle, and simple dramatic narrative into what was often little more than an elaborate ritual of flattery and ingratiation, a celebration and endorsement of the ruling culture. But disguise, dance, and the basic confrontation of masque and antimasque are not without dramatic possibilities, and some writers, Ben Jonson in particular, attempted with limited success to encompass more complex and ambitious ideas, usually in the form of a didactic moral allegory. Above all it is an intensely *political* genre, not only because of its close dependence as a form on a particular political culture but because its allegorical confrontations of Love and Honour, Virtue and Pleasure, like the structural opposition of courtly masquers and dissolute, foreign, or plebeian antimasquers, articulate in a form understandable and acceptable to spectators and participants alike the real internal tensions and external fears of that culture.

Spectators *and* participants: for in the masque the two groups are largely interchangeable. The Countess of Derby was not the only aristocratic lady to have acted in a masque; and at least two of her grandchildren who took the leading parts in *Comus* were already experienced masquers. The form is semi-amateur and domestic, and most masques were 'occasional' pieces, written for a birthday, wedding, or similar event. None the less it is a highly formal genre, elaborate and ritualized, as well as a mode of conspicuous expenditure appropriate to a class nervously determined to project itself as confidently in control even while its authority and its values are coming increasingly under attack. In 1634, the year of *Comus*, William Prynne suffered his first ear-cropping for his outspoken criticism of masquing in *Histriomastix* (1633); and the accelerating crisis of Charles I's authority occurs to the accompaniment of more and more elaborate and extravagantly expensive entertainments.

All this may make Milton's involvement with the masque performed in Ludlow Castle at Michaelmas 1634 seem rather surprising. Son of a wealthy father who had already settled some of his own investment income on him, he had no need, financially at any rate, to look for patronage; and the ideological connotations of the genre, courtly, aristocratic, and royalist, could hardly have been less congenial to his intellectual temperament and training, which was scholarly, bourgeois, and Puritan. Some critics have tried to get round this by arguing that it is not really a masque at all, but a morality play, an early opera, or a Platonic pastoral allegory. But it was printed three times in Milton's lifetime, twice by the poet himself, as a masque, and there is no reason to think that either he or his readers saw anything surprising or incongruous in the title. Jonson's editors accept the description of *Comus* as a masque, though adding that it is one 'in which the spirit of drama has broken free from the masque ... while retaining a few unimportant traces of a notional allegiance', like the songs and dances (Jonson 1925: II, pp. 208–9). But this is the direction in which the genre as a whole was developing in the 1630s, and Milton is only following Jonson in elaborating the dramatic elements of the form, however idiosyncratic the uses he makes of them.

Comus, as it has been known since the late seventeenth century (though not by Milton himself), was written to be performed, in a text probably a good deal shorter than the one he later printed, by the three children of the Earl of Bridgewater, their music-tutor the composer Henry Lawes and other members of the Bridgewater household (there is no evidence for or against the tradition that Milton himself acted Comus). John Egerton, first Earl of Bridgewater, was the son of Lord Chancellor Egerton and stepson of the Countess of Derby; and the occasion was his appointment the previous year as Lord Lieutenant of the Marches (i.e. the Welsh border country) and President of the Council of Wales, whose headquarters were in Ludlow, the Shropshire market town and the kingpin in a line of garrison castles commanding the Welsh border from Flint to Chepstow. Bridgewater was MP for Shropshire, and already a prominent figure in the Marches: one historian of seventeenth-century Wales describes him as 'a border lord with territorial interests extending into Wales and with nearly fifteen years' experience on the Council at Ludlow and five in the Privy Council' (Dodd 1952: p. 61). He was also, for the king's purposes, a loyalist. His earldom was reputed to have cost him £20,000 in payments to the Duke of Buckingham, and 'his steady support of Buckingham gave promise that he would be a faithful agent of royal policy'. A couple of years before, Charles had sent Sir Thomas Wentworth (later Earl of Strafford) to the Scottish borders as President of the Council of the North, and Bridgewater's appointment to the equivalent Welsh post reflects the same policy of extending the direct rule of king and privy council into provincial administration.

Ludlow, though in England, was effectively capital of Wales, and part of Bridgewater's job was to restore to it something of the political and cultural prestige it had enjoyed a generation earlier, during the presidency of William Herbert, Earl of Pembroke, whose periods of residence at Ludlow were brilliant social occasions, 'a round of banquets, masques and other gaieties' (Dodd 1952: p. 52), a provincial replica of the metropolitan splendours of Whitehall. At the same time the council, which under James I had dwindled to little more than a regional quarter sessions, was enlarged and its jurisdiction and authority extended to something like the viceregal proportions of the Elizabethan period, and Bridgewater's efforts in mustering and drilling the Welsh militias were matched by a greatly extended output and distribution of loyalist, devotional, and instructive literature in simple Welsh, a double prophylactic against the three-headed monster of Puritanism, popery, and rebellion.

Direct references to Bridgewater's political and military role frame the action of the masque. The Spirit's opening speech establishes his 'state/And new-entrusted sceptre' as the masque's immediate occasion in lines which hint at the realities of colonial rule beneath the formal rituals:

> And all this tract that fronts the falling sun
> A noble peer of mickle trust and power
> Has in his charge, with temper'd awe to guide
> An old and haughty nation proud in arms.

And at the end, after the country dancers have tripped the light fantastic against a backdrop of 'Ludlow town and the President's Castle', social hierarchy is reasserted ('Back, shepherds, back') in the 'court guise' of the second song, where the three children, 'nurs'd in princely lore', are reunited with their parents. Other features of the masque, too, suggest that their 'victorious dance/O'er sensual folly and intemperance' may have a political as well as a moral connotation. 'The voluptuous Comus, God of cheer' comes from Ben Jonson's *Pleasure Reconciled to Virtue*, to which for its second performance in 1618 Jonson had added an induction of comic stage Welshmen 'For the Honour of Wales' – that is, Charles, Prince of Wales, who appeared in the masque as Chief Masquer. Milton's version of the character, with his primitivistic associations of forest and witchcraft, roved 'the Celtic and Iberian fields' – France and Spain, both Roman provinces inhabited by Celts – before settling down in Shropshire; while Sabrina, redemptive water-goddess of the Severn, is the daughter of Locrine and granddaughter of Brut, so connecting the story not only with the borders and mountain fastnesses of Wales but with the ancient 'matter of Britain', the legendary prehistory of that 'old and haughty nation' that Milton found in Drayton, Spenser, and Geoffrey of Monmouth. In a less localized way, it may be that the triangle of the Spirit, the Lady, and Comus owes something to Shakespeare's masque-influenced *Tempest*, in which the magus Prospero protects his daughter Miranda from the bestial and lustful Caliban – a story even more strongly suggestive of the sexual and political anxieties of the colonial mentality.

All this is subtext, however. The main focus of the masque is on the children, and its direct concern is not the politics of colonial rule but the ethics of family life in a society threatened, perhaps even dominated, by the excess and intemperance not of its subject peoples but of its own ruling class. Staunch royalist Bridgewater may have been; but the family had Puritan inclinations, and Milton took the anxieties of pious and respectable parents over the physical and spiritual safety of their 15-year-old daughter as the central motif of the narrative, confronting her with a threat that, so far from being a generalized morality-play abstraction of 'lust' or 'intemperance', must have been all too readily identifiable. In spite of his Celtic and primitivistic associations, Comus, with his 'rout' of drunken followers (of both sexes), is primarily an allegory of the unscrupulous aristocratic libertine, like the royal favourites Somerset and Buckingham (in 1628 Milton's old schoolfriend Alexander Gill had been fined £2,000 and sentenced to life imprisonment and mutilation for proposing a toast to Buckingham's assassin, John Felton). Even closer to home than Egerton's patron Buckingham was the infamous Mervyn Touchet, second Earl of Castlehaven, hanged in May 1631 for sodomy and for prostituting his wife and daughter-in-law to his servants; for his wife was Anne Stanley, daughter of the Countess of Derby and sister of Egerton's wife Frances, and the violated daughter-in-law was Alice Egerton's cousin. The text aligns Comus with these courtly dissolutes (746), as well as with the Laudian canon law (808), the seductive hedonism of Caroline lyric (743–4), and the frivolous pseudo-rustic pastoralism of courtly 'disguises' (167). Against him it ranges the Lady's denunciation of the hypocrisy of courts (325–6) and aristocratic extravagance (768–71), the 'sage/And serious doctrine of virginity' (786–7) and the elevated Christian-Platonic pastoralism of the Attendant Spirit. The political setting – the 'temper'd awe' of the responsible governor – frames and counterpoints the moral argument – the responsibilities of parents and children; not comfortably (for the position of the upper gentry is already painfully divided between loyalty to the king, recognition of his weakness, and deep suspicion of the company he keeps) but with a compelling logic and consistency.

This consistency may help to suggest why masque, for all its courtly and royalist associations, might have struck Milton as a

154

not uninteresting genre to experiment with. In fact, the associations may have made it *more* interesting, since his attitude to established genres was often adversarial, motivated not by traditionalism but by the challenge of making them over to new purposes. Milton's ideas about poetry, and about his own future as a poet, are always *social* ideas. Intensely ambitious as he was, he never projected himself, in the romantic way, as a solitary figure. Even after 1660, 'with dangers compass'd round,/And solitude', he continues to look for a 'fit audience ... though few' (*Paradise Lost*, VII, 27–31). The 'poet soaring in the high region of his fancies' never forgets the organic obligation 'to imbreed and cherish in a great people the seeds of virtue and public civility'. Millar MacLure has written of Spenser's preoccupation in *The Faerie Queene* with 'the civilising of the new rich' (Ricks 1970: p. 79); and Milton will have been thinking in these years of families like the Egertons, a bourgeois aristocracy of merit, created by the administrative revolution of the Tudor and Jacobean state; politically conservative, no doubt, but pious, thrifty, sober, socially responsible: the stones from which, perhaps, Providence would shortly raise a new people of Abraham in England.

These values emerge directly in the Lady's reply to Comus (762–79). He has coupled sexuality and money in a natural economy of uninhibited expenditure ('Beauty is Nature's coin, must not be hoarded'); and she too invokes Nature ('good cateress') in lines that develop some of the key themes of what will later be called the 'Protestant ethic', uniting public and private moralities in a concept of personal integrity ('chastity') based on virtuous husbandry. Fine, in theory. But many readers have felt, with F. R. Leavis, that while 'the Lady has all the arguments, Comus has all the life'. Much of the critical debate about the masque has revolved around its adequacy as a dramatic narrative. Samuel Johnson called it 'a suite of speeches', lacking dramatic tension and plausibility. This in turn reflects uncertainty about its genre: masques and moralities *are* more static and ritualized than stage-plays (Johnson objects to the Spirit's first speech being addressed to the audience, standard practice in masques); and if we expect *Comus* to provide the dramatic excitements of *Hamlet*, we may well feel cheated.

There has been debate, too, about the ideas themselves. How

far does the Lady's defence of the 'doctrine of virginity' constitute the central meaning of the text? What is the significance of
the Sabrina episode? Of the Spirit's epilogue? For some, like A.
S. P. Woodhouse, virginity is central, and the masque articulates an orthodox Augustinian asceticism (Woodhouse 1968):
we live in a fallen world, in which, with effort, we can achieve
virtue. But virtue alone is not enough to save us. For that we
need grace. The symbolic link between nature and grace is the
sacraments (Sabrina's baptismal 'drops ... from my fountain
pure'). The Lady can withstand Comus's charms because she is
virtuous; but to rise from her seat she needs a supernatural
intervention. The epilogue stresses the separation of the two
orders: Venus, goddess of natural love, pines unrequited 'on
the ground' for her wounded Adonis, while 'celestial Cupid'
(symbol of divine love) is reunited 'far above' with his beloved
Psyche (Greek for 'soul').

This reading has a good deal to recommend it. It is consistent. It makes sense of a lot of difficult details. It also conscripts
Milton to a reassuringly traditional kind of Anglo-Catholic
orthodoxy, rather as C. S. Lewis does with *Paradise Lost* (Lewis
1942). This *may* have been Milton's position in 1634, or he may
have thought it wise to give the impression that it was (like
Marlowe pretending to be piously shocked at the end of *Doctor
Faustus*), or he may have somehow conveyed these ideas in the
masque without really intending to. But as R. M. Adams and
others have pointed out, this makes difficulties with the closing
lines: there, Virtue 'can teach ye how to climb/Higher than the
sphery chime' (i.e. to Heaven); and grace, far from being a
necessary condition of salvation, stands ready to help as a last
resort only 'if Virtue feeble were'. The conditional form here,
which Adams says has 'thoroughly embarrassed' the orthodox
camp (Adams 1968), suggests a transitional position somewhere between the doctrine of grace and the do-it-yourself
salvationism (really a kind of humanism) of the mid-1640s,
when education 'can repair the ruins of our first parents' (Yale:
II, pp. 366–7), and although we bring the impurity of original
sin into the world, what purifies us is not grace but 'trial, and
trial is by what is contrary' (see below, p. 88). In a similar
way, E. M. W. Tillyard, revising his own earlier reading,

rejects the stress on virginity and places the climax of the narrative not in the Lady's defeat of Comus but in the Spirit's epilogue (lines probably added after the Ludlow performance), where the consummated and fruitful love of Cupid and Psyche symbolizes not the spiritual union of redeemed soul and divine love but, simply, marriage, the 15-year-old Alice Egerton's real social destination. The Lady's resistance, he argues, 'is not final. The setting is aristocratic; the Lady, though but young, will one day be a great lady. She must take her place in society and do what is expected of her' (Tillyard 1951: p. 95). Rosamund Tuve, in turn, has challenged this, arguing that the central Platonic myths that structure the narrative, in particular the story of Circe, are too powerful and fixed in their connotations to be manipulated 'to show ... that "the meaning was marriage"' (Tuve 1957: p. 112). For her, Comus is 'leagues away from problems of social or religious contract or some single human institution'. Rather, the masque dramatizes 'the great traditional metaphors' of the neo-Platonic and hermetic canon: traditional, and therefore, she implies, immutable. What Milton himself would have thought of this awed deference to 'tradition' is another matter (he called his first pamphlet for the Council of State Eikonoklastes, 'the breaker of images'); and it should be added that Tuve's reading, as well as being un-Miltonic in tone and emphasis, is also entirely undramatic. Learned and often informative, she is even less interested than most academic commentators (and in marked contrast to the journalist and frustrated dramatist Johnson) in music, dance, performance. For her, Comus is a poem written by a scholar for scholars to read, a learned message in code.

Some of these disagreements, naturally enough, represent deep divergences of opinion not just about Milton but about poetry, history, and the world; and once again, there is no simple question of 'right' or 'wrong' interpretations, though every reader is likely to find some more interesting and plausible than others. But readings that ignore the practical circumstances and functions of texts, or abstract them completely from their historical settings, or hold them to be embodying views wholly unrelated to those of the author but strikingly similar to those of the critic: these also reflect the unhistorical and conservative bias of much post-war Milton criticism, and of the British and American universities out of which it has generally come. Many of the interpretations of *Comus* that I have mentioned were published in the 1940s and 1950s, and a Milton bookishly neo-platonic (Tuve), traditionally Anglican (Lewis), and harmlessly non-political (both) is a much more comfortable sort of person to have around in a reactionary and conformist period like the 1950s than Johnson's 'acrimonious and surly republican' or Shelley's 'bold enquirer into morals and religion'.

Much of the recent debate has turned on the final scene: the summoning of Sabrina, the releasing of the Lady from the enchanted seat, and the Spirit's concluding speech. Most people are likely to find these passages difficult. The allegory is obscure and ambiguous, and the classical references come thick and fast. Who or what are 'scaly Triton', 'fair Ligea', or 'th'Assyrian queen'? More to the point, who cares? A couple of things need to be said about this. Individual references of this kind *do* matter in Milton. Far more than merely decorative (as in some Renaissance poetry), they constitute a level of meaning in the text which it can be very rewarding to disentangle. The speech with which the Spirit calls on Sabrina's help, for instance, invokes a group of female water-deities who, escaping from rape and violence, are all in some way transfigured or immortalized. This has obvious relevance to Sabrina, to whom the same thing happened. It frames the Lady's similar predicament in an ancient folklore of violence, death, and transfiguration through water. It may well have reminded the Egertons, as tactfully and consolingly as possible, of the Castlehaven horrors. And it looks forward to *Lycidas*, where male counterparts of Leucothea and Parthenope, like Orpheus, Melicertes, and Lycidas himself, figure in a comparable sequence, with even stronger hints of a general underlying symbolism. The effect is richly pictorial, too (and masque is as much a visual as a verbal form). The golden apples of the Hesperides, Mercury and the three Graces, Venus, Cupid, and 'the spruce and jocund Spring' all appear in Botticelli's magnificent and mysterious *Primavera* ('Spring'), a painting as complex and scholarly in its allegory, as simple and sensuous in its primary impact, as anything in Milton.

At the same time, it would be a mistake to be too daunted by the difficulty of understanding all this. It is possible to find Botticelli's painting beautiful and moving without understanding any of the references; and while all the details in Milton's mythologizing passages contribute to the meaning, the *structural* effect is broad. Remember the occasion and purpose: the education of a class, the civilizing of the new rich. The emergence of a new social order – for I am suggesting that Milton is already envisaging something of this kind as early as 1634 – calls for more than the straightforward didacticism of the Lady's replies to Comus. It requires too a fresh repertoire of images and stories, a new *culture* that will express its energy and confidence. And although the raw materials of that culture will inevitably be drawn from this past, their real meanings and uses will belong to the future. All Milton's writings can be seen to serve this project in one way or another. The mythological allegories of *Comus* – the Graces and Hours, the garden of the daughters of Hesperus, Venus and Adonis, Psyche and Cupid: images of unity and reconciliation but also of suffering, endurance, and heroic struggle – gather up the past to reinvent it, investing the Lady's bourgeois virtue and her father's bourgeois wealth and power with the glamour and resonance of 'a secular ritual' (to quote MacLure once again) 'expressing the permanence and variety of the European inheritance' (Ricks 1970: p. 79).

Permanence does not mean lack of change, and the 'inheritance' that informs seventeenth-century writing is the opposite of static. Just how mobile those traditions are can be seen in the genre that above all others enabled Milton in the 1630s to connect private and public, secular and religious themes through a network of interconnecting myths and linking devices: *pastoral*. Tracing its origins from Sicilian Greeks writing in the third century BC through the Latin *Eclogues* of Virgil two hundred years later, pastoral had been developed during the sixteenth century into an unusually flexible form, encompassing erotic, idyllic, political, satirical, and devotional modes.

Once more Spenser is a key figure, displaying in his early *Shepheardes Calendar* (1579) a virtuoso range of pastoral styles and subjects. Most interesting to Milton is his elaboration, with the 'good shepherd' passages of scripture in the background, of the shepherd figure into an analogue of both poet and priest, an identification absent from the classical and continental antecedents that draws the genre directly into the heart of Protestant polemic. In the 1641 *Animadversions*, the third of his five pamphlets attacking the Laudian bishops, Milton quotes in full the passage from the fifth eclogue of the *Calendar* ascribing the depredations of the Catholic 'wolves' to the greed and negligence of the Anglican prelates, adding that it is 'not without some presage of these reforming times' (Yale: I, pp. 722–3).

One misapprehension needs to be cleared away. Just about the only subject-matter that is definitely out of bounds for pastoral is shepherds – real ones, that is. 'To understand pastoral as a genre', declares J. B. Broadbent, 'don't read books about it but think about sheep' (Broadbent 1975: p. 185). But though this may work for insomnia, it will not help at all with pastoral, which has got no more to do with sheep than westerns have to do with cows or *Animal Farm* with pigs. Even the earliest pastorals, the 'Sicilian muses' of Theocritus and Moschus, are creatures not of the sun-baked hillsides and high windswept pastures of Sicily but of courtly, literary, cosmopolitan Alexandria; and Renaissance pastoral is no Tudor version of *The Archers*, but (like modern science fiction) an inherently allegorical genre, its meanings coded and oblique. Its simple swains with their oaten pipes, their proud Phyllises and false Corinnas, are a heuristic device, an exploratory metaphor for prising open the packed complexities of the urban and courtly world with a sophisticated naivety that can say the unsayable, like Lear's Fool. The shepherd's equivalent in a later period, William Empson has suggested, is a child like Alice, allowed to say things about adults which they cannot say about themselves, because she is supposed not to understand what she is saying (Empson 1966: pp. 203–33).

It was the conventionality of pastoral, its coded, often cryptic character, that annoyed Samuel Johnson in *Lycidas*:

we know that they never drove afield, and that they had no flocks to batten; and though it be allowed that the representation may be allegorical, the true meaning is so uncertain and remote, that it is never sought because it cannot be known when it is found.

(Johnson 1906: p. 116)

Modern readers may be inclined to agree; but that is because for us, as for Johnson, pastoral itself has become 'uncertain and remote'. It may in fact already have been approaching the end of its useful life when Milton employed it, and perhaps it is only the political–ecclesiastical crisis of the 1630s that enabled him to rework the Spenserian motifs with a momentarily recharged relevance and urgency. By the 1660s it had passed out of earshot, as a serious imaginative and political mode. Dryden couldn't 'hear' it at all; and the pastorals of his eighteenth-century successors are pastiche, decorative and self-consciously silly.

Equally uncongenial to Johnson, and just as integral a feature, indeed a structure, of Protestant pastoral is the mingling together of 'trifling fictions' like the nymphs and muses with 'the most awful and sacred truths' of Christianity. In the passage from the May Eclogue that Milton quoted in *Animadversions*, Spenser notes that the pastors of the early church did not need large incomes and country houses because 'Pan himself was their inheritance', and adds a note explaining with a great show of learning that the Greek Pan, a rural deity noted principally for drunkenness and priapic incontinence, represents the founder of Christianity (Spenser 1912: 437, 439). Milton is more scrupulous, perhaps even prudish. Far from 'mingling' sacred and profane, pagan and Christian, he goes to some lengths structurally to *separate* the two ('Return, Alpheus'), and avoids explicitly syncretic figures like Spenser's Pan/Christ. Syncretism, the identification of Christian and pagan deities and cosmologies, is a central concern of the fifteenth-century neo-Platonists like Marsilio Ficino and Pico della Mirandola, whose work Milton certainly knew well before he visited the Florentine academies in 1638. Full syncretism is very unusual in his writing – as opposed to casual latinizing like 'Jove' for 'God'. Generally he prefers to let the analogies between Christianity and its Mediterranean and Levantine sister-religions resonate suggestively without conceding parity. But certain figures clearly interested him deeply: the Egyptian sun- and water-god Osiris, butchered by his brother and endlessly reassembled by his grieving wife and sister; the celestial nuptials of Cupid and Psyche; the wounding of the river-god Adonis; the story of Orpheus, who survived the underworld only to be dismembered by the Thracian maenads – all of these interpreted by the Florentine Platonists as 'vestiges' or prefigurings of the death and resurrection of Christ (see Wind 1967).

One thing is clear from *Lycidas*: that, as well as pondering the logic and justice of the 'blind Fury', Milton was by 1637 developing a powerful critique of the Anglican establishment, a critique that was bringing him close to Presbyterian dissidents like Prynne and Leighton. Both of those had suffered brutally for writing and saying no more than *Lycidas* does. Indeed the poem's promise of a terrible retribution awaiting the 'blind mouths' of the established church goes further and cuts deeper than polemics that had cost their authors an ear-cropping. Of course, 'poetry makes nothing happen', especially when it is hidden away in a collection of academic elegies, more than half of them in Latin. But the 'trifling fictions' of pastoral, like the fanciful attitudinizing of the masque, can sometimes provide a useful disguise, as Spenser knew. At the same time, the political commitment that emerges in the lines of the 'pilot of the Galilean lake' and finds apt expression in the Spenserian metaphors may already be moving Milton away from the courtly genres with their classicized Christianity and their acquiescence, complacent or elegiac, in the established order of things. Like the careful disentangling of classical and Christian motifs, the poem's structure suggests an approaching disengagement. The last eight lines, metrically as well as thematically separate (a stanza of *ottava rima*), produce a striking shift of perspective. A 'monody' (Milton's own description of the poem) is a soliloquy or dramatic scene presented raw, without explanation or commentary from author or chorus; but these lines have a 'choric' effect, framing the rest of the text in

162

quotation marks and throwing into relief the dramatic character of its shifting tenses, its passages of direct speech, its vertiginous transitions. The poem's passionate and spontaneous immediacy, it turns out, is nothing of the kind: it is in the third person. And if we imagine Milton's 'voice' behind the body of the poem, then who is speaking the ending?

Examples of this sort of thing can be found in other Renaissance poems; but the result in this case is strikingly modern, a Brechtian 'alienation effect'. As in Brecht's plays, this self-distancing of the text, drawing attention to its own writtenness, can help us to form a critical estimate and an awareness of our own responses. It can also suggest a restless distancing on the part of the poet. The 'fresh woods and pastures new' retain the pastoral convention while hinting at a movement beyond it. The precedents of Virgil and Spenser suggested that for a serious poet pastoral was an apprentice genre, a youthful preparation for more ambitious things (an *Aeneid*, a *Faerie Queene*). Whatever the reason, Milton never (the Latin 'Epitaphium Damonis' apart) used it again.

Critics rarely argue nowadays, as they once did, about Milton's 'sincerity'; but readers coming to his poetry for the first time may still feel an uncomfortable discrepancy between the supposed subject-matter of *Lycidas* ('the author bewails a learned friend, unfortunately drowned') and the elaborate architecture of the poem, agreeing with Johnson that 'where there is leisure for fiction there is little grief'. It may indeed be true, as Tillyard suggests, that its most compelling passages have more to do with Milton's own preoccupations than with the unfortunate Edward King, whose meagre handful of conventional Latin verses hardly qualifies him for Orphean status. It is hard, too, to feel that King's death provides adequate motivation or occasion for the impassioned historical vision that animates the poem's structure and imagery, the vision of a great Protestant nation, learned, pious, and guarded by a special providence against assault, betrayed by its prelates within but poised now on the threshold of a new, perhaps a final, reformation. True, elegy is a public, not a private mode. Its function is to commemorate and elevate the dead by transcending the fact of death and conferring at least a literary immortality, and neither Milton nor anyone else would have thought it an appropriate place for expressions of raw personal emotion, however sincere. But *Lycidas* remains an eccentric and disturbing example of the genre, and critics who have tried to answer Johnson's charge of insincerity by claiming that it is entirely traditional, a polished rehearsal of conventional pieties and elegiac figures of speech, are not necessarily doing Milton a favour.

John Crowe Ransom makes a similar point, though with a different emphasis, when he argues that the Renaissance genres are 'anonymous', embedded in traditional practices of writing that absorb and generalize the individual experience, raising it to a higher power of impersonality (Ransom 1938). Writing in America in the 1930s, Ransom is strongly influenced by the theories of T. S. Eliot, for whom poetry 'is not the expression of personality, but an escape from personality', and other modernist poet-critics ('All that is personal soon rots', wrote Yeats).[1] For him, *Lycidas* is flawed not (as for Johnson) because it is too conventional but because it is not conventional enough: Milton's handling of the traditional forms and topics of elegy is 'insubordinate ... a gesture of his rebellion', displaying an anger and violence that belong not to the genre or the occasion but to the poet's youthful mood and the historical moment. Other critics have shown that Ransom over-simplifies the genre here: some of Milton's 'insubordination' turns out to be standard practice for the genre. But although there is no obligation to follow him in deploring the elements of 'personality' in the poem, much of what he says is helpful, confirming Milton's restless and dynamic relationship with inherited forms, and rescuing the poem from the curse of a sterile traditionalism 'such as a college easily supplies'. Like the Tory Johnson and the atheist Empson, the agrarian fundamentalist Ransom makes Milton more interesting by attacking him than most critics do by defending.

Lycidas was published in 1638, and whether Milton intended it or not it is difficult not to feel that it marks some kind of terminus. His mother had died the previous April. The Latin elegy for his friend Charles Diodati confirms his determination to abandon pastoral. After his Italian trip – itself a sort of watershed – he moved back to London, and from then until the appearance of *Paradise Lost* twenty-eight years later he published very little new poetry (of the English poems in the 1645 collection, only three sonnets were written after his return from Italy). His reading, too, suggests a change of course at this time: the entries in the commonplace book from 1639 to 1644 record intensive study of British history, and he probably began work on his own *History of Britain* (published in 1670) some time in the mid-1640s.

Between 1639 and 1660, Milton produced nineteen substantial prose works, three in Latin and the rest in English. They fall into three chronological groups, which to some extent correspond also to their subject-matter. First come the five 'antiprelatical' pamphlets of 1641–2, the four divorce pamphlets of 1643–5, the *Education* tractate and *Areopagitica* of 1644: all dealing with aspects of 'private' liberty, though of course with important implications for the public sphere. Next are the writings directly associated with the revolutionary coup d'état of 1648–9 and with Milton's defence of it for the Council of State: the *Tenure* and *Eikonoklastes* of 1649 and the three Latin *Defences* of 1651–5. Finally, there are the pamphlets written during 1659 and 1660 in a despairing last-ditch attempt to rally dissenters and republicans to a common programme of root-and-branch reform: the *Treatise of Civil Power*, the *Likeliest Way to Remove Hirelings*, and the *Ready and Easy Way*.

Milton referred deprecatingly to his prose writings as the work 'of my left hand', believing himself 'led by the power of nature' to the higher art of poetry. In this he agrees with standard Renaissance judgement, and perhaps with modern too. True, nineteenth-century admirers of Macaulay's Whig hero enthused windily about the 'energy and richness', the 'melody, majesty and power', the 'peculiar sweetness and harmony' of Milton's prose; phrases that tell us nothing about Milton, rather more about the literary tastes of middle-class Victorians, who regarded him as a sort of prose Wagner. But Eliot's description, 'too near to half-formed poetry to be good prose', signals the decisive turn towards a cooler contemporary judgement: 'good prose' is lucid, unpretentious, to the point; Milton's is opaque, long-winded, rhetorical, a word whose damning connotations of artificiality would have surprised Milton himself. The inventor of Comus and Satan knew of course that rhetoric could lie and confuse, but he knew too that *all* language, in prose or verse, is 'rhetorical', structured by shared rules of discourse; and the question for him would not have been 'Rhetorical or not?' but 'Which of the many traditions, styles, and intentionalities of rhetoric?'

In the ideal curriculum set out in the *Education* pamphlet, writing (as opposed to functional literacy) is taught only at the end of nine years of intensive study, the final and the highest of practical accomplishments.

> And now lastly will be the time to read with them those organic arts which enable men to discourse and write perspicuously, elegantly, and according to the fitted style of lofty, mean or lowly. Logic therefore, so much as is useful, is to be referred to this due place, with all her well-couched heads and topics; until it be time to open her contracted palm into a graceful and ornate rhetoric taught out of the rule of Plato, Aristotle, Phalereus, Cicero, Hermogenes, Longinus.... From hence, and not till now, will be the right season of forming them to be able writers and composers in every excellent matter, when they shall be thus fraught with an universal insight into things; or whether they be to speak in Parliament or Council, honour and attention would be waiting on their lips.
>
> (Yale: II, pp. 401–6)

From this it is clear that for Milton, as for the classical rhetoricians, first, speaking and writing are intimately connected (his view of language is 'phonocentric', grounded in the authority of the spoken word); secondly, style is neither personal nor merely ornamental, but an inseparable extension of method (logic) and content. While still at Cambridge he had argued that the genuine orator 'must first acquire a thorough knowledge of all the arts and sciences', and here the students must be 'fraught with an universal insight into things' before they can be expected to write well.

These rather daunting standards apply to public oratory and

its written equivalents, of course. It will not be necessary to bring 'all the arts and sciences' or 'an universal insight' to every casual communication. But they alert us to the high formality of Renaissance prose, not as 'half-formed poetry' but as a sister art deploying comparable resources of imagery, rhythm, and sound to move and convince; and they remind us that Milton's language aims not at spontaneity and colloquial immediacy but at Ciceronian *eloquence*: persuasive public argument within the styles and genres of an established rhetorical discipline. That discipline constrains, to be sure, in the same way that a twelve-bar blues or the chords of a popular song constrain a jazz musician. But there is no more reason to suppose that Milton's prose is suffocated by the conventions of rhetoric than to think that the high eloquence and inventiveness of Bessie Smith or Charlie Parker are overpowered by the far more rigid and unforgiving forms *they* worked with. As for genre, 'Milton's prose' sounds flat and colourless, acres of uninviting print; but the actual forms vary as widely as the poetry does, each with its own range of styles and shape of argument. *Of Reformation* is a 'letter to a friend' (not literally: it is a formal genre, like *Private Eye*'s 'Dear Bill' correspondence or Adrian Mole's 'Diary'). *Of Education* is a 'tractate', a scholarly monograph dealing with a single topic for a readership of insiders. *Areopagitica* and the *Tenure* are public speeches (though written to be read, not orally delivered) arguing a major issue of principle within the structure of a classical oration, the first to Parliament (though with a wider audience in view), the second to the Council of State. *Eikonoklastes* is a set of 'animadversions', a point-by-point commentary on another text, in this case the 'King's Book', *Eikon Basilike. The Ready and Easy Way* is a 'treatise' (Milton's own description), a closely argued discourse for private reading and consideration, addressed to the dwindling band of republicans and commonwealthsmen. Milton's handling of these genres is free, as might be expected. *Of Reformation*, for example, abandons the letter convention and ends with an invocation in almost epic style. *The Ready and Easy Way* breaks in its closing pages into an impassioned 'oral' mode quite different from the measured exposition of the main argument. But the breaks and improvisations grow out of the underlying genre and structure, and assume an awareness of them in the reader.

In one sense, a single argument runs through all the prose writings. In 1659 he reminded the newly recalled Rump Parliament of 'this liberty of writing which I have used these eighteen years on all occasions to assert the just rights and freedoms both of church and state' (Yale: VII, p. 274); and the historian Austin Woolrych has argued that 'beneath the inescapable inconsistencies of his political writings ... the essentials remain firm: the vision of a regenerate nation, the ideal of an aristocracy of virtue, the constant vindication of intellectual and religious liberty', stressing the positive content of the ideas, as Milton himself did (Woolrych 1974: p. 72). Johnson took a different view, claiming that 'he had determined rather what to condemn, than what to approve', that 'his predominant desire was to destroy, rather than establish, and that he felt not so much the love of liberty as repugnance to authority' (Johnson 1906: p. 112). It is true that the pamphlets contain passages of scathing satire and abuse: the prelates 'under sail in all their lawn and sarsnet, their shrouds and tackle, with a geometrical rhomboides upon their heads' (*Reformation*, 796–8), the Presbyterian clergy 'rambling from benefice to benefice like ravenous wolves seeking where they may devour the biggest' (*Tenure*, 323). But to accuse him of a destructive negativity for that reason is absurdly to ignore the period and the circumstances in which he was writing. None of Milton's major ideas (full separation of church and state, toleration of religious dissent, government by assembly, advancement by merit rather than wealth or birth) would have commanded anything like general assent in the seventeenth century, and to deplore the fact that Milton wrote under fire and on the run is like objecting that Marx is unfair to capitalism or that the Book of Revelation is a bit negative about the devil. Circumstances called for an activist not a contemplative discourse; and in any case Milton is no utopian (for all his Platonism he is unimpressed by the 'airy burgomasters' of the *Republic* and *Laws*). 'To sequester out of the world into Atlantic and Utopian polities, which never can be drawn into use, will not mend our condition', he wrote in 1644. The only way to do that is 'to ordain wisely as in this

world of evil, in the midst whereof God hath placed us unavoidably' (*Areopagitica*, 304).

But if Milton was no Whig philosopher, expatiating at his
ease on 'the love of liberty', he was no modern democrat or
egalitarian either. He may have endorsed the wish of Moses
that all the Lord's people might become prophets, but they
showed few signs of developing in that direction, and the
'misguided and abused multitude' blindly 'choosing them a
captain back for Egypt' in the spring of 1660 only confirmed
misgivings expressed much earlier. The sovereign people of the
Tenure, like the 'knowing people, a nation of prophets, of sages
and of worthies' of *Areopagitica*, remains a theoretical entity,
without sociological substance. In practical terms Milton, a
contractualist like the Anglican Richard Hooker (1554–1600)
and the absolutist Thomas Hobbes (1588–1679), always envisages the people hierarchically, their power devolved
permanently on to some representative authority. His secular
politics were those of a meritocratic elitist with a deep suspicion
of popular movements and electoral processes, which he came
to regard as fatally vulnerable to the Circean enticements of
idolatry, or ideology. But though classically republican in politics, his position is interestingly complicated by the religious
views of his maturity, which owe a good deal to the antino-
mian and anarchistic underground of the Puritan movement.
His early clerical ambitions 'church-outed by the prelates'
(Yale: I, p. 823), he never joined any church or sect (an unusual
position in this period), remaining from the mid-1640s to his
death a 'radical independent', subscribing to the priesthood of
all believers and the absolute authority of the individual conscience, underpinned by an unconditional humanism that carries
him well beyond orthodoxy to the outer limits of religious
belief itself: 'no ordinance human or from heaven can bind
against the good of man; so that to keep them strictly against
that end is all one with to break them' (Yale: II, p. 588). To
obey the law (or the commandments), if to do so goes against
the 'good of man', is the same as to break them. And who is to
decide in each case what the good of man is? The individual
conscience guided by reason. ('Where's your Good Old Cause
now?' jeered a voice from the crowd as the Fifth Monarchist

and regicide Thomas Harrison rode past to his terrible and humiliating death. 'Here in my bosom', he replied.) The fundamental distinction, in fact, is not between politics and religion, which nobody in the seventeenth century would have regarded as separate entities ('whether the war was for religion or liberty', Andrew Marvell concluded, 'is not worth the labour to decide'), but between public and private life, or rather between the *respublica*, the state, on the one hand, and civil society, the sphere of private liberty, on the other. Unlike his contemporary Hobbes, for whom the authority of the state is paramount and liberty means the freedom to do what you are told, Milton makes domestic and religious liberty the cornerstone of political practice. Between them, the two writers define the poles of a dialectic of power and freedom, public authority and individual conscience, that has continued to frame the political culture of western societies down to the present day.

One thing stands out about that culture: its overwhelming *maleness*. From Milton to Marx, from Hobbes to Habermas, the ideal citizen and active subject of the social process has been – by language and implication if not by actual prescription – a man. Mary Wollstonecraft protested that Tom Paine's *Rights of Man* said nothing (by claiming to say everything) about the rights of women. But, despite the efforts and achievements of feminists from the seventeenth century to the twentieth, the official philosophies of western societies, for all their talk of equal opportunity, are as patriarchal as *Leviathan* or the *Tenure*. As for their practice: in 1640 there were no women in the British House of Commons. In 1986 there were twenty-two, just 3.5 per cent of the membership – after three and a half centuries!

Christopher Hill, Edward Le Comte, and others have shown that Milton's ideas about women, and about sex, were a bit more complicated than the conventional Protestant patriarchalism ('He for God only, she for God in him') he sometimes expressed, and which is still occasionally presented as his entire position on the subject (Hill 1979, pp. 117–45; Le Comte 1978). Admittedly his supposed susceptibility to female charm and his advocacy of 'wedded love' against the arranged marriages and adulterous liaisons of the courtly code will hardly qualify him to be called a feminist, and in some ways his thinking falls well behind that of republican contemporaries like Gerard Winstanley, who wanted women to take a full part in public life, and John Dury, who wrote on the education of girls, something never mentioned by Milton the schoolmaster and father of three daughters. But gender and sexuality disrupt his texts repeatedly, undercutting their masculine assertiveness and qualifying their patriarchal priorities. The 'noble and puissant nation' of *Areopagitica*, 'rousing herself like a strong man after sleep, and shaking her invincible locks' (see p. 103, l. 713), superimposes a female England on a male Samson in an androgynous image of disturbing power and beauty. Stranger still, the legendary birth of Athene (Minerva) from the head of her father Zeus is conflated with a conventional childbirth and the traditional purification or 'churching' of the mother, to produce, in the *Doctrine and Discipline of Divorce*, a bizarrely witty and disconcerting accouchement:

> For Truth is as impossible to be soiled by any outward touch as the sunbeam; though this ill hap wait on her nativity, that she never comes into the world but like a bastard, to the ignominy of him that brought her forth, till Time, the midwife rather than the mother of Truth, have washed and salted the infant, declared her legitimate, and churched the father of his young Minerva from the needless causes of his purgation.

> (Yale: II, p. 225)

In the first of these, a female Samson threatens to usurp the strength and invincibility of the male hero. In the second a man gives birth, and the woman is demoted from mother to midwife. Locked firmly into patriarchal order in the doctrine and discipline of his texts, the sexes slip, merge, and metamorphose in Milton's imagery and language. Behind the contrite Eve, submissive wife and mother of the ideal Puritan household, loom the outlines of the great female deities of antiquity, the terrifying Maenads of Orphic legend, the libidinous Sirens and Nereids of Homeric water-myth, the castrating Fates and avenging Furies, and beyond them all the *magna dea*, the Great

Goddess, 'mooned Ashtaroth', source of life and bringer of death, as changeable and as constant as the moon herself.

Milton's views on the intellectual and moral inferiority of women are sometimes explained (if not excused) on the grounds that, as Christopher Hill puts it, 'no one ... in the seventeenth century claimed that women were wholly equal to men' (Hill 1979: p. 118). But even if this is true, it is beside the point if it implies that Milton shared the typical saloon-bar orthodoxies of his period. Not many people thought it was all right to execute the king either. To present Milton as a typical representative of the seventeenth-century male consensus over-looks the aggressive heterodoxy of all his ideas and the polemi-cally charged tone of many of his references to women. If he is a male chauvinist, it's pretty certain that he will be his own kind of male chauvinist. He is more like D. H. Lawrence than, say, H. G. Wells (to take an example of a modern writer in step with progressive opinion on the 'woman question'). Like Lawrence, he combined advanced views on some aspects of marriage with oppressively patriarchal ideas about women in general. Like Lawrence's, his writings often seem torn between a declarative ideological commitment (what Lawrence, like Milton, called 'doctrine') and a deeper disruptive pull of meta-phor and story. Like Lawrence, he formed strong, perhaps passionate, male attachments in early manhood, and his texts are haunted by images of female power, sufficiency, and sex-uality, against which the assertive heterosexual masculinity seems more like a defensive pose than a secure identity or conviction of principle.

In any case, it is not at all clear what a mid-seventeenth-century consensus on women would have been. Again like Lawrence, Milton was writing in a period in which the tradi-tional forms of relationship between men and women, and the ideas about them, were changing quite rapidly. Some aspects of this change, like the companionate marriage based on affection and respect rather than money and parental compulsion, Milton approved of. Others, like the homosexual and heterosexual libertinism of Rochester and Sedley, he certainly did not. Yet others, like the feminism of Bathsua Makin or the dissenting preacher Mrs Attaway (who discussed his divorce pamphlets

172

with her congregation and left her husband for another man), he probably did not think much of either. But his ideas were no more inertly 'conventional' than theirs, and his patriarchalism, uncongenial as it is likely to be to most modern readers, has the same biblical and classical weight, and the same thorny individuality, as his republicanism.[2]

The 'mooned Ashtaroth' comes from the poem 'On the morning of Christ's Nativity', where she abandons her ancient places of worship at the appearance of the Christian Messiah – though the syntax is ambiguous, and the epithet 'Heav'n's queen and mother both' makes her sound interestingly like the Virgin Mary. The 'Nativity ode', as it is often called, is the first poem in the *Poems of Mr John Milton, both English and Latin* which he published in the winter of 1645. This volume contains most of the things, the *Samson Agonistes* and the two *Paradise* poems apart, for which Milton is best known nowadays: the lines on Shakespeare, 'At a solemn music', the companion poems 'L'Allegro' and 'Il Penseroso', the early sonnets, plus reprintings with minor revisions of *Lycidas* and the Ludlow masque, here fully acknowledged for the first time. But familiar as these now are, the book must have seemed an oddity in 1645–6, coming as it did from a writer known not for poetry but for his attacks on the Anglican bishops, his opposition to censorship, and above all his advocacy of divorce, for which he had been attacked from the pulpit as a libertine and summoned to explain himself to the House of Lords. What can he possibly be thinking of, this self-styled champion of the English people, bringing out in the year of Naseby, the execution of Laud, and the disestablishment of the Church of England, a collection of decidedly old-fashioned poems (including, of all things, a masque!), half of them in Latin, and some of them written, on his own confession, when he was scarcely more than a child?

From the point of view of the publisher Humphrey Moseley the poems no doubt represented a better proposition in 1645, when Milton was enjoying minor celebrity as a pamphleteer, than they would have done in 1639, when he was a nobody. But Milton's reasons, and the real significance of the volume, may be approached through Louis Martz's suggestion that the contents 'have been arranged to convey a sense of the predestined bard's rising powers' (Martz 1980: p. 12). It is very clear from the pamphlets of the early 1640s that Milton still wished to be thought of as a poet, slender though his published output was. 'I can understand your wanting to write poems', T. S. Eliot remarked to the young Stephen Spender, 'but I don't quite know what you mean by "being a poet"' (Spender 1951: p. 146). For Milton, 'being a poet' represented something altogether more substantial, strenuous, and worthwhile than merely writing poems. *Of Reformation* (1641) looks forward to the time when 'amidst the hymns and halleluiahs of saints, some one may perhaps be heard offering at high strains in new and lofty measures to sing and celebrate thy divine mercies and marvellous judgements in this land throughout all ages' – a promise he made good twenty-six years later, his biographer Toland thought, when he published *Paradise Lost* (Darbishire 1932: p. 182); though in 1641, clearly, he was still thinking of a national epic, perhaps with an Arthurian narrative. In *The Reason of Church Government* (1642), the first of his publications to carry his full name, he introduces himself as one 'led by the genial power of nature' to poetry, and digresses at length on the subject of epic, tragedy, and 'those magnific odes and hymns wherein Pindarus and Callimachus are in most things worthy'. In the *Apology* of the same year, accused of frequenting brothels, he defends himself characteristically by recalling his early studies in 'the laureate fraternity of poets' (Dante, Petrarch, and Spenser) (Yale: I, pp. 890–1). And in the 'Captain or colonel' sonnet of 1642, the most recent poem in the 1645 collection, he invites comparison with Pindar and Euripides, in promise if not yet in achievement.

As Martz suggests, the order of the poems in the book is not straightforwardly chronological, and seems designed to display the poet's development across a range of modes and verse forms, from early metrical versions of the Psalms ('done by the author at fifteen years old') and a fragment on the Passion, abandoned as 'above the years he had when he wrote it', through to the confident control of form and subject in the pastorals of the mid-1630s, *Arcades, Lycidas*, and *Comus* (in that order). In between come the three metrically experimental 'madrigals', 'On time', 'Upon the Circumcision' and 'At a solemn music', a collection of occasional elegies and encomiums including the lines on Shakespeare and some undergraduate jocularity about the university carrier, and a group of sonnets and *canzoni* in which he falls poetically in love (in Italian) and worries that he has not yet, in his 'three and twentieth year', done much with his life. Placed pivotally in a median position between the Cambridge poems and the Italianate sonnet group, 'L'Allegro' and 'Il Penseroso', in which, as Lorna Sage has suggested, 'Milton seems to be exploring two different versions of creativity' (Broadbent 1975: p. 67), rehearse comparatively a set of contrasted literary modes and personalities, pastoral and devotional, classical and Christian, romantic and contemplative, which will be integrated and synthesized in the sonnets and pastorals that follow.

Read in this way, as oblique autobiography, a 'portrait of the artist as a young bard', the 1645 *Poems* becomes a highly dramatic text, a carefully composed narrative of poetic and personal development from the pious ambitions and overreachings of adolescence through a series of testing doubts, crises, and dilemmas to the transcendent turn at the end of *Lycidas* and the assured integrative finality of the Ludlow masque. (When he republished his poems in 1673, with *Paradise Lost, Paradise Regained*, and *Samson Agonistes* all in print and his reputation established, such a narrative no longer had any point, and he rearranged the sequence, giving pride of place to *Lycidas, Comus*, and the companion poems). Autobiography, the dramatic projection of 'self' into a formal narrative of choice, crisis, and development, is a new form in the seventeenth century, and one particularly associated with Puritanism, for the Puritan preoccupation with inner experience and personal responsibility for salvation invests each individual life with a special shape, significance, and intensity. Of all seventeenth-century poets, none is more insistently drawn to autobiography than Milton, always feeling for the structure and meaning of his life and its connection to the providential history unfolding around him. From the antiprelatical pamphlets right through to *Paradise Lost* and *Samson Agonistes* he is constantly reshaping his past as the experiential narrative rolls on. 'The author is ever distinguished from the person he introduces', he remarks in the *Apology*, succinctly recalling an important critical principle (Yale: I, p. 880). But with Milton, the author is often himself a 'person', a dramatic character in the text. Puritanism provided Milton with a particular historical formation of subjectivity, a notion of individual 'self' that enabled him to shape his own experience, including the disasters of political failure, blindness, an unhappy marriage, into a coherent narrative that runs like a subtext through everything he wrote.

For autobiography does not just chronicle a life and a personality; it *constructs* them. To Raymond Waddington the placing of the Nativity poem at the beginning of the volume 'indicates not what he has been but the way he wishes to be perceived as he embarks upon the major stage of his career' (Patrides and Waddington 1980: p. 348). Pindar and Callimachus, he had written in 1642, though 'in most things worthy', were 'in their matter most an end faulty': that is, they were pagan. So the first poem in the book announces its author as a regenerate Pindar or Callimachus, subsuming the mythic materials of the classical ode (the Golden Age, the music of the spheres) into a Christian narrative of redemption and cosmic harmony and supplanting the pagan theology of the form, its old tribal totems of water, wind, and fire, with a new imperial godhead. J. B. Broadbent regrets its lack of medieval simplicity and traditional reverence (Kermode 1960: pp. 12–31); but the poem is about power. The infant Christ is a king, indeed the 'king of kings', and Milton surrounds him with an entourage of armed courtier-angels. He represents unity out of diversity, a revolution in the historical and cultural order. In 1645 the birth of 'King Jesus', and his eventual victory over the forces of darkness and error, had an immediate and compelling political meaning, as specific and timely in the first English poem in the collection as the defeat of Comus in the last. Even the date of composition (1629) that he carefully records might well have reminded his readers of the 'old dragon' of royal prerogative, who first swinged 'the scaly horror of his folded tail' in that year.

I am not trying to suggest that the Nativity ode, or any of Milton's poems, should be read as a straightforward political allegory, though such an interpretation would very likely be closer to seventeenth-century reading practices, as well as more interesting, than much of the scholarly commentary that has been inflicted on it since. What I am suggesting is that the political struggles of the 1630s, 1640s, and 1650s saturated the writing of those decades (even a poet as seemingly unpolitical as Henry Vaughan has been shown to be caught up in them (Wilcher 1983)), and that in common with 'L'Allegro' and 'Il Penseroso' and the other substantial poems in the 1645 volume the Nativity ode is a much more dynamic and interesting thing if it is read in the context of the book as a whole and of the historical moment in which it was published. Only once does that moment obtrude directly, when Milton notes that *Lycidas* 'by occasion foretells the ruin of our corrupted clergy, then in their height'. Elsewhere it is mediated through form and image, an insistent urgency and pressure, a sense of excitement. The causes of these are far from us now; but it is not impossible to recover them, with imagination and a little effort.

'Whoever will possess his ideas', wrote his eighteenth-century biographer Jonathan Richardson, 'must dig for them, and oftentimes pretty far below the surface.' Yes, Milton *is* a 'difficult' writer, not because of his classical erudition or his Latin vocabulary or his assumption that everybody knows the Bible by heart but because his language and syntax, like his ideas, have to be encountered *actively*; they do not yield themselves up without an argument. Syllabuses and examinations have not helped here, emphasizing the wrong kinds of difficulty ('Discuss the significance of classical allusions in *Lycidas*'; 'What are the principal features of Milton's "grand style"?') and turning the activity of reading into an enforced and repetitive chore. Criticism and scholarship, too, have a way of introducing their own obstacles and inhibitions, like A. S. P. Woodhouse's proprietorial assertion, presumably intended to be helpful, that the final scenes of *Comus* exhibit 'a pattern, a vision of existence, which only the Christian can fully apprehend' (Woodhouse 1968: p. 77).

As a Marxist and non-Christian who none the less believes passionately in the historical importance and contemporary relevance of Milton's writings, I can hardly accept *that*; but my own biases and prejudices will be obvious enough, and I cannot escape the likelihood that 'my' Milton will seem as tendentious and objectionable to some readers as Woodhouse's or Lewis's does to me. What is at stake is not some unachievable 'objectivity' or finality, but the need to find new ways of posing the question of Milton, not for the sake of novelty in itself but because his texts change constantly with our ways of encountering them and the concerns that we bring to the encounter. They are, as the French poststructuralist critic Roland Barthes would have said, *writable* texts rather than *readable* ones[3]: reading them, that is, we find ourselves working on, with, sometimes even against them as if we were actually writing them ourselves, digging deep for meanings and connections that are never fixed, given, self-evident; which is perhaps only another way of saying that they remain *useful*, within our active historical and imaginative reach. This can be hard work, certainly. Whether it can also be rewarding and pleasurable is a question for every reader to decide. But of course I should not be writing this if I did not believe that it can, and should, be both.

NOTES TO THE COMMENTARY

1 T. S. Eliot (1960) *The Sacred Wood* (1920), London: Methuen, p. 58. W. B. Yeats (1961) *Essays and Introductions* (1937), London: Macmillan, p. 522.
2 There is an interesting discussion of these issues in 'Milton on sex and marriage' by David Aers and Bob Hodge, in Aers, Hodge, Kress, 1981: pp. 122–51.
3 Barthes' *S/Z* (1970) develops a distinction between *readable* texts which are immediately and conventionally intelligible and *writable* ones which 'make the reader not a consumer but a producer of the text' (p. 10). In this perspective, 'readable' is not a term of praise.

Bibliography

This is a list of all the books and articles mentioned in the introduction, commentary, and notes, to which I have added one or two standard critical texts (like J. B. Leishman's discussion of the genres and literary 'intertextuality' of the *Minor Poems*) and one or two books which have helped me to understand Milton and his period a bit better (like Hill's *Intellectual Origins* and Wolfe's *Milton in the Puritan Revolution*). It makes no attempt to be comprehensive.

Adams, Robert M. (1968) *Ikon: John Milton and the Modern Critics*, Ithaca, NY: Cornell University Press; the chapter on *Comus* is reprinted in Diekhoff 1968.

Aers, David, Hodge, Bob, and Kress, Gunther (1981) *Literature, Language and Society in England 1580–1680*, Dublin.

Blake, William (1959) *Poems and Prophecies*, edited by Max Plowman and Geoffrey Keynes, London: Dent Everyman edn (see especially 'The marriage of Heaven and Hell' and the prophetic poem 'Milton').

Breasted, Barbara (1971) '*Comus* and the Castlehaven scandal', *Milton Studies*, III, pp. 201–24.

Broadbent, J. B. (ed.) (1975) *Odes, Pastorals, Masques*, the Cambridge Milton, Cambridge: Cambridge University Press.

Carey, John (1969) *Milton*, London.

Carey, J. (1971) *Milton: Complete Shorter Poems*, London: Longman. See *A note on the texts*, p. 23.

Darbishire, Helen (1932) *Early Lives of Milton*, London. (Biographies of the poet from the seventeenth and early eighteenth centuries, including those by John Aubrey, Milton's nephew

Edward Phillips, Jonathan Richardson, and the anonymous biographer identified by Darbishire with John Phillips but now thought to be Cyriack Skinner, friend of Milton and chairman of the Rota Club.)

Diekhoff, J. S. (ed.) (1968) *A Masque at Ludlow*, Cleveland, Ohio. (A useful collection of essays on *Comus* by Tillyard, Tuve, Adams, and others.)

Dodd, A. H. (1952) *Studies in Stuart Wales*, Cardiff.

Eliot, T. S. (1951) 'The metaphysical poets' (1921), in *Selected Essays*, London. (The essay in which Eliot first floats the idea of a seventeenth-century 'dissociation of sensibility'.)

Eliot, T. S. (1957) *On Poetry and Poets*, London. (Contains Eliot's two essays on Milton, the second much more conciliatory than the first.)

Empson, William (1961) *Milton's God*, London. (About *Paradise Lost*, and so not directly relevant to the shorter poems or prose; but one of the two or three absolutely indispensable books about Milton, brilliantly trenchant, funny, and angry. The revised edition, London: 1965, contains a reply to his critics.)

Empson, William (1966) *Some Uses of Pastoral*, Harmondsworth. (First published 1935. Only obliquely about pastoral of the Renaissance kind, it contains the essay on 'Alice in Wonderland: the child as swain'.)

Fixler, Michael (1964) *Milton and the Kingdoms of God*, London.

Fletcher, Angus (1971) *The Transcendental Masque*, Ithaca, New York.

Haller, William (1955) *Liberty and Reformation in the Puritan Revolution*, New York.

Hill, Christopher (1965) *Intellectual Origins of the English Revolution*, Oxford.

Hill, Christopher (1975) *The World Turned Upside Down*, Harmondsworth. (A fascinating account, first published London: 1972, of radical Puritanism in the seventeenth century.)

Hill, Christopher (1979) *Milton and the English Revolution*, Harmondsworth (first published London: 1977).

Johnson, Samuel (1906) *Lives of the Poets*, edited by Arthur Waugh, two volumes, Oxford (first published 1779–81).

Jonson, Ben (1925–50) *Works*, edited by C. H. Herford and P. and E. Simpson, eleven volumes, Oxford.

180

Jonson, Ben (1975) *The Complete Poems*, edited by George Parfitt, Harmondsworth.

Kermode, Frank (ed.) (1960) *The Living Milton*, London. (Mostly about the epics, but contains J. B. Broadbent's interestingly disrespectful piece about the Nativity ode.)

Le Comte, Edward (1978) *Milton and Sex*, London.

Leavis, F. R. (1962) *The Common Pursuit*, Harmondsworth. (Originally published in 1952, this book contains two essays developing Eliot's attack on Milton.)

Leishman, J. B. (1969) *Milton's Minor Poems*, London.

Levey, Michael (1968) *A Concise History of Painting*, London.

Lewis, C. S. (1942) *A Preface to Paradise Lost*, London.

Lieb, M. and Shawcross, J. T. (eds) (1974) *Achievements of the Left Hand: Essays on the Prose of John Milton*, Amherst, Mass.

Macaulay, T. B. (1901) *Essay on Milton*, edited by H. B. Cotterill, London. (First published in the *Edinburgh Review* in 1825.)

Martz, Louis (1980) *Poet of Exile*, New Haven, Conn.: Yale University Press.

Otten, Charlotte (1975) 'Milton's Haemony', in *English Literary Renaissance*, 5, 81–95.

Parker, William Riley (1968) *Milton: a Biography*, two volumes, Oxford.

Patrides, C. A. (1961) *Milton's Lycidas*, New York.

Patrides, C. A. and Waddington, Raymond (eds) (1980) *The Age of Milton*, Manchester.

Pattison, Mark (1902) *Milton*, London. (First published in 1879.)

Prince, F. T. (1954) *The Italian Element in Milton's Verse*, Oxford.

Ransom, J. C. (1938) 'A poem nearly anonymous', in *The World's Body*, Baton Rouge, Louis.

Ricks, Christopher (1963) *Milton's Grand Style*, Oxford.

Ricks, Christopher (ed.) (1970) *English Poetry and Prose 1540–1674*, Volume 2 of the Sphere History of English Literature, London.

Shawcross, J. T. (ed.) (1970) *Milton: the Critical Heritage* (up to 1731), London.

Shelley, P. B. (1971) *Poetical Works*, edited by Thomas Hutchinson, Oxford.

Spender, Stephen (1951) *World Within World*, London.

Spenser, Edmund (1912) *Poetical Works*, edited by J. C. Smith and E. de Selincourt, Oxford.

Stone, Lawrence (1972) *The Causes of the English Revolution 1529–1642*, London.

Tillyard, E. M. W. (1930) *Milton*, London.

Tillyard, E. M. W. (1938) *The Miltonic Setting*, Cambridge.

Tillyard, E. M. W. (1951) *Studies in Milton*, London.

Tuve, Rosamund (1957) *Images and Themes in Five Poems of Milton*, Cambridge, Mass.

Wilcher, Robert (1983) '"Then keep the ancient way!": a study of Henry Vaughan's *Silex Scintillans*', in *Durham University Journal*, 45, 11–24.

Wilding, Michael (1977) 'Regaining the radical Milton', in *The Radical Reader*, edited by Stephen Knight and Michael Wilding, Sydney.

Wilson, A. N. (1983) *The Life of John Milton*, Oxford.

Wind, Edgar (1967) *Pagan Mysteries in the Renaissance*, Harmondsworth. (Fascinating on neo-Platonic allegory; illustrated.)

Wittreich, J. A. (1975) *Angel of the Apocalypse*, Madison, Wisconsin. (On Blake and Milton.)

Wittreich, J. A. (1979) *Visionary Poetics*, San Marino, California.

Wolfe, Don M. (1941) *Milton in the Puritan Revolution*, New York.

Woodhouse, A. S. P. (1968) 'Comus once more', in Diekhoff 1968.

Woodhouse, A. S. P. and Bush, Douglas (eds) (1972) *A Variorum Commentary on the Poems of John Milton*, Volume 2 (the minor poems), Oxford.

Woolrych, Austin (1974) 'Milton and Cromwell', in Lieb and Shawcross 1974.

Wordsworth, William (1977), *The Poems*, edited by J. O. Hayden, two volumes, Harmondsworth.

Yale: edn of Milton's prose; see *A note on the texts*, p. 23.

Notes

The lines on Shakespeare were first printed, anonymously, at the front of the second (1632) folio of Shakespeare's plays, along with poems by Ben Jonson, Leonard Digges, Hugh Holland, 'I. M.' and 'I. M. S.' (the first four reprinted from the 1623 folio). They were reprinted in Shakespeare's *Poems* (1640), and in Milton's own *Poems* (1645 and 1673), where they are dated '1630'.

1   *need*   1645/73 read 'needs'.

4   *star-ypointing*   a quasi-archaic coinage in the manner of Spenser.

5   *son of Memory*   that is, of the goddess Mnemosyne (= 'memory'), mother of the nine Muses; so the phrase makes Shakespeare their brother.

8   *lasting*   1645/73 read 'live-long'. The idea, common in Renaissance writing (including Shakespeare's own sonnets), that poetry outlasts the monuments of human fame and glory is an adaptation of the thirtieth poem in the third book of Horace's *Odes*: 'I have raised a monument more lasting than bronze.' Jonson uses the same figure: 'Thou art a monument without a tomb,/And art alive still while thy book doth live.'

10   *part*   1645/73 have 'heart'.

11   *unvalu'd*   priceless, beyond value.

12   *Delphic lines*   Apollo, god of poetry, had a shrine at Delphi (see 'Nativity', 176n). There may be a suggestion, too, of the cryptic prophecies of the Delphic oracle.

13   *herself*   1645/73 read 'itself'.

14   *make us marble*   like Niobe, who, grieving for her dead children, was transformed to marble. cf. 'Penseroso', 42.

A MASQUE PRESENTED AT LUDLOW CASTLE, 1634
[COMUS]

First performed in Ludlow Castle, Shropshire, on 29 September 1634 (for a fuller account of the circumstances, see pp. 151ff). Published anonymously, probably by the composer Henry Lawes, in 1637 (the text used here), and reprinted in Milton's *Poems* in 1645 and 1673.

7   *pinfold*   a pound or enclosure for stray cattle.

13–14   *golden key/That opes*   cf. St Peter's keys to Heaven and Hell in *Lycidas*, 111: 'The golden opes, the iron shuts amain.'

16   *ambrosial weeds*   immortal garments. For ambrosia, see 840n.

17   *mould*   earth, soil.

20   *high and nether Jove*   In ancient Greek theology, the universe was divided between three senior deities, Zeus, the god of the sky ('high'), Hades or Pluto, god of the underworld ('nether'), and Poseidon, god of the sea, rivers, and islands ('twixt'). Milton generally uses their Latin names, Jove, Dis, and Neptune. See glossary for an account of all three.

29   *blue-hair'd deities*   Tritons (see glossary); their hair and beards were traditionally sea-blue. Homer describes Poseidon as 'blue-haired' (*Odyssey*, III, 6).

30   *tract that fronts the falling sun*   western part, i.e. Wales and the Marches.

33   *old and haughty nation*   the Welsh.

38   *horror*   In Latin this word means 'bristling hairiness',

from which we get the transferred sense of a thing or sensation that 'makes your hair stand on end'. Milton's use of the word generally combines both, as in the description of Satan armed: 'on his crest/Sat horror plum'd' (*Paradise Lost*, IV, 988–9).

46–58   The story of Bacchus (see glossary) and the Tyrrhenian pirates, whom he transformed into dolphins, is from Ovid (*Metamorphoses*, III). Circe, who turned Odysseus' companions into pigs, is in the *Odyssey*, Book X. It is Milton's idea to make them the parents of Comus.

55   *blithe* cheerful.

59   *ripe* mature, adult.
    frolic merry.

60   *Celtic and Iberian fields* France and Spain.

65   *orient* originally 'rising'; then 'eastern' (from the rising sun); hence brilliant, glowing.

71   *ounce* leopard or lynx.

83   *Iris' woof* For Iris, see glossary; here, the woven fabric of the rainbow.

84   *swain* pastoral term for a shepherd or agricultural labourer.

88   *nor of less faith* to be taken with 'well knows' in the previous line; skilful and trustworthy.

89   *office* in the Latin sense of duty, responsibility.

92   *viewless* invisible, out of sight. cf. *Paradise Lost*, III, 518.

93   *star that bids the shepherd fold* Hesperus (see glossary), the evening star. Fold means 'gather [the sheep] into the fold'.

95   *gilded car of day* golden chariot of the sun. See Phoebus in glossary.

96   *allay* quench, restrain.

98   *slope* adjectival, meaning 'sliding downwards'.

115   *sounds* narrow sea-passages.
    finny drove shoals of fish.

116   *wavering morris* The tidal alternation of the sea in obedience 'to the moon' is represented as the patterned movements of a morris dance. See next note.

121   *wakes* festivities, especially on the eve of a saint's
       day. Wakes, like morris dancing, were a political
       issue in this period, particularly since the publication
       in May 1633 of the king's *Declaration to His Subjects
       Concerning Lawful Sports to be Used*, generally known
       as the *Book of Sports*, which enraged the Puritan cler-
       gy by forbidding interference with such traditional
       recreations, even on the Sabbath. Like his 'courts' and
       'feasts' (746) and 'canon laws' (808), these terms
       associate Comus suggestively with the royalists and
       high Anglican clergy.

123   *sweets to prove* pleasures to explore.

124   *Love* Cupid or Eros, son of Venus (see glossary).

132   *Stygian* hellish, from the river Styx (see glossary).

134   *ebon* black.

138   *blabbing eastern scout* The morning (Aurora, Eos) is
       represented as a prudish ('nice') busybody ('scout'),
       snooping on their secret nocturnal revelry from her
       mountain-top in the east. Milton may have been
       thinking of Homer's account of the adultery of Ares
       and Aphrodite, which was exposed to the other gods
       by the sun (*Odyssey*, VIII).

144   *light fantastic round* A round is a round-dance, as in
       114. cf. 'L'Allegro', 33–4: 'Come, and trip it as ye
       go/On the light fantastic toe.'

147   *shrouds* hiding-places.
       brakes hedges, shrubberies.

151   *trains* schemes, traps.

151–3 i.e. 'I shall soon turn as many humans into animals as
       my mother Circe did.'

155   *blear* of eyes, dim, misty; here transferred: making
       dim.

157   *quaint habits* unusual clothes, the 'apparel glistering'
       of the stage direction.

161   *glozing* ingratiating.

166   Comus' disguise as a 'harmless villager' parallels and
       contrasts with the Spirit's impersonation of the swain
       Thyrsis, just as his invocation of the nocturnal round-
       dance of the 'starry choir' complements the Spirit's

description in the final scene of the celestial marriage of Cupid and Psyche.

167   This line is missing from the 1645 and 1673 *Poems*, which also reverse 168 and 169.

            gear   business. Thrift keeps him up and working later than usual.

174   *hinds*   peasants, rural labourers.

178   *swill'd*   drunken.

179   *wassailers*   drinkers. A wassail (Anglo-Saxon = 'be healthy') is a toast, hence a drink.

189   *sad votarist in palmer's weed*   one who has taken a religious vow, dressed as a pilgrim. Sad = solemn, serious.

190   *Phoebus' wain*   See glossary, and 95n.

197   *dark lantern*   a lamp with a shutter or blind to cut off the light.

203   *rife*   everywhere.

            perfect   distinct, unambiguous.

212   *siding*   taking one's side, supporting. The ellipsis at the end of the line, indicating that the sentence is interrupted, like the direct address 'O welcome' and the phrase 'I see ye visibly', suggest that she does actually see some kind of vision at this point. At 221 it fades, then reappears briefly as a 'gleam' at 223–5.

213–15   *Faith ... Hope ... Chastity*   cf. 1 Corinthians 13.13: 'And now abideth faith, hope, charity, these three; but the greatest of these is charity.' On the substitution of the Platonic chastity (a major theme of the masque) for the Pauline charity (from the Greek for 'love'), compare Edgar Wind's account (Wind 1967: p. 73) of the neo-Platonic triad Pulchritudo-Amor-Voluptas (Beauty-Love-Pleasure) and its variant Castitas-Pulchritudo-Amor (Chastity-Beauty-Love). See note on 986ff.

214   *flittering*   fluttering. In 1645 and 1673 this is altered to 'hovering'.

230   For Echo and Narcissus (237) see glossary.

232   *Meander*   a river in ancient Phrygia, known for its leisurely and winding progress; hence 'meandering'.

It was supposed to have derived its name from a king who drowned himself in it after killing his own son.

234   *lovelorn nightingale*   Philomela, raped by her brother-in-law Tereus, was transformed into a nightingale. Carey notes that here 'lovelorn' must mean not (as usual) forsaken by love but 'lost or ruined through love' (Carey, *CSP*: p. 188).

241   *parley*   speech. Echo was punished for talking too much (see glossary).

243   *resounding*   reverberating, echoing.

251–2   *raven down/Of darkness*   cf. *Romeo & Juliet* III, ii, 17–19: 'Come, night; come, Romeo; come, thou day in night;/For thou wilt lie upon the wings of night/Whiter than new snow on a raven's back.'

254   *flowery-kirtl'd*   A kirtle is a gown or mantle.

258   *barking waves*   Scylla (see glossary) is described by Homer (*Odyssey*, XII, 86) as having 'a voice like a young puppy',and Virgil (*Aeneid*, VII, 588) has a rock surrounded by 'barking waves'.

267   *Unless the Goddess*   elliptical syntax – 'Unless you are the Goddess'.

274   *sever'd*   separated.

287   *imports*   matters.

292   *In his loose traces*   unyoked from the plough.

293   *swink'd*   To swink is to labour; hence weary after a day's work.

294   *mantling*   covering like a mantle or cloak.

297   *port*   bearing, posture.

299   *element*   the air.

301   *plighted*   pleated, bunched.

313   *bosky*   bushy.

       bourn   burn, stream; or possibly bourne = boundary, hence hedge.

315   *stray attendance*   lost companions.

316   *shroud*   shelter, hide (cf. 147).

318   *pallet*   literally, a straw mattress. The lark roosts on the ground, in grass or corn.

325   *courts*   'Courtesy takes its name from courts; but

though the pretence is practised there, the reality is more likely to be found in a humble cottage.' cf. Comus' similar etymological explanation of 'homely' (748–9).

331 *Unmuffle* remove a scarf or muffler; hence show the face.

332 *benison* blessing.

334 *Chaos* associated with darkness, as the created universe is with light. cf. *Paradise Lost*, III, 18: 'I sung of Chaos and eternal Night.'

335 *double night* the absence of both moonlight and starlight; but there may be an allusion too to the sinister trinity of Chaos, Erebus (shadow, darkness), and Night. See glossary and 581n.

340 *levell'd rule* straight line.

341–2 *star of Arcady ... Tyrian Cynosure* Callisto, daughter of the king of Arcadia, was transformed into the constellation of Ursa Major, the Great Bear or Plough, which Greek mariners used for night navigation. Phoenician ('Tyrian') sailors used the pole star or Cynosure (dog's tail), in the constellation of Ursa Minor.

349 *innumerous* countless.

359 *over-exquisite* too inquisitive or imaginative.

360 *cast* speculate (cf. forecast).

366 *to seek* deficient, inadequate.

368 *bosoms* (verb) cherishes.

378 *plumes* preens, repairs.

381 *He that has light* The 'inner light' of conscience and the assurance of salvation was a central concept of Puritanism. cf. *Paradise Lost*, III, 51–3: 'So much the rather thou celestial Light/Shine inward, and the mind through all her powers/Irradiate', where the contrast of inner and outer illumination gains added force and poignancy from the poet's blindness.

382 *centre* of the earth.

386 *affects* chooses, prefers (without any of the connotations of 'affectation').

390 *weeds* clothes.

393   *fair Hesperian tree*   See glossary under Hesperus, Hesperides; and 982n and 986n for the wider significance of the motif.

404   *it recks me not*   It doesn't concern me, I care nothing.

407   *unowned*   lost.

413   *squint*   adjectival – looking sidelong, askance.

426   *mountaineer*   not a climber but a mountain-dweller.

429   *grots*   caves, from the Italian *grotto*, from which we get 'grotesque' and 'grotty'. Grot is the older form, in English.

430   *unblench'd*   unafraid, undeterred.

436   *swart*   black.

439   *schools of Greece*   the traditions of Greek philosophy.

440   *arms*   weapons; hence the mythological weaponry in the lines that follow, Dian's bow, Cupid's bolt, Minerva's shield.

442   *silver-shafted*   a reference to her arrows; cf. the 'quiver'd nymph' in 422.

443   *brinded*   dappled.

447   *snaky-headed Gorgon-shield*   Athene, the Roman Minerva (see glossary), carried the head of the Gorgon Medusa, with its snaky locks and its ability literally to petrify anyone who looked at it, on her *aegis* (shield or breastplate). The passage is an example, of a fairly simple kind, of the neo-Platonic reading of Graeco-Roman myth as moral allegory.

459   *oft*   adjectival = frequent.

459–75   These seventeen lines summarize Plato's account in the *Phaedo* of the progressive purification of the body into spirit, and its converse, the degeneration of the corrupt soul into matter. The 'liveried Angels', 'heav'nly habitants' and 'lewd and lavish act of sin' reframe the Platonic discourse – as always in Milton – in terms of the Fall and the Pauline doctrine, itself strongly influenced by Platonic speculation, of salvation: 'For this corruptible must put on incorruption, and this mortal must put on immortality' (1 Corinthians 15.53). cf. *Paradise Lost*, V, 497–9: 'Your bodies may at last turn all to spirit,/Improv'd by tract of time, and wing'd ascend/Ethereal.'

468   *Imbodies, and imbrutes*   becomes physical, bestial.

487   *draw*   swords (the 'iron stakes' of 491).

495–512 The dialogue of *Comus*, as opposed to the songs and
the passages of rhymed trochaic tetrameter like Comus' first speech (93–144) and the last scene, is in
unrhymed iambic pentameters (blank verse), apart
from these eighteen lines of rhymed iambic penta-
meter (heroic couplets), which give the first ex-
changes between Thyrsis and the brothers a height-
ened patterning and formality and provide some metrical variety. Milton later deprecated 'the troublesome
and modern bondage of rhyming', in long poems at
least, and vindicated the blank verse of *Paradise Lost* as
an example of 'ancient liberty recovered'.

513   *'Tis not vain or fabulous*   There is an important
literary–political argument here. Picking up the
thread of neo-Platonic allegory in 441ff, the Spirit
insists, anticipating some of the arguments of *Areopagitica*, that the mythological literature of Graeco-
Roman antiquity, however fanciful and even immoral
it may appear to a devout Christian, not only embo-
dies profound moral and spiritual insights but actually
prefigures and illumines the revealed truth of scripture. This is a central axiom of the Christian humanism of the fifteenth and sixteenth centuries, and is
developed in great detail by the neo-Platonist mytho-
logues. For a fuller account, and some of the implications of the belief in the continuity of classical and
Christian mythologies, see *Critical commentary*, pp.
158, 161 and Wind 1967. In *Paradise Regained* Christ
rejects the whole argument, dismissing Greek literature and philosophy as 'false, or little else but
dreams,/Conjectures, fancies, built on nothing firm'
(IV, 291–2) and asserting the superiority and sufficiency of scripture: a passage that has been taken to
signify Milton's own repudiation of his earlier
humanist enthusiasms.

517   *Chimeras*   For the Chimera (usually singular, but
here used generically for monsters) see glossary. Virgil (*Aeneid*, VI, 288) places it at the entrance to Hades.

191

518   *rifted rocks* In antiquity the mouth of Hell was often identified with a cleft or cavern in a cliff, at Cape Taenarum, Colonus, or elsewhere.

526   *murmurs* muttered incantations.

532   *brow* (verb) grow above.

535   *Hecate* See glossary and 135. The tripartite moon-goddess was often associated, especially in the Christian era, with witchcraft and blood-sacrifice. cf. *Paradise Lost*, II, 662–5: 'Nor uglier follow the Night-hag, when call'd/In secret, riding through the air she comes/Lur'd with the smell of infant blood, to dance/With Lapland witches.'

539   *unweeting* ignorant, unsuspecting.

540   *by then* when.

547   *meditate my rural minstrelsy* either sing or play music; probably sing, since the elder brother has referred to his 'madrigal' (495), and Virgil's Thyrsis (Eclogue VII) is a singer. The use of 'meditate' to mean compose or perform is Virgilian. cf. *Lycidas*, 66.

548   *ere a close* before the end of the phrase, the cadence.

559–60 *be never more/Still to be so displac'd* The text has no punctuation after 'more', preserving Milton's typically ambiguous and contrapuntal syntax, hinging on 'still', which is both adjective (silent) and adverb (always): 'cease to exist so long as she could always be so displaced' and 'never again be silent so long as she could be so displaced'. The difference in meaning is minimal, but the equivocation and pause on 'still' syncopates the rhythm.

562   *Under the ribs of Death* in the breast (traditional seat of the soul) of a corpse, or of Death itself.

581   *triple knot* According to Hesiod, Chaos had two offspring, Erebus (a Homeric name for darkness) and Night. See 334n.

585   *period* sentence.

597   *self-fed, and self-consum'd* The idea that evil will consume itself is Shakespearean. See *Troilus and Cressida*, I, iii, 121–4 ('And appetite, an universal wolf … Must make perforce an universal prey, / And last eat

up himself') and *King Lear*, IV, ii, 49–50 ('Humanity must perforce prey on itself / Like monsters of the deep'). cf. 'On time', 10: 'last of all thy greedy self consum'd'.

604–5   See glossary for Acheron, Harpies, Hydras; and cf. *Paradise Lost*, II, where the fallen Angels explore the topography of Hell, with its 'four infernal rivers' and 'harpy-footed Furies'.

608–9   *cleave his scalp/Down to the hips*   This colourful bit of bombast is only found in 1637. In later printings Milton toned it down: 'to a foul death/Curs'd as his life'.

610   *emprise*   enterprise.

620   *Of small regard to see to*   not striking to the eye. In *Areopagitica* truth is described as 'unsightly and unplausible, even as the person is of many a great man slight and contemptible to see to'. Some readers (e.g. Le Comte in Lieb and Shawcross 1974: p. 29) think both passages allude to Milton himself, who was short and apparently touchy about his appearance. But the idea is a common one.

626   *scrip*   wallet.

627   *simples*   herbs.

635   *clouted*   a clout (French *clou*) is a hob-nail.

636   *Moly*   this magical and medicinal herb with its 'black root and flower like milk' was given to Odysseus (Ulysses) by Hermes to protect him against the enchantments of Circe (*Odyssey,* X). It is sometimes identified as a kind of wild garlic, one species of which is known to botanists as *Allium moly*.

638   *Haemony*   This has been explained as a reference to Haemonia, or Thessaly, a part of Greece associated with magic; as a combination of the Greek words for 'blood' and 'wine', and hence an allusion to the eucharist; and as *Hypericum androsaemum* or 'tutsan', a plant sometimes believed to have supernatural as well as medicinal powers (Otten 1975).

649   *necromancer*   magician, literally one who can raise the dead.

193

655   *sons of Vulcan* For Vulcan see glossary. He had several sons; Milton is probably referring to Cacus, who in his fight with Hercules belched out smoke and flames (Virgil, *Aeneid*, VIII).

665   *while Heaven sees good* implying that even Comus can only do what Heaven permits him to.

672   *cordial julep* cordial (literally: for the heart) means invigorating; julep, from the Persian for 'rose-water', is a syrup or sweet drink.

675   *Nepenthes* In the fourth book of the *Odyssey*, Odysseus and Menelaus, reminiscing about the Trojan War, are overcome with sadness at the memory of their dead comrades, and Helen mixes into their wine a drug called Nepenthes ('Grieve-not'), explaining that she was given it in Egypt by Polydamna, wife of Thone. As with other similar patternings (see 166n), this reference balances and counterpoints the Spirit's allusion forty lines earlier to another powerful Homeric drug, Moly. The purpose of these doublings may be suggested by *Areopagitica*: 'Good and evil, we know, in the field of this world grow up together almost inseparably, and the knowledge of good is so involved and interwoven with the knowledge of evil, and in so many cunning resemblances hardly to be discerned, that those confused seeds which were imposed on Psyche as an incessant labour to cull out and sort asunder were not more intermixed' (see p. 87).

681   *gentle usage and soft delicacy* Comus is a courtly figure (cf. 745–7), and 'gentle' has a strong social connotation: 'well-bred'. Delicacy means pleasure.

698   *visor'd* masked, hence deceitful.

700   *lickerish* two overlapping meanings, liquid and lustful.

701   *draught for Juno* recalling Ben Jonson's 'Drink to me only': 'But might I of Jove's nectar sup,/I would not change for thine.' Jonson's poem was a formative influence on Cavalier lyric, with its ethos of stylish dissipation and relaxed 'good breeding'.

707   *budge* Johnson's *Dictionary* defines it as 'surly, stiff, formal'.

194

707–8	*Stoic fur ... Cynic tub* The philosopher Zeno held his classes in a stoa (porch) of the market-place in Athens, and his pupils were known as Stoics. They argued that physical existence was an evil, to be treated with indifference, and that only intellectual and spiritual life had any value. The Cynics (the name comes from the Greek for dog) advocated an ascetic discipline of poverty and self-denial; and the most famous Cynic, Diogenes, lived in a barrel. Neither, of course, would have worn 'fur' (the trimming of an academic gown), but the word associates them contemptuously with the bloodless tedium of academic philosophy.
721	*pulse* beans.
722	*frieze* cheap woollen cloth.
727	*Nature's bastards, not her sons* perhaps an ironic allusion to Hebrews 12.7–8: 'If ye endure chastening, God dealeth with you as with sons; for what son is he whom the father chasteneth not? But if ye be without chastisement ... then are ye bastards, and not sons.'
730	*cumber'd* overloaded.
733–4	These two lines combine two traditional ideas about diamonds: that they shine in the dark, and that they reproduce spontaneously. 'They below' are the monstrous creatures that live beneath the surface of the earth ('the deep').
743	*neglected rose* This signals the hedonistic and Cavalier lyrical mode known to literary historians as *'carpe diem'* ('pluck the day'), in which the male lover/seducer urges his mistress not to squander her youth but to seize the chance of pleasure before it fades. Herrick's 'Gather ye rosebuds while ye may' is a well-known example.
760	*bolt* sift, separate flour from the husk and bran; here used metaphorically, to argue with precise logical discrimination.
768ff	These lines recall *King Lear*, III, iv, 33–6 ('Take physic, Pomp;/Expose thyself to feel what wretches feel,/That thou mayst shake the superflux to them,/And shew the Heavens more just') and IV, i, 71–2 ('So

distribution should undo excess/And each man have enough'). cf. also *Reformation* (p. 67). According to his biographer John Toland, Milton, asked 'what made him side with the *Republicans*', replied 'among other Reasons, because theirs was the most frugal Government; for that the Trappings of a Monarchy might set up an ordinary Commonwealth' (Darbishire 1932: p. 186).

782   *sun-clad* a reference to Revelation's 'woman clothed with the sun' (a phrase for the mother of Christ), as well as to Petrarch's *canzone* 'Beauteous virgin, who clothed with the sun', which was the metrical model for Milton's 'Upon the Circumcision' (see p. 114).

803–5   For Jove and Saturn, see glossary. Zeus (Jove) overthrew his father Cronos (Saturn) and his Titans, and chained them up in the furthest depths of the underworld. For Erebus see 581n.

808   *canon laws* Milton shared the strong Puritan hostility to the ecclesiastical canon law. As Comus' courtly prejudices link him with the Cavalier supporters and dependants of Charles I, this phrase, though of course ironic, associates him with the Anglican prelates and invokes the intense hostility felt by English Puritans towards the church of Laud.

816–17   *rod revers'd ... backward mutters* Spells can traditionally be neutralized by reading them backwards. The reversing of the rod has the same effect. Both are found in Ovid's version (*Metamorphoses*, XIV) of the Circe episode from the *Odyssey*.

822   *Meliboeus* Milton's pastoral name (taken from Virgil) for Spenser, from whom he takes the Sabrina narrative. 'The soothest shepherd that ere pip'd on plains', with its Spenserian double alliteration (s and p), associates him properly with pastoral, in the political and philosophical uses of which Spenser was a pioneer. Milton's high opinion of Spenser as a philosophical poet ('soothest shepherd') is attested by his description of him in *Areopagitica* as 'our sage and serious poet Spenser, whom I dare be known to think a better teacher than Scotus or Aquinas' (see p. 88).

826 The story of Sabrina, daughter of Locrine and granddaughter of Brute (or Brutus), legendary Trojan founder of Britain, comes from Geoffrey of Monmouth's *History of the British Kings*, via Spenser's *Faerie Queene* (II, x). Both accounts have her drowned by her stepmother Gwendolen; Milton's variation brings the story closer to those Ovidian tales of young women or men transfigured, often in or near water, in the act of escaping from violence or sexual assault (Syrinx, Daphne, Ino, Melicertes, Glaucus), for both her suicidal leap into the water and her metamorphosis into a 'goddess of the river' are Milton's invention. He gives the orthodox account, sticking closely to Geoffrey of Monmouth, in the first book of the *History of Britain* (Yale: V, 18). Sabrina is the Latin name for the river Severn, and the handling of the motif suggests that Milton may have thought that it was the Severn that flows below Ludlow Castle. (Actually it is the Teme, a tributary that joins the Severn just south of Worcester.) But the Severn, symbolic boundary between the kingdoms, suits the political as well as the mythological purposes of the text.

837 *his daughters* the fifty Nereids.

838 *lavers* basins.

  asphodel The asphodel (*Asphodelus ramosus*), from which we get the word daffodil, was associated in the ancient Mediterranean world with death and immortality. The afterworld of *Odyssey*, XI, is described as a 'field of asphodel' (539).

840 *ambrosial oils* Homer (*Odyssey*, XVIII, 192, and *Iliad*, XIV, 170) describes as 'ambrosial' a scented oil used for cleansing the skin. The word, probably from the same root-word as 'amber', was thought to mean 'deathless', and ambrosia is sometimes described as the food of the gods (as nectar is their drink). cf. 16n.

845 *Helping* curing.

  blasts infections.

869 Homer (*Iliad*, IX, 183) describes Poseidon as 'earth-embracer' and 'earth-shaker'. The sea was thought to

be the source of earthquakes. Neptune's 'mace' is his traditional trident, symbol of the thunderbolt that he shares with his brother Zeus.

872   *Carpathian wizard*   Proteus, soothsayer and 'old man of the sea' (see glossary). He was the shepherd of Poseidon's seals, hence the 'hook' (shepherd's crook).

875   *Leucothea*   Ino, daughter of Cadmus, is described by Homer (*Odyssey*, V, 334) as 'Leukotheē' ('white goddess'). In a legend strongly reminiscent of the Sabrina story, she leapt into the sea with her son Melicertes to rescue him from the insane rage of his father Athamas, and was rescued and immortalized by the Nereids. See *Lycidas*, 164n.

904   *charmed band*   the sorcery that binds her and prevents her from rising.

923   *Anchises' line*   Brute (Brutus), father of Locrine and legendary founder of Britain, was descended from Aeneas and so from his father Anchises, whom Aeneas carried on his shoulders from the burning ruins of Troy.

982   *Hesperus and his daughters three*   The garden of the Hesperides (see glossary) is here identified with the Elysian 'fields of the sky', Homeric abode of the blessed (*Odyssey*, VI, 42).

986   *Graces*   These three goddesses (see glossary), generally known in antiquity as Thalia (Generosity), Euphrosyne (Cheerfulness), and Aglaia (Splendour), and always depicted dancing together, were renamed in the Renaissance Pulchritudo (Beauty), Amor (Love), and Voluptas (Joy). In some versions, Voluptas is replaced by Castitas (Chastity). See Wind 1967: p. 73.
    Hours   another triad of goddesses, called by Hesiod Eunomia (Fairness), Dike (Justice), and Eirene (Peace), but from Ovid onwards augmented to four and identified with the seasons. The Hour of Spring plays an important part in Renaissance allegory. The Graces and Hours were associated by the neo-Platonists with the creation and mystical order of the universe itself. cf. *Paradise Lost*, IV, 266–8: 'while

universal Pan/Knit with the Graces and the Hours in dance/Led in th'eternal Spring'.

991   *nard, and cassia*   Spikenard is an aromatic plant; cassia a kind of cinnamon, the fragrant bark of an Indian shrub. Both are biblical (see Exodus 30.24; Song of Solomon 1.12).

993   *blow*   usually 'come into flower'; here, unusually, transitive, 'bring into flower'.

995   *purfled*   multi-coloured.

997   This line 'shows that Milton thought the meaning important and wanted it heeded' (Tillyard 1951: p. 95). See 513n.

1002   The epithet 'Assyrian' identifies Venus/Aphrodite with the Middle Eastern moon-goddess Ashtoreth or Astarte. In the Phoenician version of the story Adonis' place is taken by Thammuz. See 'Nativity', 200–4, and *Paradise Lost*, I, 438–52.

1004   *advanc'd*   raised, elevated from earthly to 'celestial' love.

1006   *wand'ring labours*   In Apuleius' *Golden Ass* Venus persecutes her future daughter-in-law Psyche with a series of futile tasks. See *Areopagitica*, p. 87. The humanist tradition allegorized the marriage of Cupid and Psyche as the union of the soul (Greek *psyche*) with divine love (Greek *eros*).

1011   *Youth and Joy*   In Apuleius, Psyche has one child, Voluptas (Pleasure), interpreted by Christian Platonists as the eternal bliss of the redeemed soul. Milton's twins seem to be his own variation of the motif, of which he gives a different version in *Apology against a Pamphlet* (1642): 'the divine volumes of Plato, and his equal [= contemporary] Xenophon; where if I should tell you what I learnt of chastity and love, I mean that which is truly so, whose charming cup is only virtue which she bears in her hand to those who are worthy; the rest are cheated with a thick intoxicating potion which a certain sorceress the abuser of love's name carries about; and how the first and chiefest office of love begins and ends in the soul, producing those happy twins of her divine generation Knowledge and Virtue, with such abstracted sublimities as these, it might be worth your listening' (Yale: I, 891–2).

1015   *welkin*   sky.

1021   *sphery chime*   the music of the spheres, hence the limits of the physical universe. (See 'Nativity', 102n, 131n.)

LYCIDAS

In the manuscript of Milton's poems in Trinity College, Cambridge, *Lycidas* is headed 'Novemb: 1637'. It was published in 1638, signed J. M., in *Obsequies to the Memory of Edward King*, the second part of a collection of Latin and English elegies (*Justa Edouardo King naufrago*) to a Fellow of Christ's College and an acquaintance of Milton, drowned on his way to Ireland. Reprinting the poem in 1645, Milton sharpened the political argument (see 129n) and prefaced it with the heading: 'In this monody the author bewails a learned friend unfortunately drowned in his passage from Chester on the Irish seas, 1637, and by occasion foretells the ruin of our corrupted clergy, then in their height.'

1–2   *laurels ... myrtles ... ivy*   The significance of these three evergreens has been much debated. The laurel was sacred to Apollo, the myrtle to Venus, the ivy to Bacchus. Apollo, father of the Muses, and Venus, mother of the Graces, are appropriate enough, since Edward King was young and had published some Latin poetry; Bacchus less so, since he was popularly associated with drunkenness. But the philosopher Socrates was compared with the Bacchic Marsyas and Silenus; and Horace called ivy the reward of learning (Wind 1967: pp. 172–3; Horace, *Odes*, I, i, 29). So it seems reasonable to take them as figurative of poetry, youth, and scholarship (King was a Fellow of Christ's College).

2   *never-sere*   evergreen, and thus symbolic of immortality.

3   *harsh and crude*   bitter and unripe.

200

10   *he well knew*   All the printed texts, including 1638,
        have 'he knew'. But the manuscript reading is 'he
        well knew', and one copy of 1638 has 'well' inserted
        in a handwriting thought to be Milton's own.

13   *welter*   to rock to and fro. cf. 'weltering waves' in
        'Nativity', 124.

14   *meed of some melodious tear*   tribute of a poetic elegy.

15   *Sisters of the sacred well*   the Muses (see glossary).
        Several springs were dedicated to them, including
        Pieria on Mount Olympus and Aganippe on Mount
        Helicon. Both mountains were associated with Zeus
        (Jove), but 'seat of Jove' suggests Olympus, hence
        Pieria.

19   *Muse*   here in the sense of 'poet'.

22   *peace be*   recalling the words *requiescat in pace* ('rest in
        peace'), often inscribed in abbreviated form (RIP), on
        tombstones.
        shroud   Shrouds are not usually 'sable' (black); and in
        any case an urn (containing cremated ashes) would
        not need a shroud. Milton may be using it in the
        sense
        (cf. *Comus*, 147) of 'hiding-place', hence vault or
        tomb.

24   *rill*   stream.

26   *glimmering*   1645 and 1673 have 'opening'.

27   *drove afield*   i.e. their flocks.

29   *Battening*   feeding.

30   *Oft till the ev'n-star bright*   1645 and 1673 have 'Oft till
        the star that rose, at evening, bright', and the manu-
        script is emended to 'Oft till the star that rose in
        evening bright', so it presumably represents Milton's
        preference. But it does not really make sense, since
        the evening star, which is clearly intended, does not
        rise in the evening, but simply becomes bright then.

31   *burnish'd wheel*   1645 and 1673 have 'westering'.

34   *Satyrs ... Fauns*   rural deities, half-goat and half-
        human in appearance, associated with Pan (see glos-
        sary).

36   *Dametas*   Several attempts have been made to identify

this pastoral figure with one of Milton's tutors, all pointless and inconclusive. For a summary see Carey, *CSP*: pp. 242–3.

46   *taint-worm* Some editors refer to a small spider known as a 'taint', reputedly harmful to cattle; but the word is presumably generic for parasites of domestic animals.

weanling newly weaned (cf. nestling).

50   *Where were ye, Nymphs* cf. Theocritus' first Idyll: 'Where were you, Nymphs, oh where, while Daphnis pined', imitated by Virgil, Eclogue V. For the nymphs, see glossary.

53–4   *Druids ... Mona* Anglesey (Latin Mona, Welsh Ynys Mon) was believed to be the centre of the ancient and semi-legendary priesthood of the Druids. cf. *Areopagitica*, 567n.

55   *Deva* Latin name for the Cheshire Dee. King was sailing from Chester to Ireland when he was drowned.

wizard stream In the 1628 Vacation Exercise, Milton wrote of the 'ancient hallowed Dee'. The river was thought to be able to change its course and to vary the points at which it could be forded.

58   *Muse ... Orpheus* For both, see glossary. The legendary singer-poet Orpheus was decapitated and dismembered by a group of Thracian women, and his head carried down the Hebrus (modern Evros) and south along the coast of Asia Minor to the island of Lesbos. The story is from Ovid's *Metamorphoses*, XI (Virgil has a version in *Georgics*, IV), and Fowler (p. 359) remarks that it 'seems to have focused some of Milton's deepest fears'. In *Paradise Lost*, VII, 33–8, he asks the muse Urania to 'drive far off the barbarous dissonance/Of Bacchus and his revellers, the race/Of that wild rout that tore the Thracian bard/In Rhodope, where woods and rocks had ear/To rapture, till the savage clamour drowned/Both harp and voice; nor could the Muse defend/Her son'. Lesbos was the birthplace of the poet Sappho, and Wind (1967:

pp. 161–3) has some discussion of the relationship between Sappho and Orpheus.

66   *meditate the thankless Muse* See *Comus*, 547n.

68–9   *Amaryllis ... Neaera* The names are from George Buchanan's *Pastorals*. Instead of 'hid in', 1645 and 1673 have 'or with', perhaps to remove any suggestion of a triangular relationship. But the earlier reading is certainly more erotically interesting.

73   *guerdon* reward (here, fame). For 'where', 1645 and 1673 have 'when'.

75   *the blind Fury with th'abhorred shears* Strictly speaking the blindness and the shears belong not to a Fury but to the Fate, Atropos (for Fates and Furies, see glossary). Most editions record this as a simple error; but in combining Fate and Fury into a single composite figure the passage articulates a central cosmological question; for while the Fates preside over an order of necessity entirely indifferent (hence 'blind') to human interests and values, the Furies embody a conception of primitive tribal retribution (itself to be superseded, in Aeschylus' *Oresteia*, by the Athenian concept of codified civic justice). Thus 'blind Fury' can be read as the sign of a contradiction or an unanswered question: is death simply an act of blind irrational necessity, or does it result from a cruel but comprehensible kind of justice? The Furies could be (and were) persuaded to change their minds; the Fates could not. The question is related to the great post-Reformation debate about free will and predestination, and preoccupied Milton up to and beyond his attempt in *Paradise Lost* to 'justify the ways of God' (that is, prove them just). In that poem, the more philosophical of the fallen Angels 'reasoned high/Of providence, foreknowledge, will and fate,/Fixed fate, free will, foreknowledge absolute,/And found no end, in wandering mazes lost' (II, 558–61).

76   *slits the thin-spun life* Atropos cut the thread spun by her sisters, each cut ending a human life.

79–80   *in the glistering foil/Set off* The metaphor is from jewellery. Precious stones were set with a backing of silver foil, to enhance ('set off') their brilliance with reflected light.

80   *broad rumour*   worldly reputation.

82   The Graeco-Roman Jove is conflated with the Judaeo-Christian Jehovah/Christ, here presented as presiding over the Last Judgement. The visual iconography of the two theologies was often similarly syncretic in the Renaissance, as in the Olympian Jehovah of Michelangelo's Sistine 'Creation of Adam', or the angry Christ in the same artist's 'Last Judgement', described by Michael Levey as 'beautiful and terrible like Apollo, the dealer of destruction' (Levey 1968: p. 108).

85   *Arethuse*   See glossary. This transition, like the parallel one at 132, uses the disappearance and reappearance of water in the limestone mountains of Sicily and central Greece as a structural device for the poem's different levels and 'voices'.

86   *Mincius*   Mantua, Virgil's birthplace, is on the Mincius (modern Mincio). Thus Mincius = Italian pastoral, as Arethuse = Sicilian.

88   *oat*   the pastoral reed-pipe, made from a hollow oat-stem; hence, by metonymy, poem.

89   *herald of the sea*   Triton (see glossary, and *Comus*, 24).

90   *in Neptune's plea*   either 'to plead in Neptune's defence' (against the charge of having caused Lycidas' death) or, more probably, to hold an inquiry in Neptune's name. The structuring metaphor of an inquest or judicial hearing runs down to the judgement in 130–1, with Aeolus, Camus and St Peter appearing in testimony. This striking variation of the conventional procession past the funeral bier enables Milton to address the question of responsibility (see 75n) and so to connect the personal and political implications of Lycidas' death.

91   *felon winds*   Felon can mean simply 'cruel', 'wild'; but the legal connotations work well in the context (see last note).

93   *rugged wings*   rugged = ragged. The winds are often represented as winged.

96	*Hippotades* patronym for Aeolus, son of Hippotes. For Aeolus see glossary.
99	*Panope with all her sisters* the fifty Nereids, daughters of Nereus. cf. *Comus*, 835.
100	*bark* ship. This is the first judgement, identifying the immediate cause of Lycidas' death; a naturalistic explanation appropriate to the evidence of wind and water. But this is developed into a wider social and moral indictment in the passage that follows by the linked institutions of university and church, learning and piety.
103	*Camus* the river Cam; hence the University of Cambridge.
104	*mantle hairy ... bonnet sedge* These three lines develop an elaborate allegorical metaphor based on Virgil's description of the Tiber (*Aeneid*, VIII, 31ff.). The slow-flowing ('footing') river, with its water-weed ('mantle hairy') and riverine vegetation ('bonnet sedge'), and the plants and fishes moving obscurely below the surface ('figures dim'), is represented as an ancient scholar ('reverend sire') in academic cap and gown. The flag-iris (*Iris pseudacorus*) growing along its banks recalls its Mediterranean congener *Iris germanica*, Ovid's 'hyacinth', whose flowers and leaves were thought to bear the letters AIAI ('alas'; cf. 'inscrib'd with woe') as a token of Apollo's grief at the accidental death of his lover Hyacinthus – another of Milton's metamorphic water-myths, like Sabrina and Leucothea in *Comus*, Arethusa and Alpheus, and Lycidas himself, in this poem.
107	*reft* stolen.
	pledge child. Like 'reverend sire' (103), this recalls the parent–child relationship implied in the traditional conception of the university (Alma Mater, alumnus, etc.).
109	*pilot of the Galilean lake* Some readers take this to be Christ; but the keys, the mitred locks and the pontifical tone point to St Peter, guardian of the gates of Heaven and Hell and first bishop of the church.
110	*two massy keys* Matthew 16.19: 'And I will give unto

thee the keys of the kingdom of heaven.' Milton's curious invention of one key for opening and another for closing seems to be his own, perhaps suggested by the double action of Revelation 3.7 (recalling Isaiah 22.22): 'These things saith he that is holy, he that is true, he that hath the key of David, he that openeth, and no man shutteth; and shutteth, and no man openeth.' For the golden key, cf. *Comus*, 13–14.

111   *amain*   forcibly.

112   *mitr'd locks*   a reference to the bishop's mitre.

114–15   The figure of the thief (or wolf) in the sheepfold comes from John 10, the source of the pastor/priest identification in Christian pastoral: 'Verily, verily, I say unto you, he that entereth not by the door into the sheep-fold, but climbeth up some other way, the same is a thief and a robber.... he that is an hireling, and not the shepherd, whose own the sheep are not, seeth the wolf coming, and leaveth the sheep, and fleeth: and the wolf catcheth them, and scattereth the sheep.' This parable became a cornerstone of Puritan polemic, supplying much of the language for the attack on Anglican 'hirelings' (beneficed clergy). See, for example, *Reformation*, 341. Milton draws heavily here on Spenser's version in the May Eclogue of the *Shepheardes Calender*, 103–31, a passage which he will quote aprovingly in his *Animadversions* (1641), adding that it was 'not without some presage of these re-forming times': 'Tho under colour of Shepheards some while/There crept in wolves full of fraud and guile/That often devoured their owne Sheep,/And often the Shepheard that did them keepe.' cf. too *Paradise Lost*, IV, 192–3: 'So clomb this first grand thief into God's fold:/So since into his church lewd hirelings climb', and the sonnet to Cromwell (where the distinction between idle, cowardly hireling and rapacious wolf, beneficed Anglican and proselytizing Catholic, has finally disappeared altogether): 'Help us to save free conscience from the paw/Of hireling wolves whose gospel is their maw' (see p. 136).

119	*blind mouths* John Ruskin has a celebrated explanation of this grotesque figure as a trilingual pun on 'bishop' (Greek/*episkopos* = overseer) and 'pastor' (Latin/*pascere* = to feed): a blind overseer, and a mouth that feeds only itself. 'The most unbishoply character a man can have is therefore to be blind. The most unpastoral is, instead of feeding, to want to be fed' (*Sesame and Lilies*, I, 22).
120	*sheephook* the bishop's crosier, which itself reflects the pastoral allegory of John 10.
122	*What recks it them* What do they care? (cf. *Comus*, 404).
	sped provided for.
123	*list* choose, please (with 'grate').
124	*scrannel* a Miltonic coinage; probably 'thin', 'scrawny'
128	*the grim wolf* In the Spenserian and Miltonic reading of John 10, the wolf (stepmother of Romulus and Remus, symbol of the city of Rome) represents the Roman Catholic Church, and especially the Jesuits, who were actively recruiting and proselytizing in England in the 1630s.
129	*little said* In October 1637 Archbishop Laud was driven to protest about the proselytizing activities of George Conn, papal agent at the court of the Queen, Henrietta Maria (herself a Roman Catholic); and a proclamation against Catholics was issued on 20 December. In 1645, when the question of prelacy had been greatly clarified by the arraignment and execution of Laud, Milton sharpened this to 'nothing said'.
130	*two-handed engine* Interpretations of this sinister object include the sheephook (120), the 'two massy keys' (110), the sword of the archangel Michael, the Old and New Testaments, the headsman's axe and the two Houses of Parliament: you pays yer money and you takes yer choice. But cf. *Reformation* (630): 'Let him advise how he can reject the pastorly rod and sheephook of Christ, and those cords of love, and not fear to fall under the iron sceptre of his anger,

that will dash him to pieces like a potsherd', and see
note on that passage.

131   *smites no more*   1645 and 1673 have 'smite no more'.

132   *Alpheus*   See glossary, and 85n.

133   *Sicilian muse*   Arethusa.

138   *swart*   black, hence scorching. The swart star is either
the sun or Sirius the 'dog star', in the ascendant
during the 'dog days', the hottest part of the summer.

142   *rathe*   early (obsolete; but cf. 'rather' = sooner). The
primrose dies 'forsaken' because its flower fades before the others are out. But the manuscript has the
cancelled reading 'unwedded', recalling Shakespeare,
The Winter's Tale, IV, iv, 122–4: 'pale primroses,/
That die unmarried ere they can behold/Bright
Phoebus in his strength'.

143   *crow-toe*   various possibilities; probably crowfoot,
buttercup.

          jessamine   jasmine.

144   *freak'd with jet*   marked with black.

149   *amaranthus*   The popular name for *Amaranthus cauda-
tus* is love-lies-bleeding; but it is an introduced garden
plant, and not very appropriate in a list of native wild
flowers. Whatever Milton was thinking of, it cannot
have been the 'immortal amarant' of *Paradise Lost*, III,
353, which grows only in Heaven.

151   *laureate*   strewn with laurel; cf 1n.

153   *false surmise*   false because, as the passage that follows
acknowledges, there is no hearse and no body to
strew with flowers. This is a critical point in the
structure and argument of the poem, a kind of
'alienation effect' that exposes the limits of Theocritan
and Virgilian pastoral and throws its devices into
relief as conscious fictions.

157   *humming tide*   Shakespeare, *Pericles*, III, i, 64 ('And
humming water must o'erwhelm thy corpse') may
have suggested both this adjective and its 1645
emendation, 'whelming'.

158   *monstrous world*   the ocean, traditional home of
monsters.

160   *the fable of Bellerus old*   Bellerus seems to be Milton's invention, an aetiological hero or giant whose name is intended to explain the Roman name for Land's End, Bellerium. In the manuscript, Milton first wrote 'Corineus', the legendary Trojan hero who accompanied Brutus to Britain (see *Comus*, 826n) and was given Cornwall, 'the rather by him lik'd, for that the hugest Giants in rocks and caves were said to lurk still there, which kind of monsters to deal with was his own exercise' (*History of Britain*, in Yale: V, 16).

161   *vision of the guarded Mount*   The archangel Michael was said to have appeared to the monks on St Michael's Mount in south-west Cornwall. Milton envisages him looking south towards Spain, then calls on him to turn and look with pity (163) on England.

162   *Namancos ... Bayona's hold*   Nemancos was a district, Bayona a fortified town ('hold') in Galicia in north-west Spain. Spain, though representing much less of a threat than it did in the 1580s (its place as the leading Catholic power having been assumed by France), still evoked powerful historical sentiments among Protestants. Milton writes in *Reformation* (see p. 63) of 'the Spaniard our deadly enemy'.

163   *ruth*   pity.

164   *O ye dolphins*   often taken as an allusion to Arion, who was rescued by a dolphin; but the reference is more plausibly to Melicertes (*Comus*, 875n), who, drowned at sea and carried ashore by dolphins, became under the name Palaemon a 'genius of the shore' and protector of sailors, just as Lycidas is said to do. To Christian Platonists, dolphins were spirits who carried the souls of the blessed to Paradise.

168   *daystar*   the sun. cf. 2 Peter 1.19: 'We have also a more sure word of prophesy; whereunto ye do well that ye take heed, as unto a light that shineth in a dark place until the day dawn, and the daystar arise in your hearts.' Some critics have argued that the two epistles of Peter (the 'pilot of the Galilean lake') are fundamental to the argument and imagery of the poem.

170   *ore*   gold.
173   *him that walk'd the waves*   Matthew 14.24–5: 'But the
        ship was now in the midst of the sea, tossed with
        waves: for the wind was contrary. And in the fourth
        watch of the night Jesus went unto them, walking on
        the sea.'
174   *other groves and other streams*   a reference back to the
        'fountain, shade and rill' of line 24; and an evocation
        of the Elysian fields. cf. the description of Paradise in
        similar terms, *Paradise Lost*, IV.
175   *his oozy locks he laves*   cf. *Comus*, 860–3 and 880–2.
        The streams in Paradise 'ran nectar' in *Paradise Lost*,
        IV, 240.
176   *unexpressive*   as in 'Nativity', 116, inexpressible.
        nuptial song   cf. *Comus*, 1003–11, and Critical com-
        mentary. In this passage the allusion to Christ (173),
        the reference to 'bless'd kingdoms meek' and 'saints
        above', and the quotation from Revelation (181) indi-
        cate a shift to a more explicitly biblical conception of
        redemptive afterlife; but the classical descriptions are
        still strongly present, perhaps even dominant. So
        Carey's explanation, for example, of the groves and
        streams (174) as the 'river of water of life' and the
        'tree of life' of Revelation 22 is misleading, because
        the biblical passage, like its Old Testament sources,
        envisages Heaven as a city, without any hint either of
        the pastoralism of the gospels or the ruralism of Mil-
        ton's essentially classical conception of the afterlife
        (Carey, *CSP*: p. 253).
181   Revelation 7.17 and 21.4: 'and God shall wipe away
        all tears from their eyes'.
183   *genius*   as always in Milton, a protective deity; pick-
        ing up the allusion in 164 to Melicertes/Palaemon.
186   For this striking and unexpected shift into third-
        person narration, which 'brackets' the whole poem
        up to 185 as an utterance in direct speech, see p.
        162–3.
        uncouth   unknown. The sense 'ignorant' or 'clumsy'
        is later, though 'developing during the seventeenth
        century', according to Carey (*CSP*: p. 253).

188   *stops* the finger-holes of a flute or pipe ('quill').
       'Various quills' may suggest the mixed or syncretic
       character of Christian-Platonic pastoral.

189   *Doric lay* The Sicilian Greeks came originally from
       the Peloponnese and spoke the Doric dialect; and the
       Sicilian pastoralists like Bion, Moschus, and Theocri-
       tus used a literary form of the same dialect. Hence
       generically: pastoral (with connotations of conscious-
       ly artless rusticity). cf. the letter from Sir Henry
       Wotton that Milton printed with *Comus* in 1645: 'I
       should much commend the Tragical part, if the
       Lyrical did not ravish me with a certain Dorique
       delicacy in your Songs and Odes.'

193   Most editors note the similarity to Phineas Fletcher's
       'Tomorrow shall ye feast in pastures new'; but Mil-
       ton's line, a hanging clause without a verb and hence
       with a quite different kind of grammatical suspense
       and open-endedness, has generally been read as his
       own farewell to pastoral and a determination to move
       on to a new set of genres and themes; perhaps even,
       literally, to new landscapes. *Lycidas* was finished in
       November 1637, published early the following year.
       That May Milton sailed for France, on his way to
       Italy and Greece.

OF REFORMATION TOUCHING CHURCH–DISCIPLINE
IN ENGLAND

Of Reformation, the first of Milton's five pamphlets attacking
the Anglican bishops, was published anonymously in April–
May 1641. In January, Joseph Hall, Bishop of Worcester, had
published *A Humble Remonstrance to the High Court of Parliament*, defending episcopacy and attacking its Presbyterian critics. In March a group of five Presbyterian ministers known by
the collective acronym Smectymnuus (the TY was Milton's old
tutor Thomas Young) produced *An Answer to a Book Entitled
An Humble Remonstrance*, with a historical postscript probably
by Milton. Hall replied in April with *A Defence of the Humble
Remonstrance*; and in June Smectymnuus hit back with *A Vindication of the Answer to the Humble Remonstrance*. In the mean

211

time *Of Reformation* had appeared, to be followed by the more directly polemical *Of Prelatical Episcopacy* (June–July 1641) and *Animadversions on the Remonstrant's Defence* (July 1641), *The Reason of Church Government* (January–February 1642, and the only one to appear with Milton's name) and *An Apology against a Pamphlet* (April 1642, usually known as the *Apology for Smectymnuus*). The historical treatise *Of Reformation* takes the form of an extended letter to a friend, in two books: the first an analysis of the 'hinderers of Reformation', the second a 'political discourse of episcopacy' that breaks off (534) to answer the parliamentary moderates who were urging a compromise with the bishops. This extract consists of all but the first few pages of the second book.

1   *Body*   The fable of the Body is derived not so much from Aesop (see next note) as from the story with which, according to Livy, Menenius Agrippa placated an army mutiny in 494 BC (*Histories*, II, 32). In Shakespeare's version of the incident (*Coriolanus*, I, i, 94–152) it is angry citizens rather than soldiers whom Menenius attempts to pacify with his 'pretty tale'.

2–3   *Aesop's Chronicles*   The Phrygian writer Aesop (*c.* 622–554 BC) presented his moral maxims in the form of *mythoi* or fables, often with animal characters.

5   *Wen*   a large swelling, usually a cyst or goitre on the head or neck.

20   *committee*   here a single individual.

35   *Lourdan*   sluggard, layabout.

45   *Solomon*   Proverbs 16.12: 'It is an abomination to kings to commit wickedness: for the throne is established by righteousness.'

46–7   *the universal justice that Aristotle ... praises*   Aristotle, *Ethics*, 5: 'Justice is often thought to be the chief of virtues ... we have the proverb "In justice is all virtue found in sum".'

59   *Prince*   used in this period as a general term for a ruler.

61   *whip of scorpions*   a Miltonic phrase based on 1 Kings 12.11: 'My father hath chastised you with whips, but

I will chastise you with scorpions.' Probably a kind of whip armed with steel hooks or spikes. cf. *Paradise Lost*, II, 701–2: 'Lest with a whip of scorpions I pursue/Thy lingering.'

62   *keel*   literally to cool, hence lessen, mitigate.

65   *forsake their dearest home*   As many as 20,000 people were driven by the Laudian persecutions to emigrate to the New World between 1630 and 1640.

75–6   *indifferent*   The 1640 *Constitutions and Canons* declared the position of the communion table to be 'in its own nature indifferent, neither commanded nor condemned by the Word of God'. 'Indifferency' became a focal point in the struggle between Puritanism and the bishops.

114   *the old Burgurdian league*   The fourteenth-century Burgundian League consolidated the English wool trade by regulating the commercial relations between English wool producers and Flemish weavers.

121   *East Indies*   a reference to the constant friction between the Dutch East India Company and English merchants in the Far East.

122–3   *French king*   In 1632 Louis XIII had offered to help the Dutch against the Spanish in the Thirty Years War.

127   *rochet apophthegms*   a contemptuous reference to Laud's 1640 *Canons*, which were presented in a numbered series like a collection of philosophical maxims or 'apophthegms'. A rochet is a bishop's surplice, here used adjectivally = episcopal.

130   *Gascons*   Until the fifteenth century the English kings had claimed Gascony in south-west France as part of their own territory.

134   *tympany of spaniolized bishops*   'Tympany', a malignant swelling or tumour, continues the metaphor of the 'body politic'. In 1639 the church historian Thomas Fuller accused the Puritans of wishing to 'cut off the flesh of the Church's necessary maintenance, under pretence to cure her of a tympany of superfluities'. 'Spaniolized' is a pun: Spanish (i.e. Catholic)

in style and doctrine, and fawningly obsequious like spaniels.

159   *Thus learnt Cyrus*   The story of the Persian emperor Cyrus is from the first book of Herodotus' *Histories*.

163   *drift*   a scheme or plot.

170   *one day at least*   The 1633 royal declaration *Concerning Lawful Sports*, usually referred to as the *Book of Sports*, forbade any interference with dancing and 'other harmless recreations' on Sundays. Most Puritans were strict sabbatarians, and their resentment of the *Book of Sports* enabled their opponents to exploit their reputation as sour-faced killjoys. Milton's tutor and friend Thomas Young had attacked the declaration in his *Dies Dominica* (1639).

179   *Balaam*   The story of the renegade priest Balaam is in Numbers 22.

190–1   *ceremonies ... courts*   two major causes of Puritan resentment of the bishops, the revival of liturgical ritual and the power of ecclesiastical courts.

205   *Babel*   Genesis 11.4–9: 'And they said, Go to, let us build us a city and a tower, whose top may reach unto heaven.... Therefore is the name of it called Babel; because the Lord did there confound the language of all the earth.'

207   *Antichrist*   1 John 2.18: 'as ye have heard that antichrist shall come, even now are there many antichrists; whereby we know that it is the last time'. On the basis of this passage a rich mythology of Antichrist was developed. He was the 'son of Mammon' because he was associated with 'the lust of the flesh, and the lust of the eyes, and the pride of life' (1 John 2.16), and in one tradition he was spawned from adders' eggs or the poisonous secretions of a cockatrice. In Protestant demonology, Antichrist was usually identified with the Pope.

207–8   *sour leaven*   The metaphorical opposition of leavened and unleavened bread, old superstition and new faith, derives from 1 Corinthians 5.8: 'Therefore let us keep the feast, not with old leaven, neither with the leaven

214

of malice and wickedness; but with the unleavened bread of sincerity and truth.'

221–2   *a moderate maintenance*   See *Comus*, 768ff and note.

224   *Belshazzar*   Daniel 5.1–2: 'Belshazzar the king made a great feast to a thousand of his lords, and drank wine before the thousand. Belshazzar ... commanded to bring the gold and silver vessels which his father Nebuchadnezzar had taken out of the temple ... that the king, and his princes, his wives, and his concubines, might drink therein.'

230   *harpies*   See glossary. Here used of the lay officers of ecclesiastical courts.

237   *works of holy discipline*   The *discipline* of the church refers to the day-to-day practice of Christian ministry, in accordance with the *doctrine* of scripture, and the two concepts are often coupled as 'doctrine and discipline'. The 'works of discipline' are the sanctions used to maintain the spiritual authority of the church.

245   *fees*   The bishops charged a fee for licensing preachers and schoolteachers, for ordaining clergy, and for other parochial services.

247   *truckage*   barter.

248–9   *rooks and rakeshames*   swindlers and disreputable ruffians.

259   *begin at the root*   that is, with the question of liberty, as always the central issue in Milton's writing.

261–2   *gold and silver*   The alchemists claimed to be able to produce precious metals from base ones ('drossy bullion').

268   *not sacrilegious*   because the civil magistrate does not fall under the jurisdiction of ecclesiatical law, as the clergy do.

2/8   *great Charter*   Magna Carta.

293   *emulation*   In the Old Testament (under the 'old Law' of Moses) priests often had more authority than kings.

305   *decretals*   papal decrees on matters of doctrine or ecclesiastical law.

320   *audacious Becket*   Thomas à Becket, Henry II's Arch-

bishop of Canterbury, who argued with the King about the priority of civil and ecclesiastical authority and was murdered, probably on his orders, in 1170.

330   *Pepin*   In 750 Pope Zacharias absolved all Franks of their allegiance to their king, Chilperic, and installed his own candidate, Pepin, in his place.

333   *the Emperor*   In a similar incident in 725, Pope Gregory III excommunicated Leo III, Emperor of the East, and released his Italian subjects from their allegiance to him, after Leo had published an edict forbidding the worship of images and ordering their destruction.

340-1   *started up a wolf*   See *Lycidas*, 128n.

343   *Chaucer*   a reference to the *Ploughman's Tale*, a religious polemic once attributed to Chaucer but now thought to be by William Langland, author of *Piers Plowman*.

344   *Padre Paolo*   Paolo Sarpi, dissident Venetian theologian and author of the *History of the Council of Trent* (translated into English in 1620), strongly critical of papal authority.

347   *hierarchy*   here in the original sense of 'government by priests'.

350-1   *tetrarchy ... heptarchy*   government by, or divided between, four and seven rulers; in particular, the ancient tetrarchy of Judaea and the seven kingdoms of pre-Norman England.

364-5   *dearest brothers*   since the union of the two countries under James I in 1603. The two 'Bishops' Wars' of 1639 and 1640 resulted from an attempt to impose the Anglican prayer book and liturgy on the Scottish church.

376   *Abimelech*   bastard son of Gideon, who murdered his seventy brothers to become king of Israel, but died with thousands of others in the civil war with the Shechemites, his mother's people. In Judges 9, 'God sent an evil spirit between Abimelech and the men of Shechem'.

390-1   *a surplice-brabble, a tippet-scuffle*   contemptuous terms for disputes between the clergy. A brabble is a brawl; and a tippet is a band of silk, worn round the neck and hanging down the front of the vestments.

392–3   *red cross ... guly dragons*   the cross of St George and the red ('guly') dragons of the royal standard.

409–10   *outlandish*   foreign.

414   *runagates*   a deserter or turncoat, from the Spanish *renegado*.

436   *strangeness*   coldness, unfriendliness.

445   *politicasters*   political amateurs or dilettantes, on the analogy of 'poetasters'.

453   *sequestered and collateral*   separate and equivalent.

454   *confronting mitre*   episcopal challenge (to the authority of the crown).

459   *homogeneal*   The idea is that a balanced physical and psychological constitution results from the mixture of different 'elements or humours', not from the purity and consistency of a single substance. Note the continual resurfacing of the body-metaphor.

466–7   *so much praised by ... Polybius*   The Greek historian Polybius had praised the Spartan and Roman republics as 'the best of all existing constitutions'.

490   *moiety of a scruple*   moiety = half; a scruple = 1/24 oz.

521   *same annoyances*   the twenty-six bishops who sat as 'Lords Spiritual' in the House of Lords. They were excluded by order of the Long Parliament in February 1642.

532   *vessel of the commonwealth*   the other major traditional metaphor, with the 'body politic', for political society, the 'ship of state'. cf. *The Ready and Easy Way*, p. 140.

534   *some objections*   On 9 February 1641, while Milton was writing *Of Reformation*, Lord Digby spoke in Parliament against the danger of 'flying into extremes' in the parliamentary opposition to royal prerogative.

560–1   *the good kings of Judah*   like Hezekiah, who 'removed the high places, and brake the images, and cut down the groves, and brake in pieces the brazen serpent that Moses had made', and his great-grandson Josiah, who 'put down the idolatrous priests, whom the kings of Judah had ordained to burn incense in the high places in the cities of Judah' (2 Kings 18.4, 23.5).

567   *precise Puritanism* Both words were originally applied abusively, but were adopted defiantly by the Puritans themselves.

580   *See of Canterbury* The first Archbishop of Canterbury was Augustine in 597.

597   *Ridley* Nicholas Ridley, Bishop of London and co-author with Cranmer of the prayer book of 1549; he opposed the succession of Mary or Elizabeth, and was burnt at the stake in 1555.

599   *the author of our church history* John Foxe, from whose *Acts and Monuments* (the so-called *Book of Martyrs*) the reference comes.

627   *a Pope in every parish* Digby had attacked the Presbyterian assemblies as 'a Pope in every parish' in his speech of 9 February. See 534n.

631   *iron sceptre* Psalms 2.9: 'Thou shalt break them with a rod of iron; thou shalt dash them in pieces like a potter's vessel.' See *Lycidas*, 130n.

645   *kiss each other* Psalms 85.10: 'Mercy and truth are met together; righteousness and peace have kissed each other.' cf 'Nativity', 141n.

654   *shrewd* malicious.

677–8   *Saint Ambrose ... Theodosius* In 390 the Byzantine Emperor Theodosius I slaughtered many thousands of the inhabitants of Salonica in revenge for the murder there of one of his officials. Ambrose, Archbishop of Milan, excommunicated him and banned him from the precincts of any church.

706–7   *Iscariotical* treacherous and venal, after Judas Iscariot.

731–2   *fogging proctorage* A fogger is a huckster or dishonest shopkeeper; proctors were officers of the ecclesiastical courts, the 'harpies' of line 230.

732   *Gehezi* or Gehazi, servant of the prophet Elisha, was punished with leprosy for obtaining money deceitfully (2 Kings 5).

733   *Simon Magus* (= the sorcerer) offered money to the apostles in exchange for ordination by laying on of hands. Hence 'simony', buying preferment in the church (Acts 8).

751   *Grizons* an independent Protestant canton in Switzerland.

752   *French* the Huguenots, or French Protestants.

783   *Saint Lawrence* Ordered under torture to hand over the church's wealth, he sent for cartloads of poor people, declaring 'these are the riches of the church'.

796–8   *lawn and sarsnet ... geometrical rhomboides* Lawn is a fine cotton material, sarsnet (or sarcenet) a kind of silk. The geometrical rhomboides is the bishop's mitre. For the satirical comparison of elaborate dress to a ship under sail, cf. the description of Dalila in *Samson Agonistes*, 710–21.

800–1   *in Jerusalem ... to be taxed* the annual Jewish temple tax.

802   *our tuppences* The church's poll-tax was known as the 'Easter tuppence'.
         chandlerly shop-book A chandler is a shopkeeper. The reference is to the poll-tax record.

804   *band-dogs* bloodhounds.

804–5   *pursuivants* bailiffs or court officers.

831   *tithes* Ministers were supported by a levy of a tenth ('tithe') of the produce and revenue of the parish. As a guaranteed income, often paid in return for little or no pastoral activity, tithes were a major focus of the argument for church reform.

833–4   *Christ's mystical body* the church.

859   *bottomless pit* Revelation 9.2–3: 'And he opened the bottomless pit, and there arose a smoke out of the pit, as the smoke of a great furnace: and the sun and the air were darkened by reason of the smoke of the pit. And there came out of the smoke locusts upon the earth: and unto them was given power, as the scorpions of the earth have power.'

869   *inundations* the five invasions of Britain, by the Romans, the Picts, the Saxons, the Danes, and the Normans.

	intestine war the Wars of the Roses.
884	*frozen Thule* a legendary region to the north of Britain; perhaps here referring to Shetland, where some of the Armada ships were blown.
899	*Great Whore* This figure from Revelation (17.1) was commonly identified with the Roman Catholic Church.
900	*intelligencing tyrant* the King of Spain.
901	*Ophir* a biblical source of gold (Isaiah 13.12; Job 28.16) variously identified as India, Madagascar, the Malay peninsula. Here probably Central America; but cf. *Paradise Lost*, XI, 400, 'Sofala thought Ophir', where Mozambique is intended.
926	*Principalities, Legions and Thrones* Principalities and Thrones are orders in the quasi-military hierarchy of angels. See Colossians 1.16: 'For by him were all things created, that are in heaven, and that are in earth, visible and invisible, whether they be thrones, or dominions, or principalities, or powers.' 'Legion' means 'many', and is presumably intended to include all the others. For a full list, see 'Nativity', 131n.

AREOPAGITICA

Areopagitica, Milton's speech 'for the liberty of unlicensed printing', was itself published without a licence or publisher's name (though with the author's) in November 1644. Before 1640, control of the press and of printed books had been an extension of royal prerogative exercised through the Star Chamber, which decreed it an offence for anything to be printed without a licence and an entry in the Stationers' Register. This system fell with the abolition of the Star Chamber in July 1641, but in June 1643 Parliament passed an order forbidding any 'book, pamphlet, paper' to be 'printed, bound, stitched or put to sale ... unless the same be first approved of and licensed under the hands of such person or persons as both or either of the said Houses shall appoint for the licensing of the same, and entered in the Register Book of the Company of Stationers, according to ancient custom', thus effectively reinstating not 'ancient custom' but the Elizabethan and Jacobean practice of government censorship culminating in the Star Chamber decree of 11 July 1637. This is the order against which *Areopagitica* was written, and its protests were unavailing. Parliament went on licensing (not very thoroughly), and in 1649 Milton himself was appointed licenser.

The title The title means either 'speech on the Areopagus' or 'matters concerning the Areopagus', and recalls the seventh oration of the Greek orator Isocrates (436–338 BC), which was a plea for the restoration of the powers of the ancient high court of Athens, the Areopagus (so named from the Hill of Ares (= Mars) on which it met, alongside the Acropolis). Like Milton's, Isocrates' speech was intended to be read rather than orally delivered; near the beginning of the *Areopagitica* Milton refers to the Athenian statesman as 'him who from his private house wrote that discourse to the Parliament of Athens that persuades them to change the form of democraty which was then established' (Yale: II, 489). Milton may also be alluding to another Areopagitic address, given by St Paul when he was invited 'by certain philosophers of the Epicureans, and the Stoicks' to explain Christianity to a public meeting on the hill (Acts 17.18–32).

1   *Dionysius* Bishop of Alexandria 247–65. The story comes from Pamphilius Eusebius's *Ecclesiastical Histories.*

14   *Apostle* St Paul. See 1 Thessalonians 5.21.

16   *another remarkable saying* Titus 1.15.

22   *in that ... vision* Acts 10.13–15: 'And there came a voice to him, Rise, Peter; kill, and eat. But Peter said, Not so, Lord; for I have never eaten any thing that is common or unclean. And the voice spake unto him again the second time, What God hath cleansed, that call not thou common.'

34   *Mr Selden* John Selden (1584–1654), lawyer and antiquary, was a leading member of the anti-Stuart opposition in the Long Parliament. The reference is to his Latin work, *De Jure Naturali et Gentium* (1640).

50   *tabled the Jews*   In Exodus 16.16, God provides man-
       na for the Israelites in the desert after their escape
       from Egypt, instructing them to 'gather of it every
       man according to his eating, an omer for every man'.
       An omer is helpfully defined (16.36) as 'the tenth part
       of an ephar'.

60   *Solomon*   Ecclesiastes 12.12: 'Of making many books
       there is no end; and much study is a weariness of the
       flesh.' The Authorized Version glosses 'study' as
       'reading'.

66–7   *Ephesian books*   Acts 19.19: 'Many of them also
       which used curious arts brought their books together,
       and burned them before all men.' Milton argues (a)
       that the 'curious arts' were magic, and therefore a
       special case, and (b) that the books were burnt volun-
       tarily by their owners on their conversion to Christ-
       ianity, and so cannot provide any scriptural authority
       for state censorship.

72   *practised*   used for sorcery.

79   *Psyche*   See glossary, and *Comus*, 1006n.

101   *excremental*   external, superficial.

104   *Scotus or Aquinas*   John Duns Scotus, 1265–1308, and
       Thomas Aquinas, 1225–74, most celebrated of the
       thirteenth-century 'schoolmen' or philosopher-
       theologians.

105   *Guyon*   In Book Two of Spenser's *Faerie Queene* Sir
       Guyon (representing temperance) visits the Cave of
       Mammon (wealth) and the Bower of Bliss (sexual
       pleasure), but is not tempted by either. In Spenser's
       allegory the Palmer stands for reason; but although he
       does accompany Guyon to the Bower, he does not
       visit Mammon's Cave. It has been thought significant
       that in his memory of the passage Milton gives reason
       a more important role than Spenser himself does.

123   *Epicurus*   an Athenian philosopher, 342–270 BC, who
       argued that virtue was preferable because it brought
       happiness. His emphasis on the pleasure principle led
       to his being represented as a hedonist and a libertine;
       hence the popular meaning of 'epicurean'.

222

124   *Talmudist*   a student of the Talmud, the corpus of Jewish commentary on the Old Testament.

125-7   *keri ... chetiv*   terms from Hebrew biblical scholarship, the *chetiv* being the literal text of scripture, the *keri* an emendation or euphemism (for example, for the name of God, too sacred to pronounce) recorded in the margin. The suggestion is that the Bible itself would have to be banned under any licensing order against immoral or heretical literature.

129-30   *Clement of Alexandria*   second-century church father.

130   *Eusebian book*   not his *Ecclesiastical Histories* (see 1n) but his *Evangelical Preparation*.

133   *Irenaeus, Epiphanius, Jerome*   Irenaeus (second century) and Epiphanius and Jerome (both fourth century) all attacked heresy and paganism in the name of orthodoxy, often describing them in lavish and highly coloured detail.

143   *Petronius*   Gaius Petronius, nicknamed '*Arbiter elegantiae*' (= judge of taste), author of the humorous and indecent *Satyricon*.

145   *ribald of Arezzo*   Pietro Aretino, sixteenth-century satirist and erotic writer, best known for his obscene *Postures* and *Dialogues*.

147-8   *Vicar of Hell*   Once taken as an allusion to the poet John Skelton, who was rector of Diss in Norfolk ('Dis' is Latin for Hell), it is now known to be a reference to the minor poet and courtier of Henry VIII, Sir Francis Brian.

151   *Cataio*   Cathay (China). In this period mariners were still searching for north-east ('north of Cataio') and north-west (Canada) passages to the Indies.

152   *Spanish licensing*   i.e. like the Inquisition.

162   *prophecy of Isaiah*   In Acts 8 an Ethiopian eunuch, reading the Old Testament, is puzzled by Isaiah 53.7 ('He is brought as a lamb to the slaughter'), and asks the apostle Philip to explain it. As a result of the explanation he is converted to Christianity.

165   *Sorbonnists*   The Sorbonne was the theological faculty of that university.

168   *Arminius* Jacob Hermanns (1560–1609), latinized to Jacobus Arminius, Protestant Professor of Theology at Leyden. As an orthodox Calvinist he had undertaken to reply to some dissenting pamphlets, but in doing so had himself decided that the doctrine of predestination was unacceptable, and became the leading proponent of the anti-predestinarian position. At this stage Milton identified Arminianism with the Laudian high-church establishment, but he later adopted an Arminian view himself. See Hill 1979, chapter 21 ('Radical Arminianism').

182   *cautelous* either 'precautionary' or 'deceitful'; here perhaps both.

193   *gather gold* The metaphor is from alchemy. cf. *Reformation*, 262.

201   *Aristotle* The reference is to the *Ethics*, I, 3.
         Solomon Proverbs 23.9: 'Speak not in the ears of a fool; for he will despise the wisdom of thy words.'
         our Saviour Matthew 7.6: 'Give not that which is holy unto the dogs, neither cast ye your pearls before swine, lest they trample them under their feet, and turn again and rend you.'

213   *cannot want* i.e. should not be deprived of.

223–4   *pace of method and discourse* the speed of a methodical and fully developed argument.

234   *Plato* Unlike the admittedly speculative and utopian *Republic*, the *Laws*, written for the Sicilian tyrant Dionysius, describes the institutions of a supposedly practicable and realistic city-state.

237   *airy* imaginary.

240   *academic night-sitting* Some of the Platonic dialogues (e.g. the *Symposium*, whose title means 'drinking-party') take the form of late-night conversations over wine. Plato himself taught in the Academy, a public park in Athens.

252–3   *Sophron Mimus and Aristophanes* comic dramatists; Sophron Mimus = 'Sophron the actor'.

272   *grave and Doric* Unlike *Lycidas*, 189 (see note), Doric here refers not to pastoral poetry but to the Dorian

224

mode of Greek music, which is permitted in the *Republic*, while the Lydian and Ionian modes are prohibited as decadent and unmanly. In *Paradise Lost*, I, 550–1, the fallen angels march 'In perfect phalanx to the Dorian mood/Of flutes and soft recorders'.

285   *lectures*   sermons (here ironically).
286   *rebeck*   fiddle (cf. 'L'Allegro', 94).
      gamut   the musical scale; here, music.
288   *Arcadias and … Montemayors*   The reference is to two popular sixteenth-century romances, Sidney's *Arcadia* (1590) and Jorge de Montemayor's *Diana* (1559).
304   *Atlantic and Utopian polities*   two famous imaginary commonwealths, Francis Bacon's *New Atlantis* (*c.* 1623) and Sir Thomas More's *Utopia* (1516), which gave its name to the whole genre.
324   *grammercy*   'grand merci', many thanks; hence credit, recognition.
329   *the motions*   puppet plays.
349ff.   This passage develops the arguments for thrift and just distribution in *Comus*, 768ff. See the note on that passage.
371–2   *compared in scripture to a streaming fountain*   often taken as a reference to Psalms 85.11, 'Truth shall spring out of the earth'; but Milton's own version of that psalm shows that he understood it differently: 'Truth from the earth like to a flower/Shall bud and blossom then.' More likely is John 4.14: 'But whosoever drinketh of the water that I shall give him shall never thirst; but the water that I shall give him shall be in him a well of water springing up into everlasting life.'
381   *professors*   those professing the true faith, i.e. Puritans.
382   *implicit faith*   religious belief taken on trust from a priest or other authority, rather than from the testimony of one's own conscience.
      Loreto   a centre of Catholic pilgrimage, and hence, for Milton, of superstition.

398   *dividual*   separate, divisible (cf. *Paradise Lost*, VII, 382).

404–5   *he whose morning appetite*   Christ, in Matthew 21.17–19, when he cursed the fig tree for its barrenness.

412–13   *tonnaging and poundaging*   'Tonnage (or tunnage) and poundage' was a duty paid by merchants on imported goods. In 1640 John Pym had complained of 'tunnage and poundage ... taken by prerogative, without grant of Parliament'.

430   *Hercules' pillars*   the straits of Gibraltar, once the westward limit of the known world to the peoples of the Mediterranean seaboard. Thus, metaphorically, the summit or furthest reach of ambition.

432   *concordance*   a systematic lexicon of biblical terms.

433   *topic folio*   a commonplace book.

434   *Harmony ... Catena*   anthologies of biblical quotations and commentary.

441–2   *interlinearies, breviaries, synopses*   translations and extracts of scripture.

445–6   *St Thomas ... St Martin ... St Hugh*   St Thomas and St Martin are churches in the commercial part of the city of London, and hence unofficial patrons of the reach-me-down rag trade. St Hugh is an apocryphal figure associated with the Shoemakers Company. Thus there may be a sarcastic pun in 'vestry' and 'to boot'.

450   *impaled*   fenced in.

471   *Christ urged it*   John 18.20: 'Jesus answered him, I spake openly to the world ... and in secret have I said nothing.'

478   *disinured*   estranged.

503   *mortal glass*   'For now we see through a glass, darkly; but then face to face' (1 Corinthians 13.12).

511   *as that story goes*   The allegorical treatment of Osiris, Isis, and Typhon is indebted to Plutarch's *Moralia*. For allegory cf. *Comus*, 513n; and for a very different reading of the Egyptian deities, see 'Nativity', 211–20.

529   *combust*   literally 'burnt up', hence 'close to the sun'.

541   *Zwinglius and Calvin*   founders of the Swiss reformed churches, Zwinglius (Huldrich Zwingli) in Zurich, Calvin in Geneva.

548   *syntagma*   'a systematically arranged treatise' (*OED*, which gives this as the first usage).

554   *golden rule*   the arithmetical rule of proportion.

567   *Pythagoras ... Persian wisdom*   Some antiquaries speculated that the Pythagorean doctrine of the transmigration of souls and the Zoroastrian tradition of magic might both have originated with the Druids. cf. *Doctrine and Discipline of Divorce* (Yale: II, 231): 'It would not be the first, or second time, since our ancient *Druids*, by whom This Island was the Cathedral of Philosophy to France, left off their pagan rites, that England hath had this honour vouchsafed from Heaven, to give out reformation to the world.' Milton is more guarded in the *History of Britain*: 'Their religion was governed by a sort of priests or magicians called Druids, from the Greek name of an oak.... Pliny writes them skilled in magic no less than those of Persia; by their abstaining from a hen, a hare and a goose, from fish also (saith Dion), and their opinion of the soul's passing after death into other bodies, they may be thought to have studied Pythagoras' (Yale: V, 60–1).

569   *Julius Agricola*   In the *History* Milton describes Agricola, governor of Britain from AD 78–85, as 'preferring the wits of Britain before the studies of Gallia' (Yale: V, 85); but like the account of the Druids, the reference is treated much more equivocally in the *History* than in *Areopagitica*.

572   *Transylvanian*   Transylvania had been an independent Protestant republic since 1635.

574   *Hercynian wilderness*   the mountains and forests of Central Europe, known to the Romans as Hyrcania.

584   *Wyclif*   John Wyclif (1324–84), ecclesiastical reformer and translator of the Bible. Many of Wyclif's ideas were implemented at the Reformation, a century and a half after his death.

585   *Huss ... Jerome*   John Hus (1373–1415) and Jerome of Prague (1365–1416), Bohemian reformers and followers of Wyclif. Hus was put to death for his criticisms of the church. All three are cited as precursors of Luther and Calvin, with the seniority and pre-eminence of Wyclif as evidence that the spirit of the Reformation originated in England.

600   *city of refuge*   The phrase, from Numbers 35.11–12, means here a sanctuary where justice and legality are guaranteed.

615–16   *five months yet to harvest*   The image of harvest, often associated with judgement, is taken from John 4.35: 'Say not ye, There are yet four months, and then cometh harvest? behold, I say unto you, Lift up your eyes, and look on the fields; for they are white already to harvest.' Nobody seems to know why Milton changed four months to five.

637   *Pyrrhus*   King of Epirus, he defeated a Roman army at the battle of Heraclea in 280 BC, and is reported to have said afterwards that with an army of Romans he could have conquered the world.

643   *temple of the Lord*   The account of the building of the great temple of Solomon is in 1 Kings 5–6.

658   *the time seems come*   In Numbers 11.29 Moses exclaims, 'Would God that all the Lord's people were prophets, and that the Lord would put his spirit upon them!'

671   *maniples*   A maniple is a small platoon of soldiers. In the Roman army it numbered between 60 and 120 men.

682   *suburb trenches*   defensive outworks dug around the city walls. London was fortified in this way after the royalist advance to Turnham Green in November 1642. See the sonnet 'Captain or colonel', p. 124.

693ff.   The story is from Livy's *Histories*, XXVI, 11.

698   *as in a body*   for this image, cf. *Reformation*, 1n.

707   *drooping to a fatal decay*   an allusion to the theory that time was running down and the universe sinking into a terminal lethargy. It forms the subject of Milton's

Latin poem 'Naturam non pati senium' ('That nature does not suffer from old age'), where as here he argues against it. Proponents of the theory included John Donne and Sir Thomas Browne.

713   *strong man*   Samson, before the cutting of his 'invincible locks'. See Judges 16.14. The Samson story was rich with significance for Milton, before and after his blindness. In 1641 he had compared 'the state and person of a king' to 'that mighty Nazarite Samson', suggesting that Charles I had been led astray by the 'strumpet flatteries of the Prelates' (Yale, I, 858–9). In the juxtaposition of strong man and eagle Wittreich (1979: p. 85) suggests that 'Milton conflates two symbols ... and, with them, two myths, one of individual regeneration, the other of national renewal'. And see p. 171.

714   *as an eagle*   Eagles were believed to be able to stare straight into the sun.

714–15   *mewing*   moulting, renewing.

723   *flowery crop of knowledge*   cf. Milton's translation of Psalms 85.11: 'Truth from the earth like to a flower/ Shall bud and blossom then.'

725   *engrossers*   monopolists, alluding to another major cause of grievance against the Stuarts. Christopher Hill suggests that 'we can see *Areopagitica* as Milton's attempt to focus the tolerationist case on one point, liberty of printing, using arguments from the attack on monopolies' (Hill 1979: p. 150).

753   *cote and conduct*   a tax levied to pay for the provisioning and transport of armies.

754   *nobles of Danegelt*   A noble was worth a third of a pound. The original danegelt, the basis of all modern taxation, was levied in pre-conquest England to pay for defensive measures against the invading Danes. Milton applies the term to the infamous ship tax of the 1630s, which, by being raised without reference to Parliament and by being associated with a foreign policy increasingly feared to be pro-Catholic, did much to crystallize the domestic opposition to

Charles I. The argument here is, that although the defence of 'just immunities' like the right not to be taxed without representation is important enough, the war was being fought for a far more fundamental principle, the 'liberty to know, to utter and to argue freely according to conscience'.

ON THE MORNING OF CHRIST'S NATIVITY

Probably written Christmas 1629, though Milton's datings are not always completely reliable.

5   *holy sages* the prophets of the Old Testament, especially Isaiah (7.14: 'Behold, a virgin shall conceive, and bear a son'); and perhaps also Virgil, whose fourth Eclogue was often read as a pagan prophecy of the birth of Christ and the return of the Golden Age. cf. 135n.

7   *And ... peace* Isaiah 9.7 (a continuation of the prophecy in the last note): 'Of the increase of his government and peace there shall be no end.'

8   *unsufferable* intolerably bright.

15   *heavenly Muse* Milton followed the French poet Du Bartas in adopting Urania, originally the muse of astronomy (her name means 'heavenly'), as the patroness of sacred poetry; but the ground had already been prepared by the neo-Platonic treatment of her as representative of the celestial sphere in the cosmic order of things (Wind 1967: pp. 149–50, 267–8). See 'Solemn music', 2n, and *Paradise Lost*, I, 6 and VII, 1ff.

     vein often used figuratively of literary or rhetorical style.

19   *the sun's team* the horses that pull the sun's chariot. cf. *Comus*, 95.

20   *took no print* not been marked by the hooves.

21   *spangled host* stars; but 'host' and 'squadrons' also suggest the warrior-angels of *Paradise Lost*, which are

also compared to stars (V, 620ff. and 708ff.). See too Job 38.7: 'When the morning stars sang together, and all the sons of God shouted for joy.'

23   *star-led wizards*   the three magi.

24   *prevent them*   not 'obstruct them' but 'arrive before them'.

41   *Pollute*   polluted, as a result of the Fall. The natural effects of the Fall are described in detail in *Paradise Lost*, X, 651–714.

47   *olive*   traditional symbol of peace.

49   *harbinger*   forerunner, messenger.

50   *turtle*   turtle dove.

51   *myrtle*   sacred to Venus, and hence a symbol of love. cf. *Lycidas*, 1n.

57   *hostile*   the original (Latin) sense of 'belonging to an enemy'.

64   *whist*   (adjective) silent.

68   *birds of calm*   The halcyon (usually identified as the kingfisher) was believed to nest on the surface of the sea in the middle of winter, during which time the weather remained calm (the so-called 'halcyon days').

71   *influence*   an astrological term denoting the effect of the stars at birth. Here all the stars are directing their beneficent ('precious') influence on the infant Christ.

74   *Lucifer*   the morning star (literally 'light-bringer'), but with strong suggestions of the other sense of Lucifer, as Satan: at the birth of Christ the stars will no longer obey Satan. cf. *Paradise Lost*, V, 708–10, where both senses are similarly in play: 'His countenance, as the morning star that guides/The starry flock, allured them, and with lies/Drew after him the third part of Heaven's host.'

81   *as*   = as if.

83   *greater sun*   an aural pun on sun/son.

84   *axletree*   of his chariot (see 19n).

85   *lawn*   pasture (cf. *Comus*, 568).

86   *or ere*   before.

89   *Pan*   See glossary for an account of this ancient and complex minor deity. The christianization of Pan,

based on the god's name, the Greek word for 'everything', is one of the key linking motifs of Christian pastoral. Spenser conflates Christ and Pan in the May Eclogue of his *Shepheardes Calendar* (line 54, and 'E.K.'.'s note). See p. 161.

90   *kindly*   with the sense of 'kinship' as well as 'benevolence': becoming human, Christ has become the same 'kind' as the shepherds.

92   *silly*   in the old sense – simple, unsophisticated.

100   *close*   cadence (cf. *Comus*, 548).

102   *hollow round*   the sphere. In Pythagorean cosmography, the planets, sun, moon, and fixed stars moved around the inside of a series of transparent and concentric spheres which, 'singing' or resonating to the notes of the scale, produced a music of supernatural beauty normally inaudible in the 'sublunary' realm below the moon. Here Nature, mistaking the chorus of angels for the music of the spheres, heard at last 'beneath the moon', believes that the end of the world has come. See also 131n.

103   *Cynthia*   the moon-goddess Artemis, twin sister of Apollo, the sun-god.

112   *helmed*   helmeted.

116   *unexpressive*   inexpressible (in human language), like the nuptial song in *Lycidas*, 176.

119   *sons of morning sung*   Job 38.7 (cf. 21n); and see *Paradise Lost*, VII, 180ff. for an expansion of the idea.

124   *weltering*   rocking, as in *Lycidas*, 13.
     oozy   cf. *Lycidas*, 175.

131   *ninefold harmony*   In the *Republic* (X, 617) Plato describes the motion of the planets in Pythagorean terms: 'up above on each of the rims of the circles a Siren stood, borne around in its revolution and uttering one sound, one note, and from all the eight there was the concord of a single harmony.' By augmenting the eight spheres (corresponding to sun, moon, five planets, and the fixed stars, as well as to the notes of the octave) with a ninth (the *primum mobile* or 'first mover'), Milton follows the neo-Platonic precedent

(see Wind 1967: pp. 265–9) of identifying Plato's 'Sirens' with the nine Muses. The theory behind this is expounded in his Latin prolusion (essay) 'On the music of the spheres' (Yale: I, 237). A further syncretism (as in Thomas Heywood's *Hierarchy of the Blessed Angels*, 1635) assimilated these in turn to the nine orders of angels: Seraphim (*primum mobile*), Cherubim (fixed stars), Thrones (Saturn), Dominations (Jupiter), Virtues (Mars), Powers (Sun), Principalities (Venus), Archangels (Mercury), and Angels (Moon).

135   *age of gold* the Golden Age, located by Hesiod during the reign of Zeus' father Cronos (Saturn). This Hellenic version of the myth of Eden was known in the Renaissance principally through Virgil's fourth ('messianic') Eclogue, often read as a prophecy of the coming of Christ and the restoration of the golden age.

141   *Truth and Justice* In his own version of Psalm 85 (which lies behind this passage), Milton preferred 'Justice' to the Authorized Version translation 'Righteousness' in verse 11: 'Truth from the earth like to a flower/Shall bud and blossom then,/And Justice from her heavenly bower/Look down on mortal men' (Carey, *CSP*: p. 314).

143   *enamell'd arras of the rainbow* the 1645 reading. Reprinting in 1673, Milton altered to 'Orb'd in a rainbow; and like glories wearing/Mercy will sit'. In *Comus*, 83, the Spirit wears 'sky-robes spun out of Iris' woof'.

144   *Mercy* cf. Milton's version of Psalm 85 (see 141n): 'Mercy and Truth that long were miss'd/Now joyfully are met.'

149   *wisest Fate says no* Without rejecting it altogether, this stanza distinguishes the classical Golden Age from the biblical apocalypse that follows, and avoids the full syncretism of identifying the two.

157   *horrid clang* The reference is to Exodus 19.16, where God announces himself on Mount Sinai with 'thunders and lightnings, and a thick cloud upon the

mount, and the voice of the trumpet exceeding loud'.
The description of the Last Judgement in Revelation
8–9 draws heavily on the Exodus imagery.

168   *Th'old dragon*   Revelation 12.9: 'And the great dra-
        gon was cast out, that old serpent, called the Devil,
        and Satan.'

169   *straiter*   narrower, tighter.

171   *wroth*   The wrath of the dragon at the birth of Christ
        comes from Revelation 12.17: 'And the dragon was
        wroth with the woman, and went to make war with
        the remnant of her seed.' In 12.4, 'his tail drew the
        third part of the stars of heaven', which Milton (*Para-
        dise Lost*, II, 692 and V, 710) identified with the rebel-
        lion in Heaven.

173   *The oracles are dumb*   The seven stanzas that follow
        describe the retreat of the pre-Christian deities of the
        Mediterranean world at the coming of Christ. Most
        of the gods are also found in *Paradise Lost*, I, 392–
        521.

175   *words deceiving*   because pagan; but also perhaps be-
        cause oracles like those at Delphi and Dodona always
        delivered their prophecies in a deliberately ambiguous
        and riddling form.

176   *shrine*   Apollo's temple and oracle was at Delphi, on
        the slopes of Mount Parnassus (the 'Delphian cliff' of
        Paradise Lost, I, 517).

186   *genius*   the local deity, as in *Lycidas*, 183.

191   *lars and lemures*   In Roman religion, lares were the
        spirits of ancestors, who protected the family home;
        lemures were malicious spirits like goblins.

194   *flamens*   Roman priests.

197   *Peor and Baalim*   an odd phrase. Peor was the moun-
        tain in Moab, east of the Dead Sea, where the priest
        Balaam built seven sacrificial altars to Baal-Peor
        (Numbers 23.28–30). Baal (plural Baalim) is a gener-
        ic term (meaning 'master') for a large number of
        Middle Eastern male deities, as Ashtareth (plural
        Ashtaroth) is for their female counterparts. The line
        probably means 'Baal-Peor and the other Baalim'.

199	*twice-batter'd god* Dagon, the god of the Philistines, whose idol they placed next to the ark of the covenant, where it was twice overturned and mutilated in the night (1 Samuel 4–5).
200	*Ashtaroth* See 197n. Ashtareth (the Syrian Astarte) was depicted as horned to symbolize the moon.
203	*Libyc Hammon* Zeus was worshipped in the form of a ram at Ammon in Libya.
204	*Tyrian* Phoenician, from Tyre, in modern Lebanon. *Thammuz* the Phoenician Adonis (see glossary), killed by a boar. His cult was associated with the annual flooding and discoloration of the river Adonis; cf. *Paradise Lost*, I, 450–2: 'While smooth Adonis from his native rock/Ran purple to the sea, supposed with blood/Of Thammuz yearly wounded.' cf. *Comus*, 1000.
205	*Moloch* a bull-headed deity whose idol at Rabbah, north-east of the Dead Sea, was a hollow shell in which children were roasted alive as a sacrifice. Milton always calls him a 'king', the literal meaning of his name.
212–13	*Isis and Orus ... Anubis ... Osiris* Egyptian deities. Orus, the sun-god, was the son of Isis; the dog-headed Anubis the son of Osiris. Isis herself was often represented, like Ashtareth, as horned, while Osiris, like Hammon and Moloch, had the cult-form of a horned animal; hence 'brutish gods'. cf. the allegorical reading of the Isis–Osiris legend in *Areopagitica*, p. 98.
214	*Memphian* in Memphis (modern Cairo).
217	*chest* like the 'ark' of 220, the box in which the image of the god was carried in religious ceremonies.
219	*timbrel'd anthems* hymns accompanied by tambourines.
226	*Typhon* Often confused or identified with Typhoeus, this gigantic serpent-monster, who appears in both Greek and Egyptian folklore, was the destroyer of Osiris.
227–8	*Our babe ... the damned crew* The 'snaky twine' of

Typhon (226) prepares for a comparison between the infant Christ and the young Hercules, who strangled two snakes in his cot.

234   *several*   separate.

236   *night-steeds*   the nocturnal equivalent of the 'sun's team' (19), Ovid's '*noctis equi*'. Milton supplies them with names in his Latin poem on the gunpowder plot, 'In quintum novembris' (Carey, *CSP*: p. 39).

240   *youngest-teemed*   newest-born. The star that appeared for the first time at the nativity.

241   *polish'd car*   shining chariot.

ON TIME, UPON THE CIRCUMCISION, AT A SOLEMN MUSIC

The date of composition of these three poems is not known; possibly 1633 (the Feast of the Circumcision is on New Year's Day). Metrically they are modelled closely on the *canzoni* and madrigals (poems consisting of one or more complex stanzas) of Petrarch and Tasso.

ON TIME

See the introductory note above.

2   *leaden-stepping*   the slow, mechanical movement of the lead counter-weight ('heavy plummet'), with a suggestion of 'leaden-footed'.

10   *self consum'd*   For this Shakespearean conceit, see *Comus*, 597 and note.

12   *individual*   either 'so close as to be indivisible' (the older sense) or 'separately to each of us' (the modern one, emerging in the seventeenth century). Both make sense; but Milton's known views on the theological question of general and particular resurrection suggest the later, individualistic sense.

UPON THE CIRCUMCISION

See the introductory note preceding the notes to 'On time'.

1	*Powers . . . Warriors* angels. See *Of Reformation*, 927n and 'Nativity', 131n.
2	*music and triumphant song* For the angels' song to the shepherds, see Luke 2.13–14 and 'Nativity', 85–100.
15	*love, or law* a real question – is the circumcision (itself foreshadowing the crucifixion) the culminating enactment of the Mosaic Law of the Old Testament, or the first instance of the 'Love' inaugurated in the New ('A new commandment I give unto you, That ye love one another', John 13.34)? The answer (line 16) is that it is both, but that Love predominates over Law, new over old.
17	*by rightful doom* the judgement of Adam and Eve, 'remediless' under the old Law.
21	*great covenant* not the Mosaic covenant, but the first commandment to obey (Genesis 2.16–17), which since the Fall 'we still (= continuously) transgress'.

AT A SOLEMN MUSIC

See the introductory note preceding the notes to 'On time'.

1	*Sirens* not the Homeric Sirens of *Comus*, 877–81, but the Platonic Sirens of Milton's second prolusion, 'On the music of the spheres' (Yale: I, pp. 234ff.). See 'Nativity', 131n.
	pledges probably 'children' (as in *Lycidas*, 107) rather than 'assurances'.
2	*Sphere-born* Modern editions often read 'borne'; but the Sirens, daughters of 'Heav'n's joy', may be born from the spheres (like Echo in *Comus*, 241), as well as carried on them. If the Sirens are identified with the Muses, as in the second Prolusion, Voice and Verse may correspond to Polyhymnia, muse of sacred song, and Euterpe, muse of lyric poetry, who are depicted alongside one another (and immediately below Urania, Milton's 'heavenly Muse') in Gaturius' *Practica Musice* (1496, reproduced in Wind 1967: plate 20).
6	*concent* harmony.
7	*sapphire-colour'd throne* Ezekiel (1.26) had a vision 'of

a throne, as the appearance of a sapphire stone', with God sitting on it.

14   *victorious palms*   traditional symbol of victory in the ancient world; but the salvationist context also points to Revelation 7.9, where the saved 'stood before the throne ... clothed with white robes, and palms in their hands'.

20   *Jarr'd against nature's chime*   As in 'Nativity', Greek and Hebrew cosmologies collaborate in a rich mythic texture without merging completely. Here the music of the spheres becomes inaudible as a result of the Fall. In *Paradise Lost*, IV, 680–8, Adam and Eve can hear 'celestial voices ... singing their great Creator'.

23   *diapason*   the full symphony of all the spheres (Greek: 'through everything').

L'ALLEGRO, IL PENSEROSO

Theories about the date of composition of the 'cheerful man' and his 'thoughtful' or melancholy *alter ego* range from 1629 to 1635 or even later.

L'ALLEGRO

See the introductory note, above.

2   *Cerberus*   See glossary.

3   *Stygian cave*   Virgil locates Cerberus' cave beside the river Styx (*Aeneid*, VI, 418).

5   *uncouth*   unknown.

6   *brooding Darkness*   Darkness has feathers and is associated with ravens ('raven down') in *Comus*, 251–2, but is female on that occasion.

7   *night-raven*   not a raven, in fact, but (probably) the night heron, whose scientific name, *Nycticorax*, means 'night-raven'.

8   *ebon*   black, as in *Comus*, 134.

10   *Cimmerian desert*   On his way to the underworld in *Odyssey*, XI, Odysseus passes through 'the city and

country of the Cimmerians', who live in a perpetual
mist and semi-darkness, unvisited by the sun.

12   *yclept* a Spenserian fake-archaism for 'called'.
      Euphrosyne literally 'cheerfulness', the name of one
      of the Graces. See glossary, and *Comus*, 986n.

15   *sister Graces* Thalia ('bountifulness') and Aglaia
      ('splendour').

17   *some sager* Actually Milton seems to have invented
      this variant of Euphrosyne's parentage.

18   *frolic* cheerful.

22   *fresh-blown* newly opened.

24   *buxom, blithe and debonair* obliging, cheerful, and
      graceful.

27   *cranks* jokes.

28   *becks* beckonings.

33   *trip it as ye go* The Graces were traditionally repre-
      sented dancing.

39   *with her* i.e. Liberty.

55   *hoar* white (with dew).

60   *state* the official progress of a monarch.

62   *dight* clothed.

67   *tells his tale* counts off his tally (of sheep).

75   *daisies pied* They come, like 'violets blue' (21), from
      the spring song at the end of Shakespeare's *Love's
      Labour's Lost*; but both were probably clichés by
      Shakespeare's time.

80   *cynosure* the pole star (see *Comus*, 341n); hence any-
      thing gazed at.

85   *messes* meal.

90   *tann'd* brown, like tanned leather.

94   *rebecks* fiddles (cf. *Areopagitica*, 286).

96   *chequer'd* dappled.

102   *fairy Mab* a mischievous nocturnal sprite, the subject
      of Mercutio's virtuoso fantasy in Shakespeare's *Romeo
      and Juliet*, I, iv, 53–94.

103   *She was pinch'd* i.e. the storyteller herself.

104   *Friar's lantern* the will-o'-the-wisp. The 'Friar' is
      Puck or Robin Goodfellow.

110   *lubber* clownish, clumsy.

113   *crop-full*   with full belly.
122   *Rain influence*   like stars (cf. 'Nativity', 71n).
132   *Jonson's learned sock*   The dramatist Ben Jonson was
        noted for his (largely self-acquired) classical learning.
        The sock is the light shoe worn by comic actors in
        the Roman theatre; hence 'comedy'. Tragic actors
        wore a more substantial boot, the 'buskin' of 'Penser-
        oso', 102.
136   *Lydian airs*   The Lydian mode was associated with
        relaxation, and in the *Republic* Plato prohibits its use
        as not conducive to virtue. See *Areopagitica*, 272n.

IL PENSEROSO

See the introductory note preceding the notes to 'L'Allegro'.

3   *bestead*   help, support.
10   *pensioners*   courtiers, dependants.
        Morpheus' train   the followers of the god of sleep and
        dreams.
13   *too bright*   The idea is developed in the description of
        God in *Paradise Lost*, III, 375–8: 'Fountain of light,
        thyself invisible/Amidst the glorious brightness
        where thou sitt'st/Thron'd inaccessible.'
18   *Prince Memnon's sister*   Memnon, king of Ethiopia
        and son of Eos (Aurora) the dawn-goddess, fought
        with the Trojans and was killed by Achilles. Homer
        calls him 'most beautiful' (*Odyssey*, XI, 552), but does
        not mention his sister Himera or Hemera, who
        appears in later versions of the Troy story.
19   *starr'd Ethiop queen*   Cassiopeia, queen of Ethiopia,
        who was 'stellified' (changed into a constellation of
        stars) for boasting of her beauty. In another version
        she was punished by Neptune for claiming that her
        daughter Andromeda was lovelier than the Nereids
        (the 'sea-nymphs' of line 21).
29   *woody Ida*   Mount Ida in central Crete, ancient home
        of Cronos (Saturn) and birthplace of Zeus (Jove).
31   *nun*   priestess.
35   *Cypress lawn*   black linen, a conflation of two
        Shakespearean images, 'Lawn as white as driven

snow,/Cypress black as e'er was crow' (*The Winter's Tale*, IV, iv, 215–16).

39   *commercing with the skies* looking only up to heaven.

53   *Guiding the fiery-wheeled throne* In Ezekiel's vision (Ezekiel 10.7–19) cherubim surrounded by fire transport the throne of God.

54   *The Cherub Contemplation* The Florentine neo-Platonist Giovanni Pico della Mirandola wrote that 'if we pass our time in the leisure of contemplation ... we shall be all ablaze with cherubic light' (*Oratio de Hominis Dignitate*, translated by E. L. Forbes, Chicago: 1948, p. 227).

59   *Cynthia* the moon. The moon-goddess Artemis and her twin brother Apollo were given the names Cynthia and Cynthius after the hill called Cynthus on their birthplace, the island of Delos.

73   *plat* plot of ground.

87   *outwatch the Bear* The constellation of Ursa Major, the Great Bear, never sets in northern latitudes. It was associated with immortality in the writings of the legendary Egyptian sage and magus Hermes Trismegistus ('thrice-great'). To 'outwatch the Bear' is to stay awake until sunrise, when the stars fade.

88   *unsphere* persuade it to leave the heavenly region where the 'bright aërial spirits live inspher'd' (*Comus*, 3) and revisit the earth.

93   *daemons* The Platonic concept of the 'daemon', a kind of natural spirit or genius, is developed in the apocryphal writings of Hermes Trismegistus (87n), where each element is said to have its own daemon.

99   *Thebes' or Pelops' line* the two great dynasties of Athenian tragedy, Laius, Oedipus, and Creon, kings of Thebes, and the descendants of Pelops, Agamemnon, Orestes, and Electra.

100   *tale of Troy* Plays about the Trojan campaign include Sophocles' *Ajax* and Euripides' *Hecuba*.

102   *buskin'd stage* tragic theatre (cf. 'L'Allegro', 132n).

104   *Musaeus* legendary poet-priest, son and pupil of Orpheus and reputed founder of Attic literature.

105   *Orpheus* cf. 'L'Allegro' for a parallel (but not quite

symmetrically placed) reference to the story of
Orpheus and Euridice.

110   *story of Cambuscan* Chaucer's unfinished *Squire's
Tale*.

120   *more is meant* In Spenserian allegory (which Spenser
himself called 'dark conceit') the deeper meanings are
concealed within a romantic narrative of 'tourneys
. . . and enchantments drear'.

123   *trick'd and frounc'd* dressed and coiffed.

124   *Attic boy* Cephalus, whom Eos, goddess of dawn,
fell in love with when she saw him hunting on
Mount Hymettus, north of Athens.

145   *consort* an instrumental ensemble; hence a mingling
of voices or sounds.

156   *pale* enclosure.

159   *storied windows* stained glass representing biblical
scenes.

170   *spell* read, understand.

'HOW SOON HATH TIME, THE SUBTLE THIEF OF YOUTH'

Presumably written in or soon after December 1631, when
Milton was 23.

5   *semblance* physical appearance. More than twenty
years later, in the *Second Defence*, Milton was still
claiming that 'though turned of forty, there is scarcely anyone who would not think me younger by nearly ten years'.

11   *lot* destiny. But even at this date, when Milton was
as close to Calvinist orthodoxy as he was ever to be,
he carefully avoids a fatalistic predestinarianism:
although his development corresponds 'in strictest
measure' to the outcome that time and the will of
heaven intend for him, it will come to fruition only
'if I have grace to use it so' (the colloquial 'have grace'
resonating with theological overtones).

14   *Taskmaster's eye* The wings of time (line 2) and the
all-seeing eye of God recall the powerful Renaissance

icon of the winged eye discussed by Wind (1967: pp. 231–5) as a symbol of divine omniscience.

'CAPTAIN OR COLONEL OR KNIGHT IN ARMS'

After the battle of Edgehill in October 1642, the king's army moved south towards London. Rejecting offers of negotiation at Reading and Colnbrook, the royalists seized Brentford in Middlesex and moved on the capital. At Turnham Green, on the western outskirts of London, they were met and turned back by the parliamentary militia, and the king withdrew to Oxford. The sonnet, which in the Trinity manuscript has the heading 'When the assault was intended to the City 1642', was presumably written sometime between Reading and Turnham Green, when the royalist threat was at its height.

5   *charms* in the sense of Latin *carmina*, songs, verses.
10   *Emathian conqueror* Alexander the Great (Emathia was a province of Macedonia). During the sack of Thebes in 335 BC he ordered that the house in which the poet Pindar had been born should not be damaged.
12   *repeated air* recited poetry. 'Electra's poet' is Euripides. A chorus from his *Electra*, recited at a banquet by a minstrel, is said to have so moved the Spartan conquerors of Athens in 404 BC that they decided to spare the city.

'A BOOK WAS WRIT OF LATE CALL'D TETRACHORDON'

Date of composition not known, but obviously some time after March 1645. Printed in the 1673 *Poems*.

1   *Tetrachordon* Published in March 1645, this was the third of Milton's four divorce pamphlets. The title, which is the subject of this humorous sonnet, is a Greek word meaning a four-stringed instrument or chord of four notes. The pamphlet is a 'harmony' (see *Areopagitica*, p. 96) of 'the four chief places in scripture which treat of marriage or nullities in marriage'.

4	*Numb'ring* enlisting.
7	*spelling false* mispronouncing or misconstruing.
7–8	*Mile-End Green* a mile from Aldgate on the east road out of London.
8–9	*Gordon, Colkitto, or Macdonnel, or Galasp* (= Gillespie) taken as typical Scottish names, i.e. barbaric and unpronounceable. George Gillespie was a leading Presbyterian and supporter of the Solemn League and Covenant. George Gordon and Alexander Macdonald (also known as Colkitto) were anti-covenanting royalists.
11	*Quintilian* the Greek rhetorician, who discusses foreign names and words as examples of linguistic barbarism.
12	*Sir John Cheke* Professor of Greek in Cambridge at the time of the Reformation, and tutor to Edward VI. In *Tetrachordon* Milton mentions him as 'a man at that time counted the learnedest of Englishmen, and for piety not inferior' (Yale: II, p. 716). The construction, slightly elliptical, means: 'your age did not, as ours does, hate learning ...'; and the sardonic point is that people who have no difficulty with the 'rugged names' of Scots generals and covenanters can no longer understand a simple and euphonious Greek word like *tetrachordon*.

'HARRY, WHOSE TUNEFUL AND WELL-MEASUR'D SONG'

This sonnet, dated 'Feb. 9 1645' (i.e. 1646) in the manuscript, was printed in Henry Lawes's *Choice Psalmes* (1648), a collection commemorating the death of Lawes's brother William at the battle of Chester. Lawes, who collaborated with Milton on *Arcades* and the Ludlow masque, was court composer to Charles I, and in spite of his friendship with Milton he remained a royalist. The *Psalmes* were dedicated to the king, and in 1660 he composed Charles II's coronation anthem. He died in 1662, and was buried in Westminster Abbey.

4	*Midas' ears* Midas umpired a musical contest between Pan and Apollo, and, when he gave the prize to Pan, Apollo changed his ears to an ass's.

committing bringing into conflict; that is, setting short syllables to long notes or phrases, and vice versa.

12–13 *Dante ... Casella* At the entrance to Purgatory (*Purgatorio*, II) Dante meets his friend the musician Casella, and persuades him to sing a setting of one of his (Dante's) *canzoni*.

'FAIRFAX, WHOSE NAME IN ARMS THROUGH EUROPE RINGS'

Probably written in August 1648, but not published in Milton's lifetime. Sir Thomas Fairfax was commander-in-chief of the New Model Army, and Milton was not alone in 1648 in hoping that he might play a leading part in government when the Civil War was over. But he distanced himself from the Independents in army and Parliament, withdrew from the commission trying Charles I, moved to suppress leveller radicalism in the regiments in 1649, and retired in the summer of 1650 to his estate in Yorkshire (where he hired Andrew Marvell as a tutor for his daughter Mary).

6 *new rebellions* In the summer of 1648 there were royalist insurrections in Wales, Essex, Lancashire, and Kent. Cromwell's regiments put down the uprisings in west and north, while Fairfax defeated the Kentish insurgents at Maidstone before moving north to blockade Colchester. The town surrendered on 27 August.

7 *false North* A Scottish army under the Duke of Hamilton marched south in July 1648 with the intention of helping the English royalists, in breach of the covenant between the two countries.

8 *imp* to repair a falcon's wing by grafting new feathers into it.

12–13 *public faith ... public fraud* In a digression from the account of Saxon Britain in Book III of the *History* (probably written in the early summer of 1648 but not published until after his death as the *Character of the Long Parliament*) Milton elaborated this charge against the financial dishonesty and incompetence of Parliament: 'for that faith which ought to have been kept as sacred and inviolable as any thing holy, the public faith, after infinite sums received and all the wealth of the church not better employed but swallowed up into a private gulf, was not ere long ashamed to confess bankrupt' (Yale: V, p. 444).

THE TENURE OF KINGS AND MAGISTRATES

Published in February 1649. Charles I was executed on 29 January, after a trial lasting a week (20–27 January). The Yale editor (III, p. 103) concludes that the writing of the *Tenure* 'may have begun not many days, one way or the other, from the opening of the trial'.

61   *Claudius Sesell* Claude de Seissel (1450–1520), lawyer and adviser to Louis XI. In his *Grand Monarchie de France* (1519) he wrote of 'three bridles ... by which the supreme power of kings is restrained: religion, law and the state'. Law he identified with *parlements*.

93   *the Jews* The passage reads: 'O Lord our God, other lords beside thee have had dominion over us: but by thee only will we make mention of thy name.' That is, they will only use the word 'Lord' of God himself.

94–5   *Tertullian* Quintus Septimus Tertullianus, north African theologian and a father of the early church (155–222).

130   *pagan Caesars* The Roman emperors were deified at their death.

141   *fifty-first Psalm* Hobbes (*Leviathan*, chapter 12) interpreted Psalm 51.4 in exactly the sense that Milton here calls 'absurd', as providing biblical authority for the absolutist theory that kings are not bound by secular law.

156   *tragedy of Euripides* the *Heracleidai* ('Children of Hercules'), lines 423–4.

159   *Trajan* The story is from Dio Cassius' *Roman History*, LXVIII, 16; but it was given wide circulation by

George Buchanan's *History of Scotland* (1582). At the coronation of James VI of Scotland, later James I of England, a medal was struck depicting a sword and bearing the words '*Si mereor in me*' ('Against me if I should deserve it').

170   *Justinian* Flavius Anicius Justinianus (483–565), Emperor of the East, remembered for his *Corpus Juris Civilis*, the basic textbook of Roman law, which codified the statutes of predecessors like Theodosius II (401–50).

197   *economize* administer.

205   *abrogated* rejected, annulled.

214–15 *not mortal man ... but Justice* cf. the similarly Platonic formulation in *Reformation*, 640: ''Tis not the common law, nor the civil, but piety and justice that are our foundresses.'

243   *pismires* ants.

255   *wrested laws and scriptures* cf. *Reformation*, 282: 'wrenching and spraining the text'.

259   *discover* reveal, expose.

264–5 *old and perfect enemy* The phrase makes Charles I sound ominously like the 'old enemy' Satan.

273   *Stories can inform them* These examples of the treachery and brutality of kings come from historical sources like Buchanan's *History of Scotland* and from recent memory. The massacre of Parisian Protestants by Charles IX and the Duke of Guise on St Bartholomew's Eve 1572 was the subject of a play by Marlowe. The Neapolitan revolution had been suppressed by the Spanish only a few months before Milton was writing.

292   *David* See 1 Samuel 26–27.

316   *sidesmen* supporters.

323   *pluralities* the holding of more than one living by a clergyman, widely practised in the Anglican Church and by some Presbyterians: with tithes, a major focus of Puritan critique.
       simony See *Reformation*, 734n.

329   *progging* prodding, nagging.

331   *tithes*   See *Reformation*, 832n.

332   *oblations*   gifts for devotional purposes; applied espe-
        cially to the bread and wine used in the eucharist,
        supplied by lay parishioners.

338   *presumptuous Sion*   Sion College was from 1647 until
        the Restoration the headquarters of the Presbyterian
        Assembly.

345–6   *great characters and little moment*   large letters and small
        substance.

356   *curse ye, Meroz*   Judges 5.23: 'Curse ye Meroz, said
        the angel of the Lord, curse ye bitterly the inhabitants
        thereof; because they came not to the help of the
        Lord, to the help of the Lord against the mighty.'
        This passage, which even more than most can be
        applied to practically any occasion, was one of the
        most popular sermon-texts on all sides during the
        Civil War.

'CROMWELL, OUR CHIEF OF MEN, WHO THROUGH
A CLOUD'

Not printed in Milton's lifetime (it was first published with his
1694 *Letters of State*), this sonnet appears in the Trinity manuscript with the heading 'To the Lord General Cromwell, May
1652. On the proposals of certain ministers at the Committee
for the Propagation of the Gospel.' In February 1652 a group of
Independent ministers led by John Owen proposed the establishment of a state church with a salaried clergy. Cromwell was
a member of the Parliamentary Committee for the Propagation
of the Gospel, and the sonnet urges him not to return to the
'secular chains' of an established church.

5   *crowned fortune*   Charles I and his son.

7   *Darwen stream*   The Darwen runs close to the battle-
        field of Preston, where the New Model Army routed
        Hamilton's Scots forces in August 1648.

8   *Dunbar*   Another of Cromwell's victories over the
        Scots, in September 1650.

9   *Worcester*   The battle of Worcester in September 1651
        finally destroyed any hope of a royalist counter-coup.

14   *hireling wolves*   'Hirelings' is Milton's standard term for beneficed clergy; and 'wolves', which in 1637 had denoted the Roman Catholic Church (see *Lycidas*, 128n), is here broadened to include all greedy and careerist clerics.

'WHEN I CONSIDER HOW MY LIGHT IS SPENT'

Published in the 1673 *Poems*. The date of composition is un-known, but is presumably after Milton's blindness became total in 1652. 'Ere half my days' is not much help: Milton was 43 in 1652. But his father had lived until well into his 80s, and he may have expected to do the same.

2   *half my days*   Milton was completely blind by the spring of 1652, when he was 44.

3   *one talent*   In the parable of the talents (Matthew 25.14–30), the servant who received only one talent (glossed in the Authorized Version as £187), instead of investing and increasing it like the others, hid it in the earth, and was 'cast into outer darkness' as a punishment.

4   *useless*   Perhaps, continuing the financial imagery of the talent, a pun on use = investment; the metaphor is sustained in 'true account' (6).

12   *Thousands at his bidding*   The distinction between the thousands who 'speed' and the others, perhaps fewer, who 'stand and wait' has been thought to refer to the angels, the highest orders of whom were supposed to wait in the presence of God, like the 'bright-harness'd angels' who sit 'in order serviceable' about the 'court-ly stable' (cf. 'His state/Is kingly') in the last stanza of 'Nativity'. Angel means 'messenger'.

ON THE LATE MASSACRE IN PIEDMONT

The Waldenses (Vaudois), whom Milton regarded as 'our first reformers', were followers of a religious sect founded in Lyons in the twelfth century by Peter Waldo (Pierre de Vaux). They established themselves in parts of Switzerland and in the Alps in Savoie and Piedmont in north-eastern Italy. Milton had already studied them in Pierre Gilles's *Ecclesiastical History* (1644). In the spring of 1655 the Duke of Savoy sent an army to drive them out of Piedmont, and almost two thousand of the Vaudois were killed. But they fought back, and a peace treaty that August, brought about by diplomatic pressure from England and elsewhere, restored the status quo (Milton handled the diplomatic correspondence). The sonnet was presumably written between April and June 1655, and was published in the 1673 *Poems*.

4   *worshipp'd stocks and stones* Milton regarded the Vaudois, whose sect dates from the twelfth century, as Protestants before the Reformation. Pre-Reformation England is compared to those Israelites condemned by Jeremiah (2.27, 3.9) for 'saying to a stock, Thou art my father; and to a stone, Thou hast brought me forth' and for committing 'adultery [i.e. idolatry] with stones and with stocks'.

12   *triple tyrant* the Pope, from his three-tiered crown.

14   *Babylonian woe* Revelation 17–18.

'METHOUGHT I SAW MY LATE ESPOUSED SAINT'

The date of composition of this sonnet is not known. Milton's second wife Katherine Woodcock died on 3 February 1658. It was published in 1673.

2   *Alcestis* She offered to die in place of her husband Admetus, but was rescued from Death by Hercules. The story is the subject of Euripides' *Alcestis*, in which Admetus calls Hercules 'great Zeus' son' (1136).

5   *wash'd* Like 'Purification' (6) and 'pure as her mind' (9), this may be a punning allusion to the name Katherine, from Greek *katharos* = pure, clean.

6   *th'old Law* The 'laws of purification and atonement' in Leviticus stipulate that after giving birth to a girl child a woman 'shall be unclean two weeks ... and she shall continue in the blood of her purifying

threescore and six days' (12.5). Katherine Milton died in February 1658, three months after the birth of her daughter Katherine. The child herself died six weeks later.

7–8   *I trust to have/Full sight of her*   Milton had been completely blind for over four years when he married Katherine Woodcock in November 1656.

THE READY AND EASY WAY TO ESTABLISH A FREE COMMONWEALTH

Oliver Cromwell, Lord Protector, died in September 1658. The protectorate, which passed on his death to his son Richard, was hijacked the following spring by a group of republican army officers, then abolished in May by the recalled Rump Parliament. Relations between army and Parliament, as bad as they had been in the 1640s, went downhill over the summer, and in October the army ejected the Rump once more. In the same month the Rota Club began to meet in a Westminster coffee-house to debate republican solutions to the political crisis. Meanwhile George Monck, commander-in-chief of the Scottish army, was moving south to support the ejected Parliament, enlisting help on the way from Fairfax and other north country landowners. Towards the end of the year Milton drafted his 'Proposals of certain expedients for the preventing of a civil war' (Yale: VII, pp. 334–9), arguing that the Rump should be reinstated as a perpetual Grand Council on the Venetian model. By the time he had argued the proposal more fully in the first edition of *The Ready and Easy Way* (late February 1660), Monck had forcibly restored the excluded Presbyterian members purged from the Long Parliament twelve years before, thus virtually ensuring the restoration of Charles II. Appointed commander-in-chief of the whole army, Monck purged the regiments of republicans and sectaries and presided over a new Council of State with a Presbyterian and pro-monarchist majority. By the end of March elections were being held, the first for twenty years, and in May the new Parliament invited the king to return. In April 1660, with the Good Old Cause in ruins around him, Milton brought out a second edition of *The Ready and Easy Way*, from which these extracts are taken.

18–19 *ambitious leaders in the army* major-generals Lambert and Fleetwood, who ejected the Rump Parliament in October 1659.

20–1 *other commanders* especially George Monck, who supported the Rump.

48 *not transferred but delegated* a rephrasing of *Tenure*, p. 128: 'the power of kings and magistrates is nothing else but what is only derivative, transferred and committed to them in trust from the people ... in whom the power yet remains fundamentally'.

71 *ship of the Commonwealth* cf. *Reformation*, 533n.

101 *'partial rotation'* The rotation of assemblies is a key argument of James Harrington's utopian *Oceana* (1656), though he does not actually use this phrase. Between October 1659 and February 1660 Harrington and Henry Neville convened a political society called the Rota, which met regularly at Miles's coffee-house in Covent Garden.

132 *Sanhedrim* the ancient Jewish assembly, first instituted by Moses in Numbers 11.16.

133 *Areopagus* See *Areopagitica*, note on title, p. 220.

136 *Venice* in many ways a model state for seventeenth-century republicans; but see 298n.

183 *Marius* The struggle between the populist Gaius Marius (157–86 BC) and his erstwhile lieutenant and protégé Lucius Cornelius Sulla led to the first civil war in Rome, culminating in Sulla's military dictatorship. The title-page of the second edition of *The Ready and Easy Way* carries the epigraph, adapted from Juvenal, '*Et nos/consilium dedimus Syllae, demus populo nunc*' (We have given advice to Sulla, let us now give it to the people'). Sulla in this sardonic reference has been identified with Cromwell; but it is more likely that Milton is thinking of General Monck, ambitious, and ambiguous, friend of the Rump. (See Yale: VII, p. 406.)

198–9   *sit . . . lieger*   sit as a representative or agent.

200–1   *bean or ballot*   The Athenian assembly voted with beans, the Roman with wooden tickets or 'ballots'.

211   *Tarquins*   kings of Rome in the sixth century BC, eventually thrown out by a popular uprising led by Junius Brutus.

288   *agrarian law*   The cornerstone of the society described in Harrington's *Oceana* is a law limiting the size of estates and inherited wealth, and thus distributing land and money more evenly among the landowning class.

298   *someone or other*   probably Monck, who was suspected of harbouring the ambition to be 'something like a Duke of Venice'.

302   *Nassau*   one of the family names of the house of Orange, stadtholders (regents) of the Netherlands. William III, later king of England, was stadtholder in 1660, but had been excluded from office by De Wit's republican States Party. The French ambassador to London remarked that General Monck was said to aspire to 'a post similar to that held by the Prince of Orange' (i.e. a constitutional monarchy). See Yale: VII, p. 182.

326–7   *idol queen*   the 'queen of heaven' to whom the Israelites in Egypt 'burned incense and poured out drink offerings' in Jeremiah 44.17–19.

348–9   *'the Good Old Cause'*   Already a catch-phrase, this broad term was used by a wide range of leveller, republican, and dissenting groups in the 1640s and 1650s. Henry Vane, close to Milton politically, defined it, with useful vagueness, as 'just natural rights in civil things, and true freedom in matters of conscience' (*A Healing Question*, 1656). It was often invoked, as here, to unite the fragmented opposition of army, Parliament and independency by appealing to shared memories of struggle and a common purpose.

353   *the Prophet*   Jeremiah 22.29.

361   *raise of these stones*   Matthew 3.9, where John the Baptist reproaches the Jewish elders for boasting of

their ancient traditions, and reminds them 'that God is able of these stones to raise up children unto Abraham'.

371   *precipice of destruction*   perhaps recalling the 'steep place' down which the Gadarene swine rushed headlong to their destruction (Matthew 8.32).

'CYRIACK, WHOSE GRANDSIRE ON THE ROYAL BENCH'

Probably written in the mid-1650s (line 8 refers to the military and diplomatic manoeuvres of the major Protestant and Catholic powers in the aftermath of the Thirty Years War), this sonnet was not printed until 1673. Cyriack Skinner (1627–1700) had been Milton's pupil in the 1640s, and remained a close friend. A republican, he chaired the Rota meetings in 1659–60 (see p. 250).

1   *grandsire*   Skinner's maternal grandfather was Sir Edward Coke (1552–1634), jurist and legal historian, James I's Chief Justice on 'the royal bench/Of British Themis') and lifelong opponent of ecclesiastical and royal prerogative.

2   *Themis*   Roman goddess of justice.

3   *volumes*   Coke's *Institutes* (1628) are one of the cornerstones of English legal practice.

7   *Euclid ... Archimedes*   that is, put aside your studies in geometry and physics.

8   *Swede ... French*   probably a reference to the aggressive foreign policy of Charles X of Sweden and the French foreign minister Cardinal Mazarin in 1655.

'CYRIACK, THIS THREE YEARS' DAY THESE EYES, THOUGH CLEAR'

Like the last, this sonnet, though not printed (in the posthumous *Letters of State*) until 1694, was probably written in the mid-1650s (Milton had become totally blind by 1952).

1–2   *clear ... of blemish or of spot*   In the *Second Defence* Milton claimed that the only deceit he had been guilty of was that his eyes appeared externally healthy.

10   *conscience* consciousness.

11   *Liberty's defence* the writing of the first and second
        Defences (1651 and 1654), which Milton believed had
        cost him his eyesight.

13   *mask* i.e. masque; but the spelling retains the secon-
        dary sense of 'disguise', 'empty sham'.

Glossary of classical names

Acheron One of the six rivers of the Greek underworld. The others are Styx, Lethe, Phlegethon, Cocytus, and Avernus. *Com*, 604.

Adonis A youth loved by Aphrodite, killed by a boar while hunting. At her request, he was permitted to return to life and spend part of each year with her. A vegetation and fertility god, his name derives from the Semitic *adon*, 'lord'. A Greek counterpart of the Asiatic Thammuz, with cults throughout the Near East. *Com*, 999; 'Nat', 204n.

Aeolus Greek god of the winds, which he kept in a cave. Milton coined the patronymic 'Hippotades', from his father Hippotes. *Lyc*, 96n.

Alpheus A river in southern Greece, believed to pass unmixed through the sea and emerge in the fountain Arethusa in Sicily. *Lyc*, 132.

Ambrosia The food of the gods, an incorruptible substance also used to anoint the body. Hence ambrosial = immortal. *Com*, 16, 840.

Amphitrite A Nereid, or sea-goddess; daughter of Nereus, and mother of Triton. *Com*, 921.

Anchises Father of the Trojan hero Aeneas, he accompanied his son from Troy to Italy. *Com*, 923.

Aphrodite Greek goddess of sexuality and fertility, one of the forms of the Asiatic and Near-Eastern *Magna Dea* (see Ashtareth). Identified with the Roman Venus, as her son Eros (= Love) is with Cupid. *Com*, 138n.

Apollo   Greek god of prophecy, music, poetry, the sun, twin brother of Artemis-Diana and father of the nine Muses. Often called Phoebus (= bright). *Com*, 428, 662; *Lyc*, 1n, 104n; 'Nat', 103n, 176n.

Arcadia   Mountainous kingdom in southern Greece. Regarded by the Greeks as a primitive and barbaric region, it was envisaged by later writers as an idyllic, unspoilt country inhabited by musical shepherds. *Com*, 341.

Ares   Greek god of war, the Roman Mars. *Com*, 138n.

Arethusa   A fountain and stream near Syracuse in Sicily, depicted as a nymph pursued by the river-god Alpheus (q.v.). *Lyc*, 85, 133n.

Arion   Semi-legendary poet-singer of the seventh century BC. Sailing from Greece to Italy he was attacked by the crew of the boat, and escaped by jumping overboard. A dolphin, attracted by his singing, carried him safely to land. *Lyc*, 164n.

Artemis   Greek virgin-goddess of the moon, often represented as a hunter. She and her twin brother Apollo were born on Mount Cynthus on the island of Delos, from which she is sometimes called Cynthia. Identified with the Roman Diana. 'Nat', 103n.

Astarte   The Phoenician equivalent of the Greek Aphrodite and the Asiatic Ashtareth, though with some of the attributes of Artemis (a moon-goddess) and Hecate (withcraft). *Com*, 1002n; 'Nat', 200n.

Atropos   One of the three Fates (q.v.). The name, from Hesiod, means 'implacable'. *Lyc*, 75n.

Aurora   Roman goddess of the dawn, the Greek Eos; described by Homer as 'rosy-fingered'. *Com*, 139; 'L'All', 19.

Bacchus   Graeco-Roman god of wine, drunkenness, and carnival, often identified with Dionysus. His female worshippers were called Bacchantes or Maenads (see **Orpheus**). *Com*, 46; *Lyc*, 1n, 58n; 'L'All', 16.

Cacus   Monstrous son of Vulcan, killed by Hercules, who caught him stealing cattle. *Com*, 655n.

Cerberus   The ferocious many-headed dog that guarded the entrance to the underworld in Greek folklore. 'L'All', 2.

Chaos   In Hesiod's *Theogony* ('Birth of the Gods'), the void that first appeared at the creation of the world, parent of Erebus (darkness) and Nyx (night). *Com*, 334, 581n.

Charybdis A Homeric sea-monster, narrowly avoided by Odysseus. In reality probably a whirlpool in the straits of Messina, between Italy and Sicily. *Com*, 259, cf. Scylla.

Chimera A monstrous fire-breathing creature with the fore-parts of a lion, the body of a goat, and the tail of a serpent (or, in some versions, the heads of all three). *Com*, 517.

Circe Homeric enchantress who turned Odysseus' companions into pigs. He himself was protected by the magical herb Moly, given to him by Hermes. *Com*, 50, 153, 253, 522, 816n.

Cotytto Thracian goddess associated with baptismal and orgiastic rites. *Com*, 129.

Cronos Father of the Olympian gods (Zeus, Ares, Aphrodite, Hera, Hephaistos), he was killed by his son Zeus. Assimilated to the Roman Saturn. 'Nat', 135n.

Cupid Son of Venus, generally represented as a child, blind or blindfold and carrying a bow and arrows. Roman equivalent of the Greek Eros. *Com*, 124, 445, 1004.

Cynosure Literally 'dog's tail', a Greek name for the pole star. *Com*, 342; 'L'All', 80.

Daphne Pursued by Apollo, this nymph escaped by being transformed into a laurel tree. *Com*, 661, 826n.

Diana Graeco-Roman virgin goddess of hunting, closely associated with the moon, and often identified with Artemis. Twin sister of Apollo. *Com*, 441.

Dis Roman god of the underworld, counterpart of the Greek Hades.

Dryads Wood-nymphs, living in trees (Greek *drus* = oak tree; cf. 'Druid'). *Com*, 120, 964.

Echo A nymph whose endless chatter so irritated Hera that she cut out her tongue, with the result that she could only repeat the words of others. In another version she pined away with love for the unresponsive Narcissus, until only her voice remained. *Com*, 230.

Elysium The Homeric afterworld of demigods and heroes, located sometimes in the sky, sometimes beyond the Atlantic 'river' and the setting sun. *Com*, 257, 979, 996; *Lyc*, 174n; 'L'All', 147.

Eos See **Aurora**.

Erebus Darkness, one of the sons of Chaos (q.v.). *Com*, 581n, 804.

Eros See **Aphrodite**.

Fates The Greek *moirai*, Latin *parcae*, three female deities who preside over all human life; usually represented as spinners, carding, spinning, and cutting the thread of life. Hesiod named them Clotho ('spinner'), Lachesis ('caster of lots'), and Atropos ('implacable'). *Lyc*, 75n.

Fauns Roman rural deities, like the Greek satyrs half-human, half-goat. Followers of Bacchus and Pan. *Lyc*, 34.

Furies Female deities who pursued and punished crimes against kinship. Orestes, followed and driven mad by the Furies for the killing of his mother Clytemnestra, was eventually pardoned through the intervention of Athene, who renamed them Eumenides, 'kindly ones'. *Com*, 641; *Lyc*, 75.

Glaucus Immortalized by a magic herb, he became a sea-god, noted for his prophetic powers. *Com*, 826n, 874.

Gorgon Daughter of the sea-gods Phorcys and Ceto, a monster with snakes for hair and a face that turned all living things to stone. Also called Medusa, she was eventually killed by Perseus with the help of Athene, who carried her head on her shield. *Com*, 447.

Graces Three goddesses closely associated with Aphrodite, symbolizing hospitality, and magnanimity. Hesiod calls them Euphrosyne ('cheerfulness'), Aglaia ('splendour'), and Thalia ('generosity'). Usually represented dancing in a ring. *Com*, 986; *Lyc*, 1n; 'L'All', 15.

Hades Brother of Zeus, god of the underworld. *Com*, 20n, 518, 581; 'L'All', 149.

Harpies Winged goddesses associated with sudden deaths and disappearances. Originally wind-spirits, their name means 'snatchers'. *Com*, 605; *Ref*, 230.

Hebe Cupbearer of the Olympian gods. Her name means 'youth'. *Com*, 290; 'L'All', 29.

Hebrus River in Thrace (north-eastern Greece), modern Evros. *Lyc*, 63.

Hecate Graeco-Roman moon-goddess with three forms ('triple Hecat'), corresponding to sky, earth, and underworld. Associated with crossroads, witchcraft, and child-birth, she is probably a diminished survival of an ancient primary female deity. *Com*, 135, 535.

Helen Daughter of Zeus and Leda, wife of Menelaus, her affair with Paris was responsible for the Trojan War, the subject of Homer's *Iliad*. After the war she spent some time in Egypt before returning to her husband. *Com*, 676.

Hercules Roman form of the Greek Herakles, son of Zeus, a 'hero' or demigod of great physical strength. As a baby he strangled two huge snakes sent by Hera to destroy him, and later performed twelve impossible tasks (the 'labours of Hercules') including picking the golden apples of the Hesperides (q.v.). *Com*, 655n; *Areo*, 430; 'Nat', 227n.

Hermes Greek messenger of the gods, the Roman Mercury, often depicted with winged ankles and a 'caduceus', a rod with a snake coiled around it, as well as a distinctive pointed hat. To the Florentine humanists he symbolized reason and good sense, but he was also the god of thieves.

Hesperides The three daughters of Hesperus, who lived in an orchard of golden apples guarded by an unsleeping dragon. Hercules stole the fruit as one of his twelve labours. *Com*, 393, 982.

Hesperus The evening star (Latin Vesper), personified as the father of the Hesperides, whose golden apples symbolize the stars. *Com*, 93n, 982; *Lyc*, 30.

Hippotades See **Aeolus**.

Hours Greek goddesses of the seasons. Hesiod makes them daughters of Justice, and gives them ethical-symbolic names, Dike (fairness), Eunomia (order), and Eirene (peace); but the association with the seasons persisted into the Renaissance. Botticelli's *Primavera*, the 'spruce and jocund Spring', is one of the Hours. *Com*, 986.

Hyacinthus Apollo loved him, and accidentally killed him with a discus-throw. He was transformed into a flower (not the modern hyacinth; probably a kind of iris or orchid), and the god's tears marked the leaves and flower with the word AIAI ('alas'). *Lyc*, 104n.

Hydra A many-headed monster which grew two new heads in place of every one cut off. Eventually destroyed by Hercules. *Com*, 605; *Ref*, 585.

Hymen Graeco-Roman god of marriage, usually depicted in a saffron robe and carrying candles. 'L'All', 125.

Ino See **Leucothea**.

Iris The rainbow, personified as the messenger of the gods. *Com*, 83, 992; 'Nat', 143n.

Jove Generic name, derived from Latin Jupiter, for the leading patriarchal deity (cf. Jehovah, Jahveh) of Greek, Roman, and Judaeo-Christian cosmologies. See **Zeus**. *Com*, 20, 78, 676, 803; *Lyc*, 16, 82; 'Pens', 30, 48.

Juno Roman goddess of marriage and domestic life, wife of Jupiter. More matronly and less vindictive than her Greek counterpart Hera. *Com*, 701.

Lesbos Island in the north-east Aegean, birthplace of the semi-legendary poet Sappho, whose reputed homosexuality gives us the word 'lesbian'. *Lyc*, 63.

Leucothea Ino, daughter of Cadmus and sister of Semele, in a frenzy, leapt into the sea with her son Melicertes to rescue him from the murderous fury of his father, Athamas, whereupon she was transformed into a sea-goddess and lived with the Nereids. Homer's name for her, Leucothea, means 'white goddess'. See **Melicertes**. *Com*, 875.

Ligea One of the Sirens (q.v.). *Com*, 880.

Marsyas Apollo had him skinned alive for boasting that he was a finer singer than the god. *Lyc*, 1n.

Meander River in Phrygia (southern Turkey), supposedly named after a king who drowned himself after accidentally killing his own son. Its winding course provides the word 'meander'. *Com*, 232.

Melicertes Younger son of Ino (see **Leucothea**), who like his mother was transformed into a minor local deity, worshipped by sailors as Palaemon (Greek) or Portunus (Roman). *Com*, 826n, 876; *Lyc*, 164n, 183n.

Memnon Ethiopian prince who fought with the Trojans. His beauty is mentioned by Homer. 'Pens', 18.

Menelaus King of Mycenae, brother of Agamemnon and husband of Helen, whose elopement with the Trojan prince Paris led to the Trojan war. *Com*, 675n.

Mercury Roman counterpart of the Greek Hermes, messenger of the gods. *Com*, 963.

Mincius River in north-eastern Italy, running into the Po just

261

south of Mantua, birthplace of the Roman poet Virgil. *Lyc*, 86.

Minerva   Roman goddess with the warlike and intellectual attributes of her Greek counterpart Athene. *Com*, 448.

Moly   The magic herb with a white or yellow blossom which Hermes gives to Odysseus to protect him against the enchantments of Circe. *Com*, 636.

Muses   Nine daughters of Apollo (q.v.), each responsible for a particular artistic or intellectual domain. *Lyc*, 15, 19, 58; 'Nat', 15, 131n; 'Sol Mus', 2n; 'Pens', 47.

Naiads   Water-nymphs, living in streams. cf. **Dryads**. *Com*, 254, 833.

Narcissus   Loved by the nymph Echo (q.v.), he ignored her but fell in love with his own image in a pool. Trying to embrace it, he fell in, drowned, and was transformed into a flower. *Com*, 237.

Nectar   The drink of the gods. cf. **Ambrosia**. *Lyc*, 175.

Nepenthes   A narcotic drug given to Helen during her stay in Egypt. See **Thone**. The name means 'painless'. *Com*, 675.

Neptune   Roman god of the sea, counterpart of the Greek Poseidon. *Com*, 18, 20n, 869; *Lyc*, 90.

Nereids   Sea-goddesses, daughters of Nereus and Doris. There were fifty of them. *Com*, 837, 875n; *Lyc*, 99.

Nereus   Greek sea-deity, father of the Nereids. *Com*, 835, 871.

Nymphs   Supernatural creatures like fairies, of three principal kinds: Oreads (mountains), Dryads (woodland), and Naiads (streams). The word is often used generically or unspecified female deities or nature-spirits. *Com*, 120, 254, 422, 833, 964; *Lyc*, 50; 'Nat', 188; 'L'All', 36.

Oceanus   The Homeric world was encircled by a great river called Oceanus, of which the Atlantic ocean was thought to be the western part. *Com*, 868.

Orpheus   Legendary Thracian poet and musician, son of the muse Calliope, he followed his wife Eurydice to the underworld, and would have brought her back to life if he had not disobeyed Pluto, god of death, and looked at her face. His music could charm wild animals and animate the rocks and trees, but was unable to placate the Maenads, female votaries of Dionysus (see **Bacchus**), who killed and dismembered him. *Lyc*, 58; 'L'All', 145; 'Pens', 105.

Osiris Egyptian god of death, rebirth, and the underworld, his dismemberment by his brother Typhon probably symbolizes the division of the Nile into the myriad channels of the delta. His cult, together with that of his consort Isis, spread widely throughout the Mediterranean world, and later through the Roman Empire. *Areo*, 512; 'Nat', 213.

Pan Greek god of shepherds and goatherds, himself half-goat. His name was thought to derive from the Greek word *pan*, 'everything'. In some syncretic traditions (combinations of pagan and Christian myth) he was said to have died at the birth of Christ, in others to be identical with him. *Com*, 176, 268, 986n; *Lyc*, 34n; 'Nat', 89.

Parthenope A Siren. *Com*, 879.

Philomela Raped by her brother-in-law Tereus, she was metamorphosed into a nightingale. The name means 'lover of song'. *Com*, 234n.

Phoebus An adjective meaning 'bright' often used for Apollo, especially in his role as sun-god. *Com*, 66, 190; *Lyc*, 77.

Pluto See **Hades**.

Poseidon Greek god of the sea and of earthquakes (Homer calls him 'earthshaker'), perhaps originally of the whole realm between the sky (Zeus) and the underworld (Hades). *Com*, 20n, 29n, 869n, 872n. Milton always uses the Latin form *Neptune*.

Proteus Sea-god with prophetic powers, herdsman of Poseidon's seals. He had the ability to change shape, but, if caught and held, resumed his proper form and answered questions about the future. The 'old man of the sea'. *Com*, 872.

Psyche Loved by Cupid, she was persecuted by his mother Venus with a succession of near-impossible tasks, including the sorting of a huge pile of miscellaneous seeds. Cupid and Psyche were eventually married after petitioning Jupiter, and had a daughter, Voluptas ('pleasure'). Her name means 'soul'. The story, given many symbolic readings in the Renaissance, comes from Apuleius' *Golden Ass*, following a passage in Plato's *Phaedrus* about the relationship between love and the soul. *Com*, 1005; *Areo*, 79.

Saturn Roman counterpart of Cronos (q.v.), but without the violent associations of the Greek god. God of fertility and agriculture, in some accounts he was an ancient king of Latium (central Italy), and his reign was believed to have been a golden age of peace and plenty. *Com*, 805; 'Nat', 135n; 'Pens', 24.

Satyrs Greek woodland-spirits, half-human, half-goat, closely associated with Pan and Dionysus. See **Fauns, Bacchus**. *Lyc*, 34.

Scylla Homeric sea-monster who lived in a cave opposite Charybdis (q.v.). *Com*, 257.

Silenus Sileni were elderly satyrs (q.v.), usually drunk, but also wise and capable of prophecy. One in particular was foster-father and tutor of the young Bacchus. *Lyc*, 1n.

Silvanus Roman god of woods and uncultivated land, worshipped by shepherds and sharing some of the characteristics of the Greek Pan. *Com*, 268; 'Pens', 134.

Sirens Bird-women living on a rock near Scylla and Charybdis, who lured sailors to their deaths. *Com*, 253, 878–80. Plato uses the term for the symbolic muse-like creatures who produce the music of the spheres. 'Nat', 131n; 'Sol Mus', 1, 2n.

Styx Boundary-river of Hades, the Greek underworld. See **Acheron**. *Com*, 132; 'L'All', 3n.

Syrinx Pursued by Pan, she was rescued by Naiads (q.v.), who transformed her into a bed of reeds, from which Pan, sublimating sex into art, cut his first reed-pipes. *Com*, 826n.

Thammuz Middle-Eastern river- and fertility-god, closely associated with the Adonis cult. See **Adonis**. *Com*, 1002n; 'Nat', 204.

Thetis A Nereid, mother of the Homeric hero Achilles. *Com*, 877.

Thone Guardian of the mouth of the Nile. His wife Polydamna gave Helen (q.v.) the narcotic and healing drug Nepenthes (q.v.). *Com*, 675.

Thule Sub-Arctic region of frost and fog, reputedly six days' sailing to the north of Britain (probably Iceland or Norway), and regarded as the northernmost limit of the world. *Ref*, 884.

Tritons Minor sea-deities or mermen, sons of Neptune and Amphitrite. *Com*, 24, 29, 873; *Lyc*, 89.

Typhon Monster with a hundred dragon-heads. Destroyer of Osiris, it attacked the Olympian gods and was defeated and imprisoned in Tartarus (the underworld) by Zeus. *Areo*, 511; 'Nat', 226.

Ulysses Latin form of the Homeric hero Odysseus, king of Ithaca, whose ten-year journey home is the subject of the *Odyssey*. *Com*, 637, 675n.

Urania Meaning 'heavenly', it was in ancient times one of the attribute-names of Aphrodite. Milton gives it to the ninth and highest of the Muses, patroness of divine poetry. 'Nat', 15; 'Sol Mus', 2n.

Venus Ancient Italian (i.e. pre-Roman) goddess of vegetation, identified by the Romans with the Graeco-Asiatic Aphrodite (q.v.), and assumed her functions and attributes. *Com*, 124, 1002; *Lyc*, 1n; 'Nat', 51n; 'L'All', 14.

Vesta Roman goddess of the hearth, originally a domestic deity, later a public cult with a sacred fire tended by six priestesses, the 'Vestal Virgins'. 'Pens', 23.

Vulcan Ancient Italian god of fire, identified with the Greek Hephaistos. *Com*, 655.

Zeus Greek god of sky and weather, especially thunder and rain. Father (i.e. Patriarch) of the other Olympian Gods, so-called from Mount Olympus in north-east Greece. Forms of the name are found throughout the Indo-European world, often with the suffix '*pater*', 'father', from the Indian *Dyaus pita* to the Roman *Jupiter*. Milton always uses the Latinized form *Jove*, which can also suggest the Judaeic *Yahveh*. *Com*, 20n, 803n; 'Nat', 135n, 203n; 'Pens', 48.